C-3295

THIS IS YOUR **PASSBOOK**® FOR ...

CHILD PROTECTIVE SERVICES SPECIALIST

NATIONAL LEARNING CORPORATION®
passbooks.com

COPYRIGHT NOTICE

Copyright © 2020 by

National Learning Corporation

212 Michael Drive, Syosset, NY 11791
(516) 921-8888 • www.passbooks.com
E-mail: info@passbooks.com

PUBLISHED IN THE UNITED STATES OF AMERICA

PASSBOOK® SERIES

THE *PASSBOOK® SERIES* has been created to prepare applicants and candidates for the ultimate academic battlefield – the examination room.

At some time in our lives, each and every one of us may be required to take an examination – for validation, matriculation, admission, qualification, registration, certification, or licensure.

Based on the assumption that every applicant or candidate has met the basic formal educational standards, has taken the required number of courses, and read the necessary texts, the *PASSBOOK® SERIES* furnishes the one special preparation which may assure passing with confidence, instead of failing with insecurity. Examination questions – together with answers – are furnished as the basic vehicle for study so that the mysteries of the examination and its compounding difficulties may be eliminated or diminished by a sure method.

This book is meant to help you pass your examination provided that you qualify and are serious in your objective.

The entire field is reviewed through the huge store of content information which is succinctly presented through a provocative and challenging approach – the question-and-answer method.

A climate of success is established by furnishing the correct answers at the end of each test.

You soon learn to recognize types of questions, forms of questions, and patterns of questioning. You may even begin to anticipate expected outcomes.

You perceive that many questions are repeated or adapted so that you can gain acute insights, which may enable you to score many sure points.

You learn how to confront new questions, or types of questions, and to attack them confidently and work out the correct answers.

You note objectives and emphases, and recognize pitfalls and dangers, so that you may make positive educational adjustments.

Moreover, you are kept fully informed in relation to new concepts, methods, practices, and directions in the field.

You discover that you arre actually taking the examination all the time: you are preparing for the examination by "taking" an examination, not by reading extraneous and/or supererogatory textbooks.

In short, this PASSBOOK®, used directedly, should be an important factor in helping you to pass your test.

CHILD PROTECTIVE SERVICES SPECIALIST

DUTIES
Child Protective Services Specialists, under varying degrees of supervision, with varying degrees of latitude for independent action, investigate and take appropriate action, in response to allegations of child neglect and/or abuse received by the department, in accordance with agency policies and procedures. Provides professional social services casework involving the determinations of child protective investigations and recommendations of the need for services and/or court involvement, and the formulation of plans for the individual cases or as directed by the court. The primary focus of the work is in the conducting of an independent investigation for child abuse and neglect.

EXAMPLES OF WORK
Reviews allegations and makes contact with the source of the referral; does risk assessment to ensure the safety of a child or children; prepares all appropriate petitions and submits to legal unit for review and approval; assists in the preparation of signed statements or affidavits; testifies in Family Court relative to matters pertaining to Child Protective Services; transports clients to hospitals, foster homes, Family Court and other necessary services; performs scheduled and unscheduled standby activity for after hour, weekend and holiday activities; develops plan of action and makes prompt contact with affected parties; re-interviews alleged perpetrators and alleged victims; documents in the case record all activities relative to the investigation; fulfills uniform case recording requirements; attends training conferences for self improvements and provides training for Child Protective trainees.

SCOPE OF THE EXAMINATION
The <u>written test</u> will cover knowledge, skills and/or abilities in such areas as:

1. Laws, rules and regulations related to child abuse and neglect;
2. Understanding and recognizing the dynamics and effects of child abuse and neglect;
3. Principles and practices of social casework as applied to family and children's services;
4. Interviewing; and
5. Preparing written material.

HOW TO TAKE A TEST

I. YOU MUST PASS AN EXAMINATION

A. *WHAT EVERY CANDIDATE SHOULD KNOW*

Examination applicants often ask us for help in preparing for the written test. What can I study in advance? What kinds of questions will be asked? How will the test be given? How will the papers be graded?

As an applicant for a civil service examination, you may be wondering about some of these things. Our purpose here is to suggest effective methods of advance study and to describe civil service examinations.

Your chances for success on this examination can be increased if you know how to prepare. Those "pre-examination jitters" can be reduced if you know what to expect. You can even experience an adventure in good citizenship if you know why civil service exams are given.

B. *WHY ARE CIVIL SERVICE EXAMINATIONS GIVEN?*

Civil service examinations are important to you in two ways. As a citizen, you want public jobs filled by employees who know how to do their work. As a job seeker, you want a fair chance to compete for that job on an equal footing with other candidates. The best-known means of accomplishing this two-fold goal is the competitive examination.

Exams are widely publicized throughout the nation. They may be administered for jobs in federal, state, city, municipal, town or village governments or agencies.

Any citizen may apply, with some limitations, such as the age or residence of applicants. Your experience and education may be reviewed to see whether you meet the requirements for the particular examination. When these requirements exist, they are reasonable and applied consistently to all applicants. Thus, a competitive examination may cause you some uneasiness now, but it is your privilege and safeguard.

C. *HOW ARE CIVIL SERVICE EXAMS DEVELOPED?*

Examinations are carefully written by trained technicians who are specialists in the field known as "psychological measurement," in consultation with recognized authorities in the field of work that the test will cover. These experts recommend the subject matter areas or skills to be tested; only those knowledges or skills important to your success on the job are included. The most reliable books and source materials available are used as references. Together, the experts and technicians judge the difficulty level of the questions.

Test technicians know how to phrase questions so that the problem is clearly stated. Their ethics do not permit "trick" or "catch" questions. Questions may have been tried out on sample groups, or subjected to statistical analysis, to determine their usefulness.

Written tests are often used in combination with performance tests, ratings of training and experience, and oral interviews. All of these measures combine to form the best-known means of finding the right person for the right job.

II. HOW TO PASS THE WRITTEN TEST

A. NATURE OF THE EXAMINATION

To prepare intelligently for civil service examinations, you should know how they differ from school examinations you have taken. In school you were assigned certain definite pages to read or subjects to cover. The examination questions were quite detailed and usually emphasized memory. Civil service exams, on the other hand, try to discover your present ability to perform the duties of a position, plus your potentiality to learn these duties. In other words, a civil service exam attempts to predict how successful you will be. Questions cover such a broad area that they cannot be as minute and detailed as school exam questions.

In the public service similar kinds of work, or positions, are grouped together in one "class." This process is known as *position-classification*. All the positions in a class are paid according to the salary range for that class. One class title covers all of these positions, and they are all tested by the same examination.

B. FOUR BASIC STEPS

1) Study the announcement

How, then, can you know what subjects to study? Our best answer is: "Learn as much as possible about the class of positions for which you've applied." The exam will test the knowledge, skills and abilities needed to do the work.

Your most valuable source of information about the position you want is the official exam announcement. This announcement lists the training and experience qualifications. Check these standards and apply only if you come reasonably close to meeting them.

The brief description of the position in the examination announcement offers some clues to the subjects which will be tested. Think about the job itself. Review the duties in your mind. Can you perform them, or are there some in which you are rusty? Fill in the blank spots in your preparation.

Many jurisdictions preview the written test in the exam announcement by including a section called "Knowledge and Abilities Required," "Scope of the Examination," or some similar heading. Here you will find out specifically what fields will be tested.

2) Review your own background

Once you learn in general what the position is all about, and what you need to know to do the work, ask yourself which subjects you already know fairly well and which need improvement. You may wonder whether to concentrate on improving your strong areas or on building some background in your fields of weakness. When the announcement has specified "some knowledge" or "considerable knowledge," or has used adjectives like "beginning principles of..." or "advanced ... methods," you can get a clue as to the number and difficulty of questions to be asked in any given field. More questions, and hence broader coverage, would be included for those subjects which are more important in the work. Now weigh your strengths and weaknesses against the job requirements and prepare accordingly.

3) **Determine the level of the position**

Another way to tell how intensively you should prepare is to understand the level of the job for which you are applying. Is it the entering level? In other words, is this the position in which beginners in a field of work are hired? Or is it an intermediate or advanced level? Sometimes this is indicated by such words as "Junior" or "Senior" in the class title. Other jurisdictions use Roman numerals to designate the level – Clerk I, Clerk II, for example. The word "Supervisor" sometimes appears in the title. If the level is not indicated by the title, check the description of duties. Will you be working under very close supervision, or will you have responsibility for independent decisions in this work?

4) **Choose appropriate study materials**

Now that you know the subjects to be examined and the relative amount of each subject to be covered, you can choose suitable study materials. For beginning level jobs, or even advanced ones, if you have a pronounced weakness in some aspect of your training, read a modern, standard textbook in that field. Be sure it is up to date and has general coverage. Such books are normally available at your library, and the librarian will be glad to help you locate one. For entry-level positions, questions of appropriate difficulty are chosen – neither highly advanced questions, nor those too simple. Such questions require careful thought but not advanced training.

If the position for which you are applying is technical or advanced, you will read more advanced, specialized material. If you are already familiar with the basic principles of your field, elementary textbooks would waste your time. Concentrate on advanced textbooks and technical periodicals. Think through the concepts and review difficult problems in your field.

These are all general sources. You can get more ideas on your own initiative, following these leads. For example, training manuals and publications of the government agency which employs workers in your field can be useful, particularly for technical and professional positions. A letter or visit to the government department involved may result in more specific study suggestions, and certainly will provide you with a more definite idea of the exact nature of the position you are seeking.

III. KINDS OF TESTS

Tests are used for purposes other than measuring knowledge and ability to perform specified duties. For some positions, it is equally important to test ability to make adjustments to new situations or to profit from training. In others, basic mental abilities not dependent on information are essential. Questions which test these things may not appear as pertinent to the duties of the position as those which test for knowledge and information. Yet they are often highly important parts of a fair examination. For very general questions, it is almost impossible to help you direct your study efforts. What we can do is to point out some of the more common of these general abilities needed in public service positions and describe some typical questions.

1) General information

Broad, general information has been found useful for predicting job success in some kinds of work. This is tested in a variety of ways, from vocabulary lists to questions about current events. Basic background in some field of work, such as sociology or economics, may be sampled in a group of questions. Often these are principles which have become familiar to most persons through exposure rather than through formal training. It is difficult to advise you how to study for these questions; being alert to the world around you is our best suggestion.

2) Verbal ability

An example of an ability needed in many positions is verbal or language ability. Verbal ability is, in brief, the ability to use and understand words. Vocabulary and grammar tests are typical measures of this ability. Reading comprehension or paragraph interpretation questions are common in many kinds of civil service tests. You are given a paragraph of written material and asked to find its central meaning.

3) Numerical ability

Number skills can be tested by the familiar arithmetic problem, by checking paired lists of numbers to see which are alike and which are different, or by interpreting charts and graphs. In the latter test, a graph may be printed in the test booklet which you are asked to use as the basis for answering questions.

4) Observation

A popular test for law-enforcement positions is the observation test. A picture is shown to you for several minutes, then taken away. Questions about the picture test your ability to observe both details and larger elements.

5) Following directions

In many positions in the public service, the employee must be able to carry out written instructions dependably and accurately. You may be given a chart with several columns, each column listing a variety of information. The questions require you to carry out directions involving the information given in the chart.

6) Skills and aptitudes

Performance tests effectively measure some manual skills and aptitudes. When the skill is one in which you are trained, such as typing or shorthand, you can practice. These tests are often very much like those given in business school or high school courses. For many of the other skills and aptitudes, however, no short-time preparation can be made. Skills and abilities natural to you or that you have developed throughout your lifetime are being tested.

Many of the general questions just described provide all the data needed to answer the questions and ask you to use your reasoning ability to find the answers. Your best preparation for these tests, as well as for tests of facts and ideas, is to be at your physical and mental best. You, no doubt, have your own methods of getting into an exam-taking mood and keeping "in shape." The next section lists some ideas on this subject.

IV. KINDS OF QUESTIONS

Only rarely is the "essay" question, which you answer in narrative form, used in civil service tests. Civil service tests are usually of the short-answer type. Full instructions for answering these questions will be given to you at the examination. But in case this is your first experience with short-answer questions and separate answer sheets, here is what you need to know:

1) Multiple-choice Questions

Most popular of the short-answer questions is the "multiple choice" or "best answer" question. It can be used, for example, to test for factual knowledge, ability to solve problems or judgment in meeting situations found at work.

A multiple-choice question is normally one of three types—

- It can begin with an incomplete statement followed by several possible endings. You are to find the one ending which *best* completes the statement, although some of the others may not be entirely wrong.
- It can also be a complete statement in the form of a question which is answered by choosing one of the statements listed.
- It can be in the form of a problem – again you select the best answer.

Here is an example of a multiple-choice question with a discussion which should give you some clues as to the method for choosing the right answer:

When an employee has a complaint about his assignment, the action which will *best* help him overcome his difficulty is to
- A. discuss his difficulty with his coworkers
- B. take the problem to the head of the organization
- C. take the problem to the person who gave him the assignment
- D. say nothing to anyone about his complaint

In answering this question, you should study each of the choices to find which is best. Consider choice "A" – Certainly an employee may discuss his complaint with fellow employees, but no change or improvement can result, and the complaint remains unresolved. Choice "B" is a poor choice since the head of the organization probably does not know what assignment you have been given, and taking your problem to him is known as "going over the head" of the supervisor. The supervisor, or person who made the assignment, is the person who can clarify it or correct any injustice. Choice "C" is, therefore, correct. To say nothing, as in choice "D," is unwise. Supervisors have and interest in knowing the problems employees are facing, and the employee is seeking a solution to his problem.

2) True/False Questions

The "true/false" or "right/wrong" form of question is sometimes used. Here a complete statement is given. Your job is to decide whether the statement is right or wrong.

SAMPLE: A roaming cell-phone call to a nearby city costs less than a non-roaming call to a distant city.

This statement is wrong, or false, since roaming calls are more expensive.
This is not a complete list of all possible question forms, although most of the others are variations of these common types. You will always get complete directions for

answering questions. Be sure you understand *how* to mark your answers – ask questions until you do.

V. RECORDING YOUR ANSWERS

Computer terminals are used more and more today for many different kinds of exams.

For an examination with very few applicants, you may be told to record your answers in the test booklet itself. Separate answer sheets are much more common. If this separate answer sheet is to be scored by machine – and this is often the case – it is highly important that you mark your answers correctly in order to get credit.

An electronic scoring machine is often used in civil service offices because of the speed with which papers can be scored. Machine-scored answer sheets must be marked with a pencil, which will be given to you. This pencil has a high graphite content which responds to the electronic scoring machine. As a matter of fact, stray dots may register as answers, so do not let your pencil rest on the answer sheet while you are pondering the correct answer. Also, if your pencil lead breaks or is otherwise defective, ask for another.

Since the answer sheet will be dropped in a slot in the scoring machine, be careful not to bend the corners or get the paper crumpled.

The answer sheet normally has five vertical columns of numbers, with 30 numbers to a column. These numbers correspond to the question numbers in your test booklet. After each number, going across the page are four or five pairs of dotted lines. These short dotted lines have small letters or numbers above them. The first two pairs may also have a "T" or "F" above the letters. This indicates that the first two pairs only are to be used if the questions are of the true-false type. If the questions are multiple choice, disregard the "T" and "F" and pay attention only to the small letters or numbers.

Answer your questions in the manner of the sample that follows:

32. The largest city in the United States is
    A. Washington, D.C.
    B. New York City
    C. Chicago
    D. Detroit
    E. San Francisco

1) Choose the answer you think is best. (New York City is the largest, so "B" is correct.)
2) Find the row of dotted lines numbered the same as the question you are answering. (Find row number 32)
3) Find the pair of dotted lines corresponding to the answer. (Find the pair of lines under the mark "B.")
4) Make a solid black mark between the dotted lines.

VI. BEFORE THE TEST

Common sense will help you find procedures to follow to get ready for an examination. Too many of us, however, overlook these sensible measures. Indeed, nervousness and fatigue have been found to be the most serious reasons why applicants fail to do their best on civil service tests. Here is a list of reminders:

- Begin your preparation early – Don't wait until the last minute to go scurrying around for books and materials or to find out what the position is all about.
- Prepare continuously – An hour a night for a week is better than an all-night cram session. This has been definitely established. What is more, a night a week for a month will return better dividends than crowding your study into a shorter period of time.
- Locate the place of the exam – You have been sent a notice telling you when and where to report for the examination. If the location is in a different town or otherwise unfamiliar to you, it would be well to inquire the best route and learn something about the building.
- Relax the night before the test – Allow your mind to rest. Do not study at all that night. Plan some mild recreation or diversion; then go to bed early and get a good night's sleep.
- Get up early enough to make a leisurely trip to the place for the test – This way unforeseen events, traffic snarls, unfamiliar buildings, etc. will not upset you.
- Dress comfortably – A written test is not a fashion show. You will be known by number and not by name, so wear something comfortable.
- Leave excess paraphernalia at home – Shopping bags and odd bundles will get in your way. You need bring only the items mentioned in the official notice you received; usually everything you need is provided. Do not bring reference books to the exam. They will only confuse those last minutes and be taken away from you when in the test room.
- Arrive somewhat ahead of time – If because of transportation schedules you must get there very early, bring a newspaper or magazine to take your mind off yourself while waiting.
- Locate the examination room – When you have found the proper room, you will be directed to the seat or part of the room where you will sit. Sometimes you are given a sheet of instructions to read while you are waiting. Do not fill out any forms until you are told to do so; just read them and be prepared.
- Relax and prepare to listen to the instructions
- If you have any physical problem that may keep you from doing your best, be sure to tell the test administrator. If you are sick or in poor health, you really cannot do your best on the exam. You can come back and take the test some other time.

VII. AT THE TEST

The day of the test is here and you have the test booklet in your hand. The temptation to get going is very strong. Caution! There is more to success than knowing the right answers. You must know how to identify your papers and understand variations in the type of short-answer question used in this particular examination. Follow these suggestions for maximum results from your efforts:

1) Cooperate with the monitor

The test administrator has a duty to create a situation in which you can be as much at ease as possible. He will give instructions, tell you when to begin, check to see that you are marking your answer sheet correctly, and so on. He is not there to guard you, although he will see that your competitors do not take unfair advantage. He wants to help you do your best.

2) Listen to all instructions

Don't jump the gun! Wait until you understand all directions. In most civil service tests you get more time than you need to answer the questions. So don't be in a hurry. Read each word of instructions until you clearly understand the meaning. Study the examples, listen to all announcements and follow directions. Ask questions if you do not understand what to do.

3) Identify your papers

Civil service exams are usually identified by number only. You will be assigned a number; you must not put your name on your test papers. Be sure to copy your number correctly. Since more than one exam may be given, copy your exact examination title.

4) Plan your time

Unless you are told that a test is a "speed" or "rate of work" test, speed itself is usually not important. Time enough to answer all the questions will be provided, but this does not mean that you have all day. An overall time limit has been set. Divide the total time (in minutes) by the number of questions to determine the approximate time you have for each question.

5) Do not linger over difficult questions

If you come across a difficult question, mark it with a paper clip (useful to have along) and come back to it when you have been through the booklet. One caution if you do this – be sure to skip a number on your answer sheet as well. Check often to be sure that you have not lost your place and that you are marking in the row numbered the same as the question you are answering.

6) Read the questions

Be sure you know what the question asks! Many capable people are unsuccessful because they failed to *read* the questions correctly.

7) Answer all questions

Unless you have been instructed that a penalty will be deducted for incorrect answers, it is better to guess than to omit a question.

8) Speed tests

It is often better NOT to guess on speed tests. It has been found that on timed tests people are tempted to spend the last few seconds before time is called in marking answers at random – without even reading them – in the hope of picking up a few extra points. To discourage this practice, the instructions may warn you that your score will be "corrected" for guessing. That is, a penalty will be applied. The incorrect answers will be deducted from the correct ones, or some other penalty formula will be used.

9) Review your answers

If you finish before time is called, go back to the questions you guessed or omitted to give them further thought. Review other answers if you have time.

10) Return your test materials

If you are ready to leave before others have finished or time is called, take ALL your materials to the monitor and leave quietly. Never take any test material with you. The monitor can discover whose papers are not complete, and taking a test booklet may be grounds for disqualification.

VIII. EXAMINATION TECHNIQUES

1) Read the general instructions carefully. These are usually printed on the first page of the exam booklet. As a rule, these instructions refer to the timing of the examination; the fact that you should not start work until the signal and must stop work at a signal, etc. If there are any *special* instructions, such as a choice of questions to be answered, make sure that you note this instruction carefully.

2) When you are ready to start work on the examination, that is as soon as the signal has been given, read the instructions to each question booklet, underline any key words or phrases, such as *least, best, outline, describe* and the like. In this way you will tend to answer as requested rather than discover on reviewing your paper that you *listed without describing*, that you selected the *worst* choice rather than the *best* choice, etc.

3) If the examination is of the objective or multiple-choice type – that is, each question will also give a series of possible answers: A, B, C or D, and you are called upon to select the best answer and write the letter next to that answer on your answer paper – it is advisable to start answering each question in turn. There may be anywhere from 50 to 100 such questions in the three or four hours allotted and you can see how much time would be taken if you read through all the questions before beginning to answer any. Furthermore, if you come across a question or group of questions which you know would be difficult to answer, it would undoubtedly affect your handling of all the other questions.

4) If the examination is of the essay type and contains but a few questions, it is a moot point as to whether you should read all the questions before starting to answer any one. Of course, if you are given a choice – say five out of seven and the like – then it is essential to read all the questions so you can eliminate the two that are most difficult. If, however, you are asked to answer all the questions, there may be danger in trying to answer the easiest one first because you may find that you will spend too much time on it. The best technique is to answer the first question, then proceed to the second, etc.

5) Time your answers. Before the exam begins, write down the time it started, then add the time allowed for the examination and write down the time it must be completed, then divide the time available somewhat as follows:

- If 3-1/2 hours are allowed, that would be 210 minutes. If you have 80 objective-type questions, that would be an average of 2-1/2 minutes per question. Allow yourself no more than 2 minutes per question, or a total of 160 minutes, which will permit about 50 minutes to review.
- If for the time allotment of 210 minutes there are 7 essay questions to answer, that would average about 30 minutes a question. Give yourself only 25 minutes per question so that you have about 35 minutes to review.

6) The most important instruction is to *read each question* and make sure you know what is wanted. The second most important instruction is to *time yourself properly* so that you answer every question. The third most important instruction is to *answer every question*. Guess if you have to but include something for each question. Remember that you will receive no credit for a blank and will probably receive some credit if you write something in answer to an essay question. If you guess a letter – say "B" for a multiple-choice question – you may have guessed right. If you leave a blank as an answer to a multiple-choice question, the examiners may respect your feelings but it will not add a point to your score. Some exams may penalize you for wrong answers, so in such cases *only*, you may not want to guess unless you have some basis for your answer.

7) Suggestions
   a. Objective-type questions
      1. Examine the question booklet for proper sequence of pages and questions
      2. Read all instructions carefully
      3. Skip any question which seems too difficult; return to it after all other questions have been answered
      4. Apportion your time properly; do not spend too much time on any single question or group of questions
      5. Note and underline key words – *all, most, fewest, least, best, worst, same, opposite,* etc.
      6. Pay particular attention to negatives
      7. Note unusual option, e.g., unduly long, short, complex, different or similar in content to the body of the question
      8. Observe the use of "hedging" words – *probably, may, most likely,* etc.
      9. Make sure that your answer is put next to the same number as the question
      10. Do not second-guess unless you have good reason to believe the second answer is definitely more correct
      11. Cross out original answer if you decide another answer is more accurate; do not erase until you are ready to hand your paper in
      12. Answer all questions; guess unless instructed otherwise
      13. Leave time for review

   b. Essay questions
      1. Read each question carefully
      2. Determine exactly what is wanted. Underline key words or phrases.
      3. Decide on outline or paragraph answer

4. Include many different points and elements unless asked to develop any one or two points or elements
5. Show impartiality by giving pros and cons unless directed to select one side only
6. Make and write down any assumptions you find necessary to answer the questions
7. Watch your English, grammar, punctuation and choice of words
8. Time your answers; don't crowd material

8) Answering the essay question

Most essay questions can be answered by framing the specific response around several key words or ideas. Here are a few such key words or ideas:

M's: manpower, materials, methods, money, management
P's: purpose, program, policy, plan, procedure, practice, problems, pitfalls, personnel, public relations
  a. Six basic steps in handling problems:
    1. Preliminary plan and background development
    2. Collect information, data and facts
    3. Analyze and interpret information, data and facts
    4. Analyze and develop solutions as well as make recommendations
    5. Prepare report and sell recommendations
    6. Install recommendations and follow up effectiveness

  b. Pitfalls to avoid
    1. *Taking things for granted* – A statement of the situation does not necessarily imply that each of the elements is necessarily true; for example, a complaint may be invalid and biased so that all that can be taken for granted is that a complaint has been registered
    2. *Considering only one side of a situation* – Wherever possible, indicate several alternatives and then point out the reasons you selected the best one
    3. *Failing to indicate follow up* – Whenever your answer indicates action on your part, make certain that you will take proper follow-up action to see how successful your recommendations, procedures or actions turn out to be
    4. *Taking too long in answering any single question* – Remember to time your answers properly

IX. AFTER THE TEST

Scoring procedures differ in detail among civil service jurisdictions although the general principles are the same. Whether the papers are hand-scored or graded by machine we have described, they are nearly always graded by number. That is, the person who marks the paper knows only the number – never the name – of the applicant. Not until all the papers have been graded will they be matched with names. If other tests, such as training and experience or oral interview ratings have been given, scores will be combined. Different parts of the examination usually have different weights. For example, the written test might count 60 percent of the final grade, and a rating of training and experience 40 percent. In many jurisdictions, veterans will have a certain number of points added to their grades.

After the final grade has been determined, the names are placed in grade order and an eligible list is established. There are various methods for resolving ties between those who get the same final grade – probably the most common is to place first the name of the person whose application was received first. Job offers are made from the eligible list in the order the names appear on it. You will be notified of your grade and your rank as soon as all these computations have been made. This will be done as rapidly as possible.

People who are found to meet the requirements in the announcement are called "eligibles." Their names are put on a list of eligible candidates. An eligible's chances of getting a job depend on how high he stands on this list and how fast agencies are filling jobs from the list.

When a job is to be filled from a list of eligibles, the agency asks for the names of people on the list of eligibles for that job. When the civil service commission receives this request, it sends to the agency the names of the three people highest on this list. Or, if the job to be filled has specialized requirements, the office sends the agency the names of the top three persons who meet these requirements from the general list.

The appointing officer makes a choice from among the three people whose names were sent to him. If the selected person accepts the appointment, the names of the others are put back on the list to be considered for future openings.

That is the rule in hiring from all kinds of eligible lists, whether they are for typist, carpenter, chemist, or something else. For every vacancy, the appointing officer has his choice of any one of the top three eligibles on the list. This explains why the person whose name is on top of the list sometimes does not get an appointment when some of the persons lower on the list do. If the appointing officer chooses the second or third eligible, the No. 1 eligible does not get a job at once, but stays on the list until he is appointed or the list is terminated.

X. HOW TO PASS THE INTERVIEW TEST

The examination for which you applied requires an oral interview test. You have already taken the written test and you are now being called for the interview test – the final part of the formal examination.

You may think that it is not possible to prepare for an interview test and that there are no procedures to follow during an interview. Our purpose is to point out some things you can do in advance that will help you and some good rules to follow and pitfalls to avoid while you are being interviewed.

What is an interview supposed to test?
The written examination is designed to test the technical knowledge and competence of the candidate; the oral is designed to evaluate intangible qualities, not readily measured otherwise, and to establish a list showing the relative fitness of each candidate – as measured against his competitors – for the position sought. Scoring is not on the basis of "right" and "wrong," but on a sliding scale of values ranging from "not passable" to "outstanding." As a matter of fact, it is possible to achieve a relatively low score without a single "incorrect" answer because of evident weakness in the qualities being measured.

Occasionally, an examination may consist entirely of an oral test – either an individual or a group oral. In such cases, information is sought concerning the technical knowledges and abilities of the candidate, since there has been no written examination for this purpose. More commonly, however, an oral test is used to supplement a written examination.

Who conducts interviews?

The composition of oral boards varies among different jurisdictions. In nearly all, a representative of the personnel department serves as chairman. One of the members of the board may be a representative of the department in which the candidate would work. In some cases, "outside experts" are used, and, frequently, a businessman or some other representative of the general public is asked to serve. Labor and management or other special groups may be represented. The aim is to secure the services of experts in the appropriate field.

However the board is composed, it is a good idea (and not at all improper or unethical) to ascertain in advance of the interview who the members are and what groups they represent. When you are introduced to them, you will have some idea of their backgrounds and interests, and at least you will not stutter and stammer over their names.

What should be done before the interview?

While knowledge about the board members is useful and takes some of the surprise element out of the interview, there is other preparation which is more substantive. It *is* possible to prepare for an oral interview – in several ways:

1) Keep a copy of your application and review it carefully before the interview

This may be the only document before the oral board, and the starting point of the interview. Know what education and experience you have listed there, and the sequence and dates of all of it. Sometimes the board will ask you to review the highlights of your experience for them; you should not have to hem and haw doing it.

2) Study the class specification and the examination announcement

Usually, the oral board has one or both of these to guide them. The qualities, characteristics or knowledges required by the position sought are stated in these documents. They offer valuable clues as to the nature of the oral interview. For example, if the job involves supervisory responsibilities, the announcement will usually indicate that knowledge of modern supervisory methods and the qualifications of the candidate as a supervisor will be tested. If so, you can expect such questions, frequently in the form of a hypothetical situation which you are expected to solve. NEVER go into an oral without knowledge of the duties and responsibilities of the job you seek.

3) Think through each qualification required

Try to visualize the kind of questions you would ask if you were a board member. How well could you answer them? Try especially to appraise your own knowledge and background in each area, *measured against the job sought*, and identify any areas in which you are weak. Be critical and realistic – do not flatter yourself.

4) Do some general reading in areas in which you feel you may be weak

For example, if the job involves supervision and your past experience has NOT, some general reading in supervisory methods and practices, particularly in the field of human relations, might be useful. Do NOT study agency procedures or detailed manuals. The oral board will be testing your understanding and capacity, not your memory.

5) Get a good night's sleep and watch your general health and mental attitude

You will want a clear head at the interview. Take care of a cold or any other minor ailment, and of course, no hangovers.

What should be done on the day of the interview?

Now comes the day of the interview itself. Give yourself plenty of time to get there. Plan to arrive somewhat ahead of the scheduled time, particularly if your appointment is in the fore part of the day. If a previous candidate fails to appear, the board might be ready for you a bit early. By early afternoon an oral board is almost invariably behind schedule if there are many candidates, and you may have to wait. Take along a book or magazine to read, or your application to review, but leave any extraneous material in the waiting room when you go in for your interview. In any event, relax and compose yourself.

The matter of dress is important. The board is forming impressions about you – from your experience, your manners, your attitude, and your appearance. Give your personal appearance careful attention. Dress your best, but not your flashiest. Choose conservative, appropriate clothing, and be sure it is immaculate. This is a business interview, and your appearance should indicate that you regard it as such. Besides, being well groomed and properly dressed will help boost your confidence.

Sooner or later, someone will call your name and escort you into the interview room. *This is it.* From here on you are on your own. It is too late for any more preparation. But remember, you asked for this opportunity to prove your fitness, and you are here because your request was granted.

What happens when you go in?

The usual sequence of events will be as follows: The clerk (who is often the board stenographer) will introduce you to the chairman of the oral board, who will introduce you to the other members of the board. Acknowledge the introductions before you sit down. Do not be surprised if you find a microphone facing you or a stenotypist sitting by. Oral interviews are usually recorded in the event of an appeal or other review.

Usually the chairman of the board will open the interview by reviewing the highlights of your education and work experience from your application – primarily for the benefit of the other members of the board, as well as to get the material into the record. Do not interrupt or comment unless there is an error or significant misinterpretation; if that is the case, do not hesitate. But do not quibble about insignificant matters. Also, he will usually ask you some question about your education, experience or your present job – partly to get you to start talking and to establish the interviewing "rapport." He may start the actual questioning, or turn it over to one of the other members. Frequently, each member undertakes the questioning on a particular area, one in which he is perhaps most competent, so you can expect each member to participate in the examination. Because time is limited, you may also expect some rather abrupt switches in the direction the questioning takes, so do not be upset by it. Normally, a board member will not pursue a single line of questioning unless he discovers a particular strength or weakness.

After each member has participated, the chairman will usually ask whether any member has any further questions, then will ask you if you have anything you wish to add. Unless you are expecting this question, it may floor you. Worse, it may start you off on an extended, extemporaneous speech. The board is not usually seeking more information. The question is principally to offer you a last opportunity to present further qualifications or to indicate that you have nothing to add. So, if you feel that a significant qualification or characteristic has been overlooked, it is proper to point it out in a sentence or so. Do not compliment the board on the thoroughness of their examination – they have been sketchy, and you know it. If you wish, merely say, "No thank you, I have nothing further to add." This is a point where you can "talk yourself out" of a good impression or fail to present an important bit of information. Remember, *you close the interview yourself.*

The chairman will then say, "That is all, Mr. _____, thank you." Do not be startled; the interview is over, and quicker than you think. Thank him, gather your belongings and take your leave. Save your sigh of relief for the other side of the door.

How to put your best foot forward

Throughout this entire process, you may feel that the board individually and collectively is trying to pierce your defenses, seek out your hidden weaknesses and embarrass and confuse you. Actually, this is not true. They are obliged to make an appraisal of your qualifications for the job you are seeking, and they want to see you in your best light. Remember, they must interview all candidates and a non-cooperative candidate may become a failure in spite of their best efforts to bring out his qualifications. Here are 15 suggestions that will help you:

1) Be natural – Keep your attitude confident, not cocky

If you are not confident that you can do the job, do not expect the board to be. Do not apologize for your weaknesses, try to bring out your strong points. The board is interested in a positive, not negative, presentation. Cockiness will antagonize any board member and make him wonder if you are covering up a weakness by a false show of strength.

2) Get comfortable, but don't lounge or sprawl

Sit erectly but not stiffly. A careless posture may lead the board to conclude that you are careless in other things, or at least that you are not impressed by the importance of the occasion. Either conclusion is natural, even if incorrect. Do not fuss with your clothing, a pencil or an ashtray. Your hands may occasionally be useful to emphasize a point; do not let them become a point of distraction.

3) Do not wisecrack or make small talk

This is a serious situation, and your attitude should show that you consider it as such. Further, the time of the board is limited – they do not want to waste it, and neither should you.

4) Do not exaggerate your experience or abilities

In the first place, from information in the application or other interviews and sources, the board may know more about you than you think. Secondly, you probably will not get away with it. An experienced board is rather adept at spotting such a situation, so do not take the chance.

5) If you know a board member, do not make a point of it, yet do not hide it

Certainly you are not fooling him, and probably not the other members of the board. Do not try to take advantage of your acquaintanceship – it will probably do you little good.

6) Do not dominate the interview

Let the board do that. They will give you the clues – do not assume that you have to do all the talking. Realize that the board has a number of questions to ask you, and do not try to take up all the interview time by showing off your extensive knowledge of the answer to the first one.

7) Be attentive

You only have 20 minutes or so, and you should keep your attention at its sharpest throughout. When a member is addressing a problem or question to you, give him your undivided attention. Address your reply principally to him, but do not exclude the other board members.

8) Do not interrupt

A board member may be stating a problem for you to analyze. He will ask you a question when the time comes. Let him state the problem, and wait for the question.

9) Make sure you understand the question

Do not try to answer until you are sure what the question is. If it is not clear, restate it in your own words or ask the board member to clarify it for you. However, do not haggle about minor elements.

10) Reply promptly but not hastily

A common entry on oral board rating sheets is "candidate responded readily," or "candidate hesitated in replies." Respond as promptly and quickly as you can, but do not jump to a hasty, ill-considered answer.

11) Do not be peremptory in your answers

A brief answer is proper – but do not fire your answer back. That is a losing game from your point of view. The board member can probably ask questions much faster than you can answer them.

12) Do not try to create the answer you think the board member wants

He is interested in what kind of mind you have and how it works – not in playing games. Furthermore, he can usually spot this practice and will actually grade you down on it.

13) Do not switch sides in your reply merely to agree with a board member

Frequently, a member will take a contrary position merely to draw you out and to see if you are willing and able to defend your point of view. Do not start a debate, yet do not surrender a good position. If a position is worth taking, it is worth defending.

14) Do not be afraid to admit an error in judgment if you are shown to be wrong

The board knows that you are forced to reply without any opportunity for careful consideration. Your answer may be demonstrably wrong. If so, admit it and get on with the interview.

15) Do not dwell at length on your present job

The opening question may relate to your present assignment. Answer the question but do not go into an extended discussion. You are being examined for a *new* job, not your present one. As a matter of fact, try to phrase ALL your answers in terms of the job for which you are being examined.

Basis of Rating

Probably you will forget most of these "do's" and "don'ts" when you walk into the oral interview room. Even remembering them all will not ensure you a passing grade. Perhaps you did not have the qualifications in the first place. But remembering them will help you to put your best foot forward, without treading on the toes of the board members.

Rumor and popular opinion to the contrary notwithstanding, an oral board wants you to make the best appearance possible. They know you are under pressure – but they also want to see how you respond to it as a guide to what your reaction would be under the pressures of the job you seek. They will be influenced by the degree of poise you display, the personal traits you show and the manner in which you respond.

ABOUT THIS BOOK

This book contains tests divided into Examination Sections. Go through each test, answering every question in the margin. At the end of each test look at the answer key and check your answers. On the ones you got wrong, look at the right answer choice and learn. Do not fill in the answers first. Do not memorize the questions and answers, but understand the answer and principles involved. On your test, the questions will likely be different from the samples. Questions are changed and new ones added. If you understand these past questions you should have success with any changes that arise. Tests may consist of several types of questions. We have additional books on each subject should more study be advisable or necessary for you. Finally, the more you study, the better prepared you will be. This book is intended to be the last thing you study before you walk into the examination room. Prior study of relevant texts is also recommended. NLC publishes some of these in our Fundamental Series. Knowledge and good sense are important factors in passing your exam. Good luck also helps. So now study this Passbook, absorb the material contained within and take that knowledge into the examination. Then do your best to pass that exam.

EXAMINATION SECTION

EXAMINATION SECTION
TEST 1

DIRECTIONS: Each question or incomplete statement is followed by several suggested answers or completions. Select the one the BEST answers the question or completes the statement PRINT THE LETTER OF THE CORRECT ANSWER IN THE SPACE AT THE RIGHT.

1. In general, the most serious decision a CPS agency (or inter-agency board) can be called upon to make is

   A. when to intervene in a case of neglect
   B. whether to make a home visit in response to a report
   C. when to return a child from a foster home to a natural home
   D. whether to begin termination of parental rights

1.____

2. Which of the following is/are defined by the Child Abuse Prevention and Treatment Act as a form of child neglect?
     I. Failure to seek periodic medical and dental check-ups that have the potential to prevent disease
     II. Punishment involving close confinement
     III. Failure to seek necessary health care for a sick child
     IV. Failure to enroll a school-age child in an educational program

   A. I only
   B. II and III
   C. III and IV
   D. I, II, III and IV

2.____

3. The first task that a worker faces in making judgements about clients is

   A. predicting the likelihood of abuse or neglect
   B. determining relationships between events
   C. describing the general situation and family interactions
   D. testing theories about assumptions

3.____

4. Inflicted bruises on a child are so common at certain body sites that discovering them there is diagnostic of abuse. Which of the following is LEAST likely to be the site of an inflicted bruise?

   A. Forehead
   B. Neck
   C. Genitals
   D. Buttocks and lower back

4.____

5. The most frequently reported type of child maltreatment is

   A. physical abuse
   B. physical endangerment
   C. sexual abuse
   D. neglect

5.____

6. The final phase of an interview with a child who has suffered sexual abuse should be devoted to   6.____

    A. gathering as much concrete evidence as possible against the perpetrator
    B. making sure the child understands that he or she should never let the abuse happen again
    C. telling the child emphatically that the abuse was not his or her fault
    D. compiling a list of physical and behavioral symptoms

7. What is the legal term for an individual who assumes parental obligations and status without a formal, legal adoption?   7.____

    A. Parens patriae
    B. In loco parentis
    C. Ad litem
    D. In re

8. Of the forms of maltreatment listed below, the one that generally causes the greatest number of child fatalities is   8.____

    A. emotional abuse
    B. physical abuse
    C. neglect
    D. sexual abuse

9. Major indications that an agency should initiate the termination of parental rights include   9.____
    I. Voluntary placement of a child without visits, correspondence, or other contact for one year
    II. Repetitive moderate injuries
    III. Untreatable psychopathology in the child
    IV. Untreatable psychopathology in one or both parents

    A. I and II
    B. I, II and IV
    C. II, III and IV
    D. I, II, III and IV

10. Which of the following is the minimum required to trigger the mandatory reporting requirements of the Child Abuse Prevention and Treatment Act?   10.____

    A. Reasonable suspicion
    B. Suspicion shared by at least one other witness
    C. Clear and convincing evidence
    D. A preponderance of evidence

11. When a child is abandoned or orphaned and the state must step in, it is usually the case that an attempt is made to first place the child   11.____

    A. in a suitable institution
    B. with an adoption agency
    C. with foster parents
    D. with relatives

12. Which of the following parties is generally <u>not</u> involved in the pretrial or trial stages of a dependency and neglect proceeding?   12.____

    A. CPS or social services agency
    B. Child through guardian *ad litem*
    C. Concerned party seeking custody
    D. Parents or custodians

13. In a typical risk assessment instrument, which of the following variables would most likely be classified as constituting no risk or a low risk?   13.____

    A. Family is geographically isolated from community services
    B. A caretaker who is overly compliant with the investigator
    C. An injury on the child's torso
    D. One previous report of abuse

14. Once a placement has occurred, the worker's next immediate responsibility is generally to   14.____

    A. conduct observations at the foster home
    B. make a post-placement family assessment
    C. begin the implementation of in-home services
    D. develop an individual case plan

15. Which of the following cases would typically require the most time for review by a CPS board or staff?   15.____

    A. Failure to thrive
    B. A child younger than 1 year old in an unheated home
    C. School-age child exhibiting antisocial behavior
    D. A child younger than 1 year old with physical abuse

16. In taking a child's history of alleged sexual abuse, it's important to remember that there's little evidence to suggest that children's reports are unreliable. In the rare instances that a child makes a false accusation, it's usually for one of a limited number of reasons. Which of the following is <u>not</u> one of these?   16.____

    A. The child wants to please or anger the parents
    B. The child has misinterpreted innocent behavior by the alleged perpetrator
    C. The child hopes to obtain an objective (dating, custody change
    D. The child perceives him/herself to be in trouble, and wants to protect him/herself from incrimination

17. During the first year of a child's life, about _____% of all serious intracranial injuries that occur are the result of abuse.   17.____

    A. 15
    B. 45
    C. 75
    D. 95

18. Often, the task of determining an appropriate level of intervention in cases of child neglect tends to be most difficult in cases where _____ is/are a main factor in the family's inability to maintain safe housing and adequate food.

    A. drug abuse
    B. poverty
    C. an abusive family of origin
    D. differing cultural values

18._____

19. Each of the following elements is generally common to all family preservation programs, except

    A. services are delivered according to routinely designated case categories
    B. they are crisis-oriented
    C. length of involvement is typically limited to between 2 and 5 months
    D. the staff maintains flexible hours, 7 days a week

19._____

20. Adequate foster care standards were established in the United States by

    A. *Miller v. Youakim (1979)*
    B. *G.L. v. Zumwalt(1980)*
    C. the Child Abuse Prevention Treatment Act
    D. the Adoption Assistance and Child Welfare Act

20._____

21. A worker begins an investigation of a report by visiting the home of a family and observing that a child has several bruises on her back, arms, and legs. In order to maintain an objective stance, the worker should describe the child as

    A. self-destructive
    B. clumsy
    C. abused
    D. bruised

21._____

22. A CPS agency based in an institutional or resident-care facility must meet requirements for minimally adequate care. Which of the following is generally not one of these requirements?

    A. Individualized treatment plans
    B. A sufficient number of qualified staff
    C. Planned therapeutic programs and activities
    D. Planned educational instruction

22._____

23. During an interview with a 3-year-old child who is suspected to be a victim of sexual abuse, the interview asks a series of questions, each of which the child immediately answers *Yes* while playing with some dolls that have been placed in front her. The child does not appear to be paying attention to the interviewer's questions. The interviewer should then

    A. abruptly terminate the interview and begin again later
    B. explain to the child how important it is that she pay attention and answer the questions as truthfully as she can
    C. ask another question to which the answer is known
    D. ask the child to demonstrate the abuse using the dolls with which she is playing

23._____

24. Which of the following is true of a guardianship?   24.____

    A. A guardianship obtained outside dependency court does not require r eunification efforts.
    B. A guardian is eligible for federal AFDC, regardless of familial relation to the child.
    C. Parents permanently lose their right to a child.
    D. A guardian of the child's person is automatically considered to be the guardian of the child's estate.

25. Generally, incorporating emotional abuse and neglect into juvenile codes is made espe-   25.____
cially difficult because

    A. neglect is almost always a civil rather than criminal matter
    B. there is a lack of agreement on whether certain forms of neglect require treatment
    C. they can result from a lack of interaction as often as an interaction
    D. the terms that define cause, treatment and consequences are vague

---

KEY (CORRECT ANSWERS)

1.	C		11.	D
2.	C		12.	C
3.	C		13.	C
4.	A		14.	B
5.	D		15.	D
6.	C		16.	B
7.	B		17.	D
8.	C		18.	B
9.	B		19.	A
10.	A		20.	B

21.	D
22.	D
23.	C
24.	A
25.	D

TEST 2

DIRECTIONS: Each question or incomplete statement is followed by several suggested answers or completions. Select the one the BEST answers the question or completes the statement. *PRINT THE LETTER OF THE CORRECT ANSWER IN THE SPACE AT THE RIGHT.*

1. Research has demonstrated that probably the greatest benefit involved in group classes focusing on child development and care is   1._____

   A. the learning of a few concrete skills
   B. an improvement in families' overall living environment
   C. the alleviation of social isolation
   D. acquisition of new insights and attitudes

2. Programs such as individual behavior therapy, group therapy, and therapeutic day care have been found to be especially beneficial to families when they can continue for at least _____ months   2._____

   A. 3-6
   B. 6-18
   C. 12-24
   D. 18-36

3. Which of the following conditions is most likely to necessitate the attempt to place a child outside of his or her home and away from parents?   3._____

   A. Child is younger than 2
   B. Munchausen syndrome by proxy
   C. Both parents unemployed
   D. Sibling suffered severe past abuse

4. Signs exhibited by a child that may be indicative of sexual abuse include   4._____
   I. Headaches
   II. Wetting/soiling of underwear
   III. Seductive behavior
   IV. Impulsiveness

   A. I and III
   B. II and III
   C. II, III and IV
   D. I, II, III and IV

5. An initial report contains allegations of educational neglect, but no claim of abuse or other forms of neglect. Generally, the investigating worker is required to   5._____

   A. interview only the child and the primary caretaker
   B. interview all involved child and adult subjects of the report, along with the reporter
   C. establish a collateral contact with another professional
   D. visit the home

6. An accidental fall will generally <u>not</u> cause a bruise on the   6._____

    A. soft tissue of the cheek
    B. forehead
    C. cheekbone
    D. elbow

7. Under federal law, an individual case plan for a child must be developed within _____   7._____
after the initial removal of a child or after an emergency in-person response.

    A. 48 hours
    B. 10 days
    C. 30 days
    D. 60 days

8. In forming judgements about clients, a worker should generally use information or behav-   8._____
iors that are most

    A. recent
    B. vivid
    C. consistent
    D. available

9. In general, which of the following factors has been demonstrated to be the most influen-   9._____
tial in determining whether a report of abuse or neglect will be confirmed, and whether
placement will be initiated?

    A. The nature of the incident
    B. The age of the child
    C. Agency staffing patterns
    D. Parental characteristics

10. In general, what is the likelihood that a report of child abuse or neglect will be confirmed   10._____
by a worker's investigation?

    A. 10-20%
    B. 25-50%
    C. 40-60%
    D. 60-80%

11. Which of the following is true of child custody petitions initiated by a CPS worker?   11._____

    A. It is generally filed by a named individual
    B. The child is generally removed from the home pending a hearing
    C. Preliminary hearings on the need to take immediate custody are generally held
       within 24 hours
    D. Only one copy of the petition is served to a set of parents

12. In most states, professionals who are required to report the possibility of child maltreat-   12._____
ment to the proper authority include
      I. Law enforcement personnel, such as police officers
     II. Child care providers
    III. Medical or hospital personnel
    IV. Attorneys

A. I and II
B. I, II and III
C. III only
D. I, II, III and IV

13. As a general rule, children who have been in foster care for _____ or more should be evaluated by a mental health professional.

13.____

A. 3 months
B. 6 months
C. 1 year
D. 2 years

14. The most commonly encountered hand marks left on a child in cases of physical abuse are

14.____

A. hand prints
B. linear marks-parallel bruises marking the edges of fingers
C. grab marks-oval-shaped bruises resembling fingerprints
D. pinch marks-crescent-shaped bruises facing each other

15. According to the National Center on Child Abuse and Neglect, emotional abuse includes each of the following, except

15.____

A. threatened harm
B. close confinement
C. refusal to provide essential care
D. verbal assault

16. In the Families model of home-based intervention,

16.____

A. very few, if any, support services are involved
B. the main objective is to eliminate the symptom
C. the average intervention period is just over 4 months
D. a strategic therapist assesses the family for a period of 30 days

17. Which of the following is LEAST likely to be an area of particular concern regarding the decision-making processes of child welfare workers?

17.____

A. Lack of training in methods for predicting behavior
B. Inability to predict client behavior with accuracy
C. Lack of consistency over time
D. Lack of agreement between workers on the same case information

18. Many states and localities have established a priority system for responding to initial reports of abuse or neglect. In a system based primarily on the type of allegation reported, which of the following would be given *priority two* status-dangerous and perhaps requiring emergency services?

18.____

A. Internal injuries
B. Suicidal child
C. Sprains/dislocations
D. Malnutrition/failure to thrive

19. In general, until more information is known, CPS workers should avoid the initiation of a criminal investigation of the perpetrator in cases involving   19.____

    A. Munchausen syndrome by proxy
    B. deliberate poisoning with intent to kill
    C. premeditated by not potentially lethal physical abuse
    D. nonsevere physical abuse, but where a previous sibling was killed or died under suspicious circumstances

20. The surrender of care, custody and earnings of a child, as well as the renunciation of parental duties, is known by the legal term   20.____

    A. Emancipation
    B. Quitclaim
    C. Surrender
    D. Relinquishment

21. Generally, infants who have been placed in foster care should be visited at least _____ by their biological parents.   21.____

    A. once a day
    B. 3 times a week
    C. weekly
    D. every two weeks

22. A parent or guardian fails to provide necessary physical, affectional, medical, or institutional care for a child is guilty of neglect if that failure is due to   22.____
    I. financial inability
    II. mental incapacity
    III. immorality
    IV. cruelty

    A. I, III and IV
    B. II, III and IV
    C. III and IV
    D. I, II, III, and IV

23. When faced with a situation requiring the immediate alleviation of risks, a worker may rush to pace a child without considering possible alternatives. This is an example of   23.____

    A. Hypervigilance
    B. Unconflicted change
    C. Unconflicted inertia
    D. Defensive avoidance

24. Approximately what percentage of children living in foster care are adopted each year?   24.____

    A. 10
    B. 25
    C. 45
    D. 60

25. Which of the following is LEAST likely to be included in the behavioral profile of an abused or neglected child?   25.____

    A. Excessive attention to physical appearance
    B. Immaturity
    C. Self-hatred
    D. Sexual sophistication (beyond age level)

———

KEY (CORRECT ANSWERS)

1.	C		11.	C
2.	B		12.	B
3.	D		13.	C
4.	D		14.	C
5.	B		15.	C
6.	A		16.	C
7.	C		17.	A
8.	C		18.	C
9.	A		19.	A
10.	C		20.	A

21.	B
22.	B
23.	B
24.	A
25.	A

———

TEST 3

DIRECTIONS: Each question or incomplete statement is followed by several suggested answers or completions. Select the one the BEST answers the question or completes the statement. *PRINT THE LETTER OF THE CORRECT ANSWER IN THE SPACE AT THE RIGHT.*

1. The most important factor in determining whether a parent or guardian is guilty of child neglect is   1.____

   A. the degree of the child's suffering
   B. whether the negligent behavior is intentional or the consequence of other factors such as financial trouble
   C. whether the child's suffering is physical or emotional
   D. whether the child has suffered an injury as a result of the neglect

2. When burns are inflicted on a child, the most commonly-used agent is   2.____

   A. hot water
   B. a cigarette
   C. a stove or hot plate
   D. a lighter or match

3. Which of the following legal terms refers to the role of the state as guardian of legally disabled individuals?   3.____

   A. Parens patriae
   B. Vis major
   C. Eminent domain
   D. In loco parentis

4. When documenting the effects of intervention in a case of child neglect, the worker's records must include   4.____
   I.   notations on the child's progress
   II. assessments of other concerned professionals regarding the child's situation
   III. the parents' cooperation and compliance with requests regarding problems

   A. I only
   B. I and II
   C. I and III
   D. I, II and III

5. A worker who feels that an agency's resources are not adequate to help a particular child is at risk for performing the unproductive behavior known as   5.____

   A. Defensive avoidance
   B. Unconflicted inertia
   C. Hypervigilance
   D. Unconflicted change

6. Which of the following items of information is most relevant to a domestic hearing?   6._____

    A. Treatment plan for all members of household
    B. Statement of child
    C. Why safety of the child can't be insured in the home
    D. Comparison of parents

7. Among the general population, regardless of other factors, the chances that a person will   7._____
exhibit abusive behavior is about_____%.

    A. 0-1
    B. 1-10
    C. 5-15
    D. 10-25

8. For an 8-year-old child who is sexually abused, the most likely presentation would be   8._____

    A. stranger anxiety
    B. baby talk
    C. a significant change in attitude or grades
    D. separation anxiety

9. A CPS worker may avoid the placement of a child by making use of certain emergency   9._____
services. Which of the following is generally not available in such situations?

    A. Emergency shelters for families about to be separated as a result of evictions, con-
        demned housing, etc.
    B. Emergency homemakers available 24 hours a day both to maintain children at
        home and to teach parents
    C. Outreach and follow-through with immediate casework assistance in the crisis and
        follow-through beyond the crisis stage
    D. Emergency short-term employment for out-of-work parents, accompanied by qual-
        ified day-care services

10. If parents are assigned to parenting classes in cases of neglect, it should be expected   10._____
that those who benefit from the classes will benefit after remaining with a group for at
least

    A. 3 months
    B. 6 months
    C. 1 year
    D. 2 years

11. The use of objective risk-assessment instruments in the investigation of reports has   11._____
proven difficult for each of the following reasons, except

    A. the assignment of weights to scale factors based solely on professional judgement
    B. the difficulty in making scales sensitive enough to identify all true cases of abuse or
        neglect
    C. overbroad or vague classifications of situations and behaviors
    D. the fact that incidence of abuse and neglect in the general population is not a very
        frequent occurrence

12. When launching an investigation of an initial report, a worker usually focuses first on the   12._____

    A. parental characteristics
    B. characteristics of the child or children subjects of the report
    C. incident and presenting problem
    D. physical environment in which the child lives

13. The purposes of a civil child abuse proceeding include   13._____
    I. Punishment
    II. Treatment
    III. Protection
    IV. Deterrence

    A. I and IV
    B. II and III
    C. III and IV
    D. I, II, III and IV

14. What is the approximate risk that a sibling of a physically abused child has also been   14._____
abused at the same time?

    A. 20%
    B. 40%
    C. 60%
    D. 80%

15. If a worker decides to use a rating scale to determine the risk to a child, which of the fol-   15._____
lowing factors would be LEAST likely to be included in the scale?

    A. Age of parents
    B. Age of the child
    C. Parental attitude
    D. Health of the child

16. Which of the following cases would typically require the most time for review by a CPS   16._____
board or staff?

    A. Aggressive behavior by a school-age child
    B. Re-abuse or failure
    C. Developmental delays in a 3-year-old
    D. Temporary abandonment of an 8-year-old

17. Probably the most pervasive and long-term consequence of sexual abuse for a child is   17._____

    A. phobic behaviors
    B. a poor self-image
    C. over-assertiveness
    D. nightmares

18. A home visit to a client's house reveals an environment that is less than ideal, but there   18._____
isn't enough evidence to support a finding of abuse or neglect. Which of the following are
options for the case worker?
    I. Closing the file with no referrals
    II. Referring the family to voluntary protective services
    III. Emergency placement
    IV. Solicitation of the police to conduct surveillance for evidentiary purposes

A. I and II
B. II only
C. II or III
D. I, II, III and IV

19. In general, parental alcohol and/or drug abuse is present in about_____% of all cases   19._____
of child neglect.

    A. 20-30
    B. 40-60
    C. 70-80
    D. 90-100

20. In a dependency and neglect proceeding,   20._____

    A. the purpose is to rehabilitate the offending parent or custodian
    B. the burden of proof is a preponderance of evidence
    C. the issue is whether a specific individual injured the child at a specific time
    D. the maximum penalty may involve imprisonment

21. During an interactional assessment of a parent and children, the questioner should   21._____

    A. adopt a formal style
    B. focus on issues rather than specific inquiries
    C. only question the parent after the children have been removed
    D. use closed-ended questions

Questions 22 and 23 and refer to the information below.

A 12-year-old girl reports that her stepfather has fondled her. A physical examination revealed no evidence, and the father denied any misconduct. In an interview with the CPS worker, the girl repeated her account of what happened. The mother is unsure whom to believe. She reports that the girl has been having trouble in school lately, and that she suspects the girl might be using drugs. The whole family has been under strain because of a recent move. The mother and stepfather both work full time, and interviews with co-workers reveal no evidence of family trouble.

22. Each of the following items of information is needed to make a decision about the risk to   22._____
the girl, except

    A. the girl's account of family interaction and the stepfather's ongoing behavior
    B. concrete proof (urinalysis or blood test) confirming or disproving drug use by the girl
    C. previous reports on stepfather from last state of residence
    D. the mother's attitudes toward her daughter, the stepfather, and the reported incident

23. In order to accurately assess this situation, a worker must have knowledge about each of   23._____
the following, except

    A. demographics which are predictive of sexual abuse
    B. child development
    C. family dynamics in sexual abuse
    D. risk factors for sexual abuse

14

24. Which of the following is LEAST likely to be included in the behavioral profile of an abused or neglected child?   24._____

    A. Anxiety
    B. Withdrawal
    C. Extreme aggression
    D. Arrogance

25. In general, criminal filing in cases of child abuse should be strongly considered as a way of enforcing treatment when the offender is   25._____

    A. a sibling
    B. an unrelated adult such as a teacher or boyfriend
    C. a single parent
    D. mentally or emotionally impaired

KEY (CORRECT ANSWERS)

1.	B		11.	C
2.	A		12.	B
3.	A		13.	B
4.	D		14.	A
5.	A		15.	A
6.	D		16.	B
7.	B		17.	B
8.	C		18.	A
9.	D		19.	C
10.	D		20.	B

21.	B
22.	B
23.	A
24.	D
25.	B

15

EXAMINATION SECTION
TEST 1

DIRECTIONS: Each question or incomplete statement is followed by several suggested answers or completions. Select the one the BEST answers the question or completes the statement. *PRINT THE LETTER OF THE CORRECT ANSWER IN THE SPACE AT THE RIGHT.*

1. In most states, minors must be at least _____ and able to prove to the court that they can provide their own support and make mature decisions before the court will emancipate them.

    A. 10
    B. 12
    C. 14
    D. 16

1.____

2. An initial report contains allegations of environmental neglect, but no claim of abuse or any other form of neglect. Generally, the investigating worker is required to
    I. interview all subjects of the report and the reporter
    II. contact local law enforcement
    III. visit the home
    IV. establish a collateral contact with a professional person

    A. I only
    B. I and III
    C. II and IV
    D. I, II, III and IV

2.____

3. The first use of the "best interests of the child" standard in a custody decision occurred in

    A. *Chapsky v. Wood (1881)*
    B. *Meyer v. Nebraska (1923)*
    C. *In re Gault (1967)*
    D. *Wisconsin v. Yoder (1972)*

3.____

4. Many states and localities have established a priority system for responding to initial reports of abuse or neglect. In a system based primarily on the type of allegation reported, which of the following would be given "priority three" status--a non-emergency situation that may not require CPS intervention?

    A. Excessive corporal punishment
    B. Torture
    C. Drug/alcohol abuse
    D. Chronic truancy

4.____

5. Each of the following is a potential sign of neglect in a school-age child, <u>except</u>

    A. poor self-discipline
    B. unreceptiveness to concepts of caring and respect for peers
    C. delayed language development
    D. bullying

5.____

6. The confidentiality provisions of the Child Abuse Prevention and Treatment Act require   6._____
    states to make unauthorized disclosures of child abuse and neglect reports a criminal
    offense. These provisions apply to
        I.   physicians
        II.   CPS caseworkers
        III. step-parents
        IV. divorce attorneys

    A. I and IV
    B. II, III and IV
    C. III and IV
    D. I, II, III and IV

7. During an interactional assessment of parents and their children, a questioner wants to   7._____
    assess the parents' current life satisfaction. The issue is best addressed by the question

    A. If you could change one thing in your lives right now, what would it be?
    B. Do you ever wish you'd never had children?
    C. Why do you think you're here answering these questions?
    D. Are you both happy right now?

8. Signs of neglect in infants and toddlers include each of the following, <u>except</u>   8._____

    A. delayed gross motor development
    B. behavioral abnormalities
    C. poor self-discipline
    D. growth failure

9. A CPS agency is attempting to prioritize its caseload. In general, which of the following   9._____
    types of cases should be addressed <u>first</u>?

    A. Reabuse cases, after initial report and intervention
    B. Foster care considered or indicated
    C. Chronic neglect families
    D. Mentally ill/mentally retarded parents

10. When interviewing a child who is suspected to be a victim of sexual abuse, it is impor-   10._____
    tant to remember that developmentally, after a child is able to answer questions regard-
    ing who and what happened to them, the next question to which children will be able to
    express an answer is

    A. Why did this happen?
    B. Where did this happen?
    C. For how long has this been happening?
    D. When did this happen

11. In a typical risk assessment instrument, which of the following variables would most likely   11._____
    be classified as constituting an intermediate risk?

    A. An injury that does not require medical attention
    B. A home environment in which a perpetrator has complete access to a child
    C. An injury to a child's knees
    D. A family that has recently experienced the birth of a child

12. Physical discipline by a parent is permitted in all states, provided that it is reasonable and   12.____
not excessive. The "reasonableness" standard is largely dependent on

    A. the size of the child
    B. whether the child is seriously hurt
    C. the culture in which the parent was raised
    D. the age of the child

13. In an official sense, "lack of supervision" usually refers to children _____ or younger   13.____
who are left without an adult or babysitter in attendance.

    A. 8
    B. 12
    C. 14
    D. 16

14. Among CSP workers, the inability of a child to make eye contact with an adult interviewer   14.____
is often cited as a sign of neglect. Workers should be careful when applying this to children from some cultures, however--especially those of _____ heritage.

    A. Hispanic
    B. African-American
    C. Native American
    D. Asian

15. Which of the following statements about dependency and neglect proceedings is true?   15.____

    A. The court issues interim orders for child custody and care pending resolution
    B. It can directly result in the termination of parental rights
    C. The child is represented by the parents' attorney
    D. A trial takes place immediately after a dependency or neglect action is filed

16. Most states have a(n) _____ -month time frame for reunification efforts before a petition   16.____
is filed to terminate parental rights.

    A. 6
    B. 12
    C. 18
    D. 24

17. The legal term for a person over whom a guardian is appointed to manage his or her   17.____
affairs is

    A. dependent
    B. curate
    C. ward
    D. protege

18. In cases involving out-of-home placement, a worker's planning for reunification begins   18.____

    A. coincident with the placement
    B. as soon as the parents accept the prescribed services
    C. as soon as the parents demonstrate a willingness to be reunited with the child
    D. 30 days after the placement

19. In a typical risk assessment instrument, which of the following variables would most likely   19._____
    be classified as constituting a high risk?

    A. A caretaker with a moderate mental handicap
    B. A minor unexplained injury
    C. An inconsistent display of necessary parenting skills by a caretaker
    D. A child younger than 5

20. Which of the following living arrangements is generally considered to be most restrictive?   20._____

    A. Group home
    B. Specialized foster care
    C. Supervised independent living
    D. Adoptive home

21. In cases of neglect, authorized state intervention must be based clearly on   21._____

    A. living conditions demonstrably inferior to the local standard
    B. the availability of a service or services to meet the particular needs of the child
    C. a substantial need to protect the child from specific harm by a parent
    D. reasonable suspicion

22. If a priority system is established for responding to initial reports, workers should use it   22._____
    primarily to determine

    A. the level of intervention required
    B. the relative risk to the child
    C. the parties guilty of the abuse or neglect
    D. whether a home visit is justified

23. Generally, the time a child stays in foster care may be litigated under each of the follow-   23._____
    ing, except

    A. section 1983 of the Federal Civil Rights Act
    B. the Child Abuse Prevention and Treatment Act
    C. Titles IV and XX of the Social Security Act
    D. common law principles

24. In cases involving placement, it is generally believed that a span of _____ gives most   24._____
    parents motivating time pressure to respond to interventions or court orders before the
    next court hearing.

    A. 30 days
    B. 3 months
    C. 6 months
    D. 12 months

25. An initial report, coming from a school, alleges that a child frequently comes to school   25._____
    with both burns and bruises, and recently suffered a sprained wrist. Viewing this a "prior-
    ity two" report, the worker must do each of the following, except

A. interview all other persons who may have interviewed the abuse or neglect
B. notify the State's Attorney of the existence and content of the report
C. interview each adult and child subject of the report
D. interview at least two other professional persons (school personnel, nurse, etc.) who are believed to have first-hand knowledge of the child's situation

---

KEY (CORRECT ANSWERS)

1.	C	11.	D
2.	B	12.	D
3.	A	13.	B
4.	D	14.	A
5.	D	15.	A
6.	C	16.	C
7.	A	17.	C
8.	C	18.	A
9.	C	19.	D
10.	B	20.	A

21.	C
22.	B
23.	B
24.	B
25.	B

TEST 2

DIRECTIONS: Each question or incomplete statement is followed by several suggested answers or completions. Select the one the BEST answers the question or completes the statement. *PRINT THE LETTER OF THE CORRECT ANSWER IN THE SPACE AT THE RIGHT.*

1. Examples of parental behaviors that would be classified as emotional abuse include   1.____
    I. Burning a child as a form of punishment
    II. Locking a child in a dark closet for several hours as a form of punishment
    III. Grounding a disobedient child for an extended period of several months for a relatively minor offense
    IV. Leaving a preschooler alone in the home

   A. I and II
   B. I, II and IV
   C. II and III
   D. I, II, III and IV

2. The clinical definition of "failure to thrive" refers simply to a child's failure to   2.____

   A. perform academically at grade level
   B. respond to normal nurturing behaviors
   C. gain weight adequately
   D. develop physically and socially

3. Of the following, the most likely reason for out-of-home placement is   3.____

   A. physical abuse
   B. severe general neglect
   C. sexual abuse
   D. absent or incapacitated caretaker

4. Which of the following factors is LEAST important in determining whether or not a parent   4.____
   or guardian is guilty of physical endangerment?

   A. Whether the child was injured or not
   B. The child's age
   C. The child's maturity level, subjectively assessed
   D. The danger involved in the situation

5. Most of the U.S. agencies established prior to 1980 to respond to the problems of abuse   5.____
   and neglect were based on the _____ model.

   A. Social-political
   B. Psychoanalytical
   C. Ecological
   D. Medical-legal

6. The Child Abuse Prevention and Treatment Act provides a definition of mental injury to a   6.____
   child that serves as a general guideline for states to follow if they want to receive federal
   funding for child protective services. The definition includes each of the following specifi-
   cations, <u>except</u>

A. The parent's behavior must cause or perpetuate the mental difficulty of the child
B. A connection exists between the parent's behavior and the child's mental problems
C. "Mental" refers to emotional, intellectual, or psychological functioning
D. The parent's behavior must be obvious or explicit

7. For a 12-year-old child who is sexually abused, the most likely presentation would be   7.____

    A. abdominal pain
    B. eating disturbances
    C. regressive behavior
    D. fear of falling asleep

8. According to Summit (1983), child sexual abuse accommodation syndrome includes   8.____
each of the following characteristics, <u>except</u>

    A. delayed disclosure
    B. regression
    C. secrecy
    D. helplessness

9. In making judgements about clients, which of the following would a worker typically do   9.____
<u>last</u>?

    A. Speculate about causes of a child's behavior
    B. Investigating the child's and the family's medical and social history
    C. Observing a series of different interactions
    D. Determining which factors and behaviors are related in family interactions

10. In an infant who has learned to crawl, the type of fracture that is almost certainly diag-   10.____
nostic of abuse is

    A. a comminuted fracture of the fingertip
    B. a transverse fracture of the radius
    C. a chip fracture of the cheekbone
    D. a spiral fracture of the femur

11. What is the legal term used to denote any conduct that may imply consent?   11.____

    A. Capitulation
    B. Sufferance
    C. Surrender
    D. Acquiescence

12. In most cases, the worker's first assessment of a child's risk for abuse or neglect is made   12.____

    A. when the initial report is taken
    B. after interviews with members of the household
    C. after the first home visit
    D. upon conclusion of a prescribed number of home visits

13. When the doctrine of informed consent is applied to the treatment of children, it must   13.____
include the elements of

    A. voluntariness, coincidence, and nonsolicitation
    B. selectivity, legitimacy, and documentation
    C. legitimacy, capacity, and nonsolicitation
    D. capacity, voluntariness, and relevancy

14. When a worker has insufficient knowledge about a situation or its possible conse-   14.____
quences for a child, he or she may fail to alter the ordinary course of assessment
because there is no perceived risk. This is an example of

    A. Learned helplessness
    B. Unconflicted change
    C. Defensive avoidance
    D. Unconflicted inertia

15. Which of the following features is not commonly associated with Munchausen syndrome   15.____
by proxy?

    A. Perpetrator is the father
    B. Most victims are infants and toddlers
    C. Perpetrator is in a medical-related line of work
    D. Perpetrator has a history of symptoms and signs similar to those which are simulated or produced in the child

16. An initial report alleges that a child who is three years old is inadequately cared for. View-   16.____
ing this as a "priority one" report, the worker must
     I. immediately contact the police
     II. notify the State's Attorney of the existence and content of the report
     III. interview each adult and child subject of the report
     IV. interview all other persons who may have interviewed the abuse or neglect

    A. I only
    B. I, II and III
    C. III and IV
    D. I, II, III, and IV

17. In the last two decades or so, the orientation of foster care has changed its orientation   17.____
from child welfare to

    A. family treatment
    B. alternative living arrangements
    C. crisis intervention
    D. punishment of perpetrators

18. Each of the following criteria are useful in assessing the reliability of a child's statements   18.____
regarding sexual abuse, except

    A. drawings or play with retrieval props (dolls, etc.) is consistent with the child's verbal history
    B. the association of the child's statements with an appropriate affect

C. the ability of a child to answer questions consistently, using the same words each time
D. the ability of the child to give specific details about what took place

19. In most states, the age of assent for treatment begins at 19.____

A. 7
B. 9
C. 12
D. 14

20. Which of the following cases established tort liability for professionals who fail to report suspected child abuse? 20.____

A. *Canterbury v. Spence (1972)*
B. *Landers v. Flood (1976)*
C. *Krikorian v. Barry (1987)*
D. *White v. North Carolina State Board of Examiners of Practicing Psychologists (1990)*

21. In cases of emotional abuse, the severity of the abuse is typically determined by each of the following, except 21.____

A. the willingness of the parents to cooperate and make progress in treatment
B. the nature of the child's psychopathology or disturbed behavior
C. the nature of the child's physical environment
D. the age of the child

22. Many states and localities have established a priority system for responding to initial reports of abuse or neglect. In a system based primarily on the type of allegation reported, which of the following would be given "priority one" status? 22.____

A. Sexual abuse
B. Bone fractures
C. Poisoning
D. Human bite marks

23. In an investigation of an initial report, a worker visits the home of the family and makes observations about the child, the incident described in the report, and the parents; Usually, the worker should then focus on 23.____

A. locating available community resources
B. determining the risk of future harm to the child
C. listing applicable agency policies and procedures
D. identifying family stressors

24. Generally, when a worker begins an investigation of an initial report of abuse or neglect, the first question that must be investigated is 24.____

A. How serious is the current situation?
B. What level of intervention in indicated?
C. What has actually happened to the child or children in question?
D. What is the risk of future harm to the child?

25. The family treatment model, a placement-prevention model,   25.____

    A. is generally least successful with neglectful families
    B. generally makes use of fewer concrete support services than other models
    C. provides in-home services for a period of about 90 days
    D. provides a corrective intervention

_____

KEY (CORRECT ANSWERS)

1.	A	11.	D
2.	C	12.	A
3.	B	13.	D
4.	A	14.	D
5.	D	15.	A
6.	D	16.	D
7.	D	17.	A
8.	B	18.	C
9.	A	19.	A
10.	D	20.	B

21.	C
22.	A
23.	D
24.	C
25.	A

_____

TEST 3

DIRECTIONS: Each question or incomplete statement is followed by several suggested answers or completions. Select the one the BEST answers the question or completes the statement. *PRINT THE LETTER OF THE CORRECT ANSWER IN THE SPACE AT THE RIGHT.*

1. In a hearing to decide the termination of parental rights,　　　　　　　　　　　　1.____

    A. the parents are represented by a defense attorney
    B. the applicable law is embodied in the state's criminal codes
    C. the child is represented by a guardian *ad litem*
    D. the burden of proof is evidence beyond a reasonable doubt

2. In general, courts have the authority to sever the legal relationship between a parent and child　　2.____

        I. as part of the finding of a dependency and neglect hearing
        II. as the conclusion of a termination hearing
        III. in criminal cases involving wrongs against children

    A. I only
    B. II only
    C. II and III
    D. I, II and III

3. Typically, when a case of neglect has resulted in an emergency placement, a period of　　3.____
_____ is assigned as the time period by which parents must be ready for the return of the child or children into an improved environment.

    A. 3 months
    B. 6 months
    C. 1 year
    D. 2 years

4. Which of the following items of information is most relevant to a dependency and neglect　　4.____
hearing?

    A. Other children in home and their probable safety
    B. Comparison of parents
    C. Recommendation regarding custody
    D. Information regarding alleged perpetrator(s)

5. The Homebuilders model of family preservation　　　　　　　　　　　　　　5.____

    A. has been found to be most successful with children who have not suffered physical abuse
    B. is motivated primarily by the goal of correction
    C. uses long-term interventions of 90-180 days
    D. is based on social learning theory

6. Which of the following items of federal legislation provides for services aimed to reduce foster care placement?   6.____

   A. Child Abuse Prevention and Treatment Act
   B. Adoption Assistance and Child Welfare Act
   C. Uniform Reciprocal Enforcement of Support Act
   D. Omnibus Budget Reconciliation Act of 1993

7. If a child is placed under the supervision of dependency court, or in custody of the county or state, court reviews are generally mandated every   7.____

   A. 3 months
   B. 6 months
   C. 1 year
   D. 2 years

8. Of the following, the most appropriate choice for a family preservation effort would be a   8.____

   A. case involving a child older than 2 in which there is not a strong likelihood of further risk
   B. family who resists in-home services
   C. case of sexual abuse in which the perpetrator cannot be removed from access to the child victim
   D. family in which the parent is severely developmentally or psychiatrically disabled

9. As a general rule, children who have been in an emergency shelter for _____ or more should be evaluated by a mental health professional.   9.____

   A. 3 months
   B. 6 months
   C. 1 year
   D. 2 years

10. The decision to confirm a report of child abuse or neglect is likely to rely on each of the following, except   10.____

   A. the intent of the perpetrator
   B. the availability of community resources that may help reduce the risk of abuse or neglect
   C. the degree to which the worker is certain that an injury was caused by willful or negligent acts of the caretaker or perpetrator
   D. information regarding past incidents or reports

11. Accidental bruises or cuts on the _____ of a child are extremely rare, and should always be looked upon with suspicion by an investigating worker.   11.____

   A. lower extremities
   B. shoulder
   C. back
   D. neck

12. Courts generally define _____ as intentional conduct by a parent showing an intent to forgo all parental duties.   12.____

    A. acquiescence
    B. abandonment
    C. emancipation
    D. neglect

13. For a 4-year-old child who is sexually abused, the most likely presentation would be   13.____

    A. nightmares
    B. thumb-sucking
    C. eating disturbances
    D. sleeping unusually long hours

14. Which of the following is a guideline that should be followed in the oversight of parental visitations of a child who has been placed in foster care?   14.____

    A. Visitations should be irregularly spaced
    B. The caseworker should take a passive role in promoting regular contact once visitation rights have been granted
    C. In general, visitations should be monitored closely at first
    D. Recommendations for visitation should be as specific as possible regarding duration and frequency

15. In a typical risk assessment instrument, which of the following variables would most likely be classified as constituting a high risk?   15.____

    A. A recent change in marital or relationship status
    B. Water and/or electricity inoperative
    C. A child between 5 and 9 years of age
    D. Family does not belong to a church or social group

16. Which of the following elements is generally common to all family preservation programs?   16.____

    A. Staff members are not required to have a degree in social work.
    B. They focus their efforts on the symptomatic family member or members.
    C. Workers carry a small caseload at any given time.
    D. They accept families of any status, regardless of the perceived risk of placement.

17. A CPS agency is attempting to prioritize its caseload. In general, which of the following types of cases would be addressed after the others have been considered?   17.____

    A. Resistant or uncooperative parents
    B. Children with emotional/psychological disorders
    C. Recommendations of different professionals or agencies are in conflict
    D. Children with moderate to severe physical injuries

18. According to the Adoption Assistance and Child Welfare Act of 1980, a placement can be made   18.____

    A. completely at the discretion of the courts
    B. only after a worker makes a real effort to seek out alternative resources and to avoid placement
    C. only if all living relatives at the age of majority or older agree
    D. completely at the discretion of the investigating agency

19. The most frequently used protocol for interactional assessments of parents and children includes eight major areas of inquiry. Which of the following is one of these?   19.____

    A. Previous legal troubles
    B. Records from family of origin
    C. Education and work experience
    D. Feeding experiences from newborn to present

20. Which of the following is LEAST likely to be a long-term consequence of emotional mal-treatment of a child?   20.____

    A. Apathy
    B. Extreme violence
    C. Impaired physical development
    D. Anxiety and anger

21. Absent special circumstances, long-term foster care is generally considered an inappropriate plan for any child aged _____ or under.   21.____

    A. 19
    B. 12
    C. 15
    D. 18

22. When interviewing a child who is suspected to be a victim of sexual abuse, it is important to remember that younger children--children under the age of 3--are generally able to answer questions regarding   22.____

    I. who the perpetrator was
    II. where the abuse happened
    III. when the abuse happened
    IV. why the abuse happened

    A. I only
    B. I and III
    C. I, II and III
    D. I, II, III and IV

23. The length of time children remain in foster care in the United States is broadly limited under the provisions of the federal   23.____

    A. Child Abuse Prevention and Treatment Act
    B. Adoption Assistance and Child Welfare Act
    C. Uniform Reciprocal Enforcement of Support Act
    D. Omnibus Budget Reconciliation Act of 1993

24. The first home visit of a CSP worker reveals a physical environment that presents immi- 24.____
nent danger to the children of the house: there is no heat (the visit occurs in a cold winter
month); no functional plumbing; and several windows are broken. The worker should

    A. seek immediate placement for all children in the household
    B. seek immediate placement for children in the household younger than 3
    C. try to find temporary alternative housing for the entire family
    D. begin the application process for financial aid that might help fix these problems

25. Which of the following conditions is most likely to necessitate the attempt to place a child 25.____
outside of his or her home and away from parents?

    A. Child is extremely fearful of parents
    B. Unhealthy or unlivable physical environment
    C. Child exhibits seductive and sexualized behavior
    D. Failure to thrive

KEY (CORRECT ANSWERS)

1.	C	11.	D
2.	B	12.	B
3.	B	13.	B
4.	A	14.	D
5.	D	15.	A
6.	D	16.	C
7.	B	17.	C
8.	A	18.	B
9.	A	19.	D
10.	B	20.	B

21.	C
22.	A
23.	B
24.	C
25.	A

EXAMINATION SECTION
TEST 1

DIRECTIONS: Each question or incomplete statement is followed by several suggested answers or completions. Select the one that BEST answers the question or completes the statement. *PRINT THE LETTER OF THE CORRECT ANSWER IN THE SPACE AT THE RIGHT.*

1. According to the United States Centers for Disease Control and Prevention (CDC), the neglect of children is generally about _____ as common as physical abuse and _____ as common as sexual abuse.

    A.   one-fourth; half
    B.   twice; twice
    C.   three times; six times
    D.   ten times; twenty times

1.____

2. Which of the following is LEAST likely to be observed in a child with post-traumatic stress disorder?

    A.   Increased physical arousal
    B.   Diminished interest in home and school environments
    C.   Aggression
    D.   Exaggerated startle response

2.____

3. The most common weapons in physical child abuse cases are

    A.   belts or cords
    B.   paddles, spoons, or similar implements
    C.   knives or other cutting instruments
    D.   hands and fists

3.____

4. Informing a caretaker or family members that Child Protective Services has been notified in a case of suspected child maltreatment is

    A.   required by law in all cases of child maltreatment
    B.   required by law only in cases in which the caretakers or family members are implicated
    C.   not usually required by law, but it recommended in all cases of child maltreatment
    D.   not usually required by law and is not recommended

4.____

5. Of the following, children are most likely to be abused or neglected by

    A.   day care staff
    B.   their natural parents
    C.   a mother's boyfriend
    D.   foster parents

5.____

6. Key characteristics of Munchausen-by-proxy syndrome (MBPS) include
      I.   involves the presentation of a child for frequent medical care and evaluation
    II.   a need for the parent or caretaker to assume the "patient" role through the child

6.____

III. a child illness that is intentionally induced, simulated, or exag gerated
IV. short-term symptoms that stop when the caretaker isn't around

A. I and II
B. II and III
C. II and IV
D. I, II, III and IV

7. In cases of child sexual abuse, the collection of forensic evidence via rape kit may be indicated if the child presents within _____ hours of the last sexual contact with the perpetrator, and if a belief exists that the perpetrator may have left evidence on the child's body.

7._____

A. 24
B. 48
C. 72
D. 96

8. Children who are neglected tend to have peer relationships marked by

8._____

A. dependence and "clinginess"
B. overinvestment in relationships
C. avoidance and withdrawal
D. anger and aggression

9. The average age of a child sexual abuser in the incident of a first attack is

9._____

A. in their teens
B. in their early 20s
C. between 25 and 45
D. between 46 and 65

10. Dissociation is a psychological defense mechanism that serves as an adaptive mechanism in abusive situations. However, if left unchecked, it may develop into

10._____

A. borderline personality disorder
B. schizophrenia
C. bipolar disorder
D. post-traumatic stress disorder

11. During a physical examination, a child spontaneously discloses that she was abused. Ideally, the medical record should clearly document

11._____

I. the exact words spoken by the child, recorded in quotation marks
II. what question or activity prompted the disclosure
III. who was present when the child disclosed the information
IV. any prior suspicions held by the health care professional about the possibility of abuse

A. I only
B. I and III
C. I, II and III
D. I, II, III and IV

12. Of the following, which environmental or historical factor tends to involve the LOWEST risk for child abuse?

    A. Foster care
    B. Ethnic minority status
    C. Developmental disabilities
    D. Premature infant

12.____

13. The differential diagnosis for child sexual abuse involves 4 key physical findings. Which of the following is NOT one of these findings?

    A. Vaginal discharge
    B. Genital bleeding
    C. Anogenital redness
    D. Abdominal bruising

13.____

14. Of the following types of burns, the one MOST likely to be regarded suspicious for an inflicted injury is a burn

    A. caused by chemicals
    B. on the back of the hand
    C. that covers the entire foot and stops at a distinct line above the ankle (a "stocking" burn)
    D. with an irregular, splattered pattern

14.____

15. Many states and localities have established a priority system for responding to initial reports of abuse or neglect. Of the following, the child most likely receive a "Priority Two" designation by CPS, as dangerous and perhaps requiring emergency services would be one

    A. who has been sexually abused and is in danger of being abused again.
    B. with internal injuries
    C. with a sprain or dislocation
    D. who is malnourished or failing to thrive

15.____

16. When a child tells an adult that they have been abused or molested, the most appropriate first response is to

    A. clearly register your disapproval of the abuser's behavior
    B. press the child to reveal as many specifics as possible in order to gather evidence
    C. let the child know that you believe and trust them
    D. approach it matter-of-factly, as if it is no great crisis

16.____

17. Because child abuse and neglect frequently occur in concert with other forms of family violence, reportable incidents to Child Protective Services typically include violence
    I. by the father against the mother
    II. between two or more siblings other than the reporting child
    III. by the mother against the father
    IV. by one sibling against the reporting child

    A. I only
    B. I and III
    C. I, II, III and IV
    D. None of the above

17.____

18. The Muram diagnostic categorization system offers insight into how a variety of prepu-   18._____
    bertal genital examinations may assist in the diagnosis of child sexual abuse. In the
    Muram system, "Category I" refers to

    A. strongly suggestive findings that have a high likelihood of being caused by sexual
       abuse
    B. nonspecific findings that are minimally suggestive of sexual abuse but also may be
       caused by other etiologies
    C. genitalia with no observable abnormalities
    D. definitive findings that have no possible cause other then sexual contact

19. The clinical definition of "failure to thrive" refers to a child's failure to   19._____

    A. fit in socially with peers
    B. achieve important milestones for mental and social development
    C. respond to normal nurturing behaviors
    D. gain weight

20. Which of the following types of head injuries in a child is most likely to be the result of a   20._____
    fall, rather than an inflicted injury?

    A. Subdural hematoma
    B. Skull fracture
    C. Epidural hematoma
    D. Subarachnoid hemorrhage

21. In which of the following situations would a nurse NOT be mandated to file a report of   21._____
    suspected abuse?

    A. Hearing a parent or caretaker state from personal knowledge that the child has
       been abused
    B. As supervisor, being notified by a staff member who suspects abuse and ultimately
       agreeing with the suspicion
    C. Seeing the same patient in the emergency room several times in a span of several
       weeks
    D. Having reasonable cause to suspect that a child is abused

22. When communicating with a suspected child victim, it is important for the health care   22._____
    professional to remember that
        I.   "old" and "young" classifications are not recommended in conversations with
             child victims
        II. children usually don't care about the impression they make on adults
        III. young children tend to repeat the end of a prior sentence if they are unsure
             of an answer
        IV. the use of pronouns is often confusing to children

    A. I only
    B. I, III, and IV
    C. II and III
    D. All of the above

23. Preparation of the child and family should be a part of every examination for sexual abuse, and the discussion may generally include each of the following, EXCEPT   23._____

    A. the health care professional's opinion about the likely cause of such injuries
    B. the fact that almost all prepubertal children do not need a speculum or internal examination
    C. the need for photographs for legal documentation
    D. an explanation of why an external examination of the genitalia is necessary

24. Which of the following is LEAST likely to be a behavioral presentment of a child who suffers from abuse or neglect?   24._____

    A. Generalized anxiety
    B. Extreme aggression
    C. Withdrawal and timidity
    D. Intellectual precociousness or arrogance

25. When determining whether a child is suspicious for maltreatment, it is important to consider   25._____

    I.   evidence of other past injuries
    II. the child's developmental level
    III. the parent's or caretaker's explanation
    IV. the nature of the injury

    A. I and III
    B. I and IV
    C. I, III and IV
    D. I, II, III and IV

KEY (CORRECT ANSWERS)

1.	C		11.	C
2.	C		12.	B
3.	D		13.	D
4.	C		14.	C
5.	B		15.	C
6.	D		16.	C
7.	C		17.	C
8.	C		18.	C
9.	A		19.	D
10.	A		20.	C

21.	C
22.	B
23.	A
24.	D
25.	D

TEST 2

DIRECTIONS: Each question or incomplete statement is followed by several suggested answers or completions. Select the one that BEST answers the question or completes the statement. *PRINT THE LETTER OF THE CORRECT ANSWER IN THE SPACE AT THE RIGHT.*

1. The most frequent result of child maltreatment in the victim is

    A. low self-esteem
    B. phobias
    C. post-traumatic stress disorder
    D. attention deficit disorder

1.____

2. Shaken-baby syndrome may typically present with several symptoms. Which of the following is LEAST likely to be one of these symptoms?

    A. Retinal hemorrhage
    B. Fractures of posterior or anterolateral ribs
    C. Diffuse axonal injury
    D. Oral lacerations

2.____

3. Boys are more likely to be sexually abused by:

    A. siblings
    B. their mothers
    C. their fathers
    D. male non-family members

3.____

4. Of the following behaviors, which is most likely to be an indicator of possible child neglect?

    A. Obsessive behaviors
    B. Offering food from home to friends at school
    C. Enjoying school more than other classmates
    D. Wearing clothing inappropriate for existing weather conditions

4.____

5. Which of the following is LEAST likely to be a medical sequela of child sexual abuse?

    A. neurologic conditions
    B. cardiovascular disorders
    C. functional gastrointestinal disorders
    D. STDs

5.____

6. Bruising or other skin manifestations of child abuse
    I. are always very conspicuous and strongly suggest physical abuse
    II. often are clearly hand-shaped in cases of spanking or swatting
    III. should be investigated if they leave marks that are unusual or have the shape of a specific object
    IV. should be considered suspicious if they are vertical marks that appear on the child's back

    A. I and II
    B. II, III and IV

6.____

C. II and IV
D. I, II, III and IV

7. During a physical examination, a 5-year-old child makes a statement that strongly sug-   7.____
gests he was sexually abused. As the health care professional, you are taught in such
situations to ask questions that are focused but not leading. The best example of this
type of question is

A. Did he touch you with his fingers?
B. Did he really touch you?
C. Did his touching make you uncomfortable?
D. What did he touch you with?

8. Child Protective Services is usually compelled to take a case to court when   8.____

A. the mandated reporter believes that the parent or caretaker poses an immediate
threat to the child
B. a parent or caretaker is older than 21 years of age
C. parents or caretakers refuse services or are uncooperative
D. the abuse is a repeat occurrence

9. Which of the following statements about child abuse is TRUE?   9.____

A. Boys are slightly more likely to be sexually abused than girls.
B. Girls are more likely to be abused by women within the family.
C. Boys are more likely to be killed or seriously injured as a result of abuse.
D. Boys are more likely to be physically abused by males outside the family.

10. Apathy-futility syndrome is a disorder that is   10.____
    I. seen among children who are chronically neglected
    II. often indicated by children who are very attached to their par ents, but inhib-
        ited in their emotional responses
    III. often indicated by a total lack of normal separation response when separated
         from caretakers

A. I and II
B. II only
C. I and III
D. I, II and III

11. Physical findings in sexually abused prepubertal girls may include bleeding and lacera-   11.____
tions of the genital area. Though most such findings are inconclusive for abuse, which of
the following would most strongly suggest sexual abuse in a prepubertal girl?

A. A healed transection of the hymen
B. A fresh laceration of the hymen without a history of accidental trauma
C. A fimbnated hymen
D. A labial hymen

12. Which of the following is NOT a criterion that should be used in assessing the reliability   12.____
of a child's statements regarding sexual abuse?

A. The child's ability to answer questions consistently and in the same words
B. The child's ability to give specific details about what happened

C. The association of the child's statements with an appropriate affect or facial expression

D. Drawings or enactments with props consistent with the child's verbal history

13. Admission laboratory tests for a child in which the health care professional suspects Munchausen-by-proxy syndrome (MBPS) should always include a(n)   13.____

A. complete toxicology screen
B. MRI or PET scan
C. rape kit examination
D. urine culture

14. In diagnosing suspected child sexual abuse, a colposcope can be used to _____ the genital area.   14.____
    I. magnify
    II. light
    III. photograph
    IV. examine the recessed portions of

A. I and II
B. I, II and III
C. II and III
D. I, II, III and IV

15. Which of the following is LEAST likely to be a characteristic of a parent or caretaker who is at risk for perpetrating child abuse?   15.____

A. Close association with one or more abusers
B. Poor impulse control
C. Unmet emotional needs
D. Isolation

16. Which of the following is included in the definition of "child sexual abuse?"   16.____
    I. Penetrative sex
    II. Fondling
    III. Sexualized kissing
    IV. Exposing oneself or masturbating in front of the child

A. I only
B. I and II
C. I, II and IV
D. I, II, III and IV

17. In most states, the legal standard for neglect applies when a parent or caretaker's failure to provide care is due to any of the following, EXCEPT   17.____

A. antisocial personality disorder
B. cruelty
C. mental incapacity
D. financial inability

18. Which of the following is LEAST likely to be the site of an inflicted bruise?   18.____

    A. Genitals
    B. Forehead
    C. Upper back
    D. Buttocks

19. Of the reported sexual assaults on children in the United States, about _____ percent   19.____
are committed by perpetrators who were previously known to the victim.

    A. 30
    B. 50
    C. 70
    D. 90

20. When abuse is likely or strongly suspected by a health care professional, the medical   20.____
history
      I.   may be coordinated with a forensic interview by representatives from Child
          Protective Services and law en forcement
      II. should be confrontational
      III. should focus on questions that are clearly related to law en forcement
      IV. should allow the health care professional a chance to share an opinion with
          the child's caretakers about the believed etiology of the child's injury or condi-
          tion

    A. I only
    B. I or II
    C. III or IV
    D. I, II, III or IV

21. According to the U.S. Department of Health and Human Services, a child from a single-   21.____
parent family is about _____ likely to be abused or neglected than those from two-par-
ent families.

    A. 87 percent more
    B. 36 percent more
    C. 55 percent less
    D. 12 percent less

22. The Muram diagnostic categorization system offers insight into how a variety of prepu-   22.____
bertal genital examinations may assist in the diagnosis of child sexual abuse. In the
Muram system, a finding of a transected hymen would be classified as a Category
_____ finding.

    A. I
    B. II
    C. III
    D. IV

23. In infants and toddlers, signs of possible child neglect may include each of the following,   23.____
EXCEPT

    A. poor self-discipline
    B. growth failure

C. behavioral abnormalities
D. delayed gross motor development

24. Of the following, a victim of child abuse is MOST likely to be 24._____

    A. needy and demanding
    B. cold and withdrawn
    C. talkative and outgoing
    D. passive and compliant

25. Typically, "child neglect" could be legally substantiated in cases in which a parent or car- 25._____
egiver
    I. fails to provide adequate clothing for a dependent child
    II. does not provide shelter for a child
    III. used physical punishment on a child
    IV. does not compel a child to attend school

    A. I only
    B. I, II or IV
    C. II or III
    D. I, II, III or IV

KEY (CORRECT ANSWERS)

1.	A		11.	B
2.	D		12.	A
3.	D		13.	A
4.	D		14.	B
5.	B		15.	A
6.	B		16.	D
7.	D		17.	D
8.	C		18.	B
9.	C		19.	D
10.	C		20.	A

21.	A
22.	B
23.	A
24.	A
25.	B

TEST 3

DIRECTIONS: Each question or incomplete statement is followed by several suggested answers or completions. Select the one that BEST answers the question or completes the statement. *PRINT THE LETTER OF THE CORRECT ANSWER IN THE SPACE AT THE RIGHT.*

1. Abnormal physical findings that are suspicious for sexual abuse   1._____

    A. are most often caused by something else
    B. are rare
    C. include a crescent-shaped hymen in prepubertal girls
    D. are visible in about half the cases

2. Physical warning signs of child emotional abuse include   2._____

    A. below-average weight
    B. speech disorders
    C. unexplained bruises
    D. hypersexualized play

3. The role of law enforcement in child abuse investigations is to   3._____

    A. evaluate the credibility of the reporter
    B. determine whether a crime has been committed
    C. determine placement of the child
    D. prosecute abusers

4. Which of the following is a frequent contributing factor to child abuse?   4._____

    A. History of family violence
    B. Spousal encouragement
    C. Overworked parents
    D. Academic underperformance

5. In making a report of suspected child abuse, a nurse or other health care practitioner should   5._____

    A. avoid mentioning the identity of the suspected perpetrator
    B. make his or her best guess as to the identity of the perpetrator
    C. document the suspected perpetrator, if known, for the purposes of ensuring the safety of the child
    D. document the suspected perpetrator, if known, and provide detailed information substantiating his or her suspicions

6. Children who are suspected of being sexually abused may need an examination emergently, urgently, or electively scheduled for a later time with their own physician. Emergent examinations should be conducted for a child   6._____
    I. in severe emotional or psychological crisis
    II. with a history of sexual contact within 96 hours of presentation
    III. with acute bleeding or injury
    IV. who may be pregnant

A.   I and II
B.   I, II, and III
C.   II and III
D.   I, II, III and IV

7.   Of the following, which is LEAST likely to be a behavioral sign exhibited by an abused or   7._____
     neglected child?

A.   Self-loathing
B.   Sexual precocity
C.   Immaturity
D.   Overfamiliarity with strangers

8.   Excessive bruising may be a sign of multiple inflicted injuries, or it may be a sign of an   8._____
     underlying medical condition. Which of the following medical conditions is LEAST likely
     to present with this symptom?

A.   Keratosis pilaris
B.   Thrombocytopenia
C.   Leukemia
D.   Hemophilia

9.   If a child has been taken into protective custody, which of the following typically occurs?   9._____

A.   Efforts are made to inform the parent/caretaker about the child's location along
     with written notice.
B.   The child is taken to family court within 24 hours for disposition to a foster home
C.   The alleged abuser is taken into immediate police custody
D.   The parent or caretaker is informed that they may not visit the child under any cir-
     cumstances

10. Of the following, which is LEAST likely to be a long-term consequence of emotional mal-   10._____
     treatment of a child?

A.   Anxiety and anger
B.   Apathy/lethargy
C.   Impaired physical development
D.   Extreme violence

11. Most of the morbidity associated with sexual abuse is related to   11._____

A.   emotional and psychological trauma
B.   perforated and torn tissues
C.   sexually transmitted diseases (STDs)
D.   bruising

12. Which of the following is LEAST likely to be the reason why a child who has been sexu-   12._____
     ally abused is reluctant to tell others about the incident?

A.   The child was a willing participant in the activity
B.   The child does not understand what happened.
C.   The child is afraid that the person involved will withdraw and break up the family
D.   The child is too young to be able to verbalize what happened.

13. Which of the following is LEAST characteristic of parents who maltreat their children?   13.____

    A.   Mental or physical disability
    B.   Lack of familiarity with developmentally appropriate expectations for children
    C.   Difficulty in processing information
    D.   Lack of familiarity with parenting role

14. Overall, about _____ percent of the injuries to the back of a child's body turn out to be   14.____
child abuse.

    A.   10
    B.   30
    C.   50
    D.   70

15. In the anogenital examination of a child suspicious for sexual abuse, it is important for the   15.____
health care professional to

    A.   note the child's emotional status
    B.   begin by visualizing the more recessed genital structures
    C.   end with a general observation and inspection
    D.   begin by noting the presence and character of pubic hair

16. Which of the following warning signs of physical abuse is LEAST common?   16.____

    A.   Problems in school
    B.   Unexplained burns, cuts, bruises or welts.
    C.   Bite marks
    D.   Fear of adults

17. Among children of all ages, approximately _____ percent of bone fractures are inflicted.   17.____

    A.   10
    B.   30
    C.   50
    D.   70

18. In the United States, many helping professionals consider the reluctance of a child to   18.____
make eye contact with an adult to be a sign of possible child neglect. Any professional
who interviews a child generally should be more cautious about applying this criterion to
children who are of _____ cultural heritage.
       I.   African American
      II.   Latino
     III.   Native American
     IV.   Asian

    A.   I and II
    B.   I, II and IV
    C.   II and III
    D.   I, II, III and IV

19. In incidents of child sexual abuse, the most valuable component of the medical evalua-   19.____
tion is usually the

    A. physical examination
    B. laboratory results
    C. interview with the child
    D. interview with the caretaker(s)

20. Which of the following is a disease that causes multiple fractures and whose symptoms   20.____
may be mistaken for child abuse?

    A. Osteogenesis imperfecta
    B. Klippel-Feil syndrome
    C. Osteomyelitis
    D. Juvenile rheumatoid arthritis

21. Statistically, most abusers involved in Munchausen-by-proxy syndrome (MBPS) are   21.____

    A. fathers
    B. mothers
    C. caretakers outside the family
    D. step-parents

22. Acute findings attributable to recent sexual abuse may include each of the following,   22.____
EXCEPT

    A. scars on genital skin and mucous membranes
    B. friability
    C. subtle erythema (inflammation)
    D. bleeding

23. Health care providers may wonder, in cases that involve custody disputes, whether an   23.____
allegation of sexual abuse by one parent or caretaker against another may warrant the
same degree of comprehensive evaluation. A study conducted and reported in the journal Pediatrics in 1988, it was found that in cases of custody disputes, allegations of sexual abuse were substantiated _____ percent of the time.

    A. 3
    B. 33
    C. 50
    D. 67

24. Nonaccidental hot water immersion burns typically   24.____
      I. are bilateral
     II. are symmetrical
    III. have well-demarcated lines
    IV. have splash marks or speckling patterns

    A. I and II
    B. I, II and III
    C. II and III
    D. IV only

25. A child is admitted to the emergency department after suffering a sudden trauma.   25.____
    Regarding the physiological response to trauma, a child who _____ in the period soon
    after the trauma is more likely to develop post-traumatic stress disorder.

    A. bleeds profusely
    B. suffers digestive problems
    C. is unconscious
    D. has an elevated heart rate

─────────

KEY (CORRECT ANSWERS)

1.	B	11.	A
2.	B	12.	A
3.	B	13.	A
4.	A	14.	D
5.	C	15.	A
6.	B	16.	C
7.	D	17.	B
8.	A	18.	C
9.	A	19.	C
10.	D	20.	A

21.	B
22.	A
23.	D
24.	B
25.	D

─────────

EXAMINATION SECTION
TEST 1

DIRECTIONS: Each question or incomplete statement is followed by several suggested answers or completions. Select the one that BEST answers the question or completes the statement. *PRINT THE LETTER OF THE CORRECT ANSWER IN THE SPACE AT THE RIGHT.*

1. Of the following clinical situations, which is MOST suspicious of child abuse on the basis of physical signs and patient history?

    A. A 6-month old with many facial scratches that go in different directions.
    B. A year-old Native American child with a livid, irregularly shaped spot on her lower back. The parents say the mark has been there since birth.
    C. A 2-month old who is constantly crying and passing gas. Her mother says the baby will not nurse.
    D. A 4-month old infant with several bruises on his back. The child's mother says he is always crying.

1.____

2. In terms of child abuse, "tertiary prevention" is

    I. targeted to families that have confirmed or unconfirmed reports of child abuse and neglect
    II. is considered to be the same as treatment by most prevention advocates
    III. targeted to the community at large
    IV. targeted to families that have one or more risk factors

    A. I and II
    B. II only
    C. III only
    D. I, II, III or IV

2.____

3. A nurse is taking a history for a child with pediatric growth failure and malnutrition. For the purpose of evaluating whether child neglect ought to be suspected, the most important part of the history will be the

    A. environmental and psychosocial history
    B. medical-based history
    C. growth and developmental progress
    D. feeding and nutritional history

3.____

4. The health care evaluation of suspected child physical or sexual abuse includes each of the following, EXCEPT a

    A. physical examination
    B. laboratory assessment
    C. history
    D. forensic interview

4.____

5. Among children who are younger than 1 year of age, about _____ percent of fractures are likely to have been inflicted by someone else.

    A. 10   B. 25   C. 50   D. 75

5.____

6. The minimum circumstance required to invoke the mandatory reporting requirements of the Child Abuse Prevention and Treatment Act (CAPTA) as reauthorized by the Keeping Children and Families Safe Act of 2003, is

    6.____

    A. reasonable cause to suspect abuse
    B. suspicion of abuse that is shared by at least one other mandatory reporter
    C. clear and convincing evidence
    D. a preponderance of evidence

7. The "Primary Target Zone" for child abuse on a child's body includes the

    7.____

    I.   thighs
    II. cheeks
    III. backside of the hands
    IV. shoulders

    A. I only
    B. I and III
    C. I, II and IV
    D. I, II, III and IV

8. When burns are inflicted on a child, the most commonly used burn agent is

    8.____

    A. a cigarette
    B. household chemicals
    C. hot water
    D. a lighter or match

9. The American Academy of Pediatrics (AAP) views _____ as "suggestive," rather than "diagnostic," of child abuse.

    9.____

    A. gonorrhea
    B. HIV
    C. T. vaginalis
    D. syphilis

10. Parental behaviors that would be classified as emotional abuse include

    10.____

    I.   leaving a kindergartner alone in the home
    II. burning a child as a form of punishment
    III. locking a child in a bathroom for several hours as a form of punishment
    IV. grounding a child for several months as punishment for a relatively minor offens

    A. I only
    B. I or II
    C. II or III
    D. II, III or IV

11. In most states, a mandated reporter of child abuse is subject to civil liability   11.____
       I.   if it can be proven that he or she did not act in good faith
      II.   if the suspicion turns out to be unfounded
      III.   if the parent or caretaker is penalized
      IV.   under no circumstances

    A. I only   B. I or II   C. I, II or IV   D. IV only

12. Of the following types of burns, the one LEAST likely to be regarded suspicious for an   12.____
inflicted injury is a burn

    A. on the child's back
    B. that is in a small-area and penetrates deeply
    C. that covers the complete circumference of the hand and extends to the wrist (a "glove" burn)
    D. on the fingertip or palm of the dominant hand

13. An infant who has suffered a head injury may present with nonspecific symptoms such   13.____
as
      I.   hyperactivity
      II.   irritability
      III.   persistent, unexplained vomiting
      IV.   apnea

    A. I and II   B. II only   C. II, III and IV   D. I, II, III and IV

14. Failure to thrive is a condition that is more likely to be correlated with each of the follow-   14.____
ing, EXCEPT

    A. female children
    B. child neglect
    C. interactional failures or dysfunctions between the child and caretaker
    D. poverty

15. Of the following, the _____ of a parent or caretaker is the factor that is MOST likely to   15.____
be correlated with the occurrence of child maltreatment.

    A. sexual orientation   B. national origin
    C. annual income   D. religion

16. Children who are suspected of being sexually abused may need an examination emer-   16.____
gently, urgently, or electively scheduled for a later time with their own physician. Indications for an urgent examination include each of the following, EXCEPT

    A. the possibility of STD
    B. pregnancy, if the child is pubertal
    C. severe psychological shock
    D. vaginal discharge

51

17. The Child Abuse Prevention and Treatment Act (CAPTA), as reauthorized by the Keeping Children and Families Safe Act of 2003, provides a specific definition for   17.____

      I.   sexual abuse
      II. physical abuse
      III. neglect
      IV. emotional abuse

    A. I only
    B. I and II
    C. I, II and III
    D. I, II, III and IV

18. Characteristics common to Munchausen-by-proxy syndrome (MBPS) include each of the following, EXCEPT that the   18.____

    A. victim is an infant or toddler
    B. perpetrator is the father
    C. perpetrator has a history of symptoms and signs similar to those being simulated or produced in the child
    D. case occurs in outpatient, rather than inpatient setting

19. A health care professional is attempting to closely observe the hymen and labia minora of a young girl. This can generally be done by applying gentle _____ traction to the labia majora.   19.____

    A. medial
    B. lateral
    C. anterior
    D. posterior

20. The Childhelp National Child Abuse Hotline (1-800-4-A-CHILD) may be useful for   20.____

      I.   mandatory reporters who seek a single place to report suspect ed child abuse, without having to worry about state guidelines
      II. mandatory reporters who want advice about how to proceed with a report
      III. parents who seek crisis intervention
      IV. any professional who wants a referral for a child

    A. I or II
    B. II only
    C. III or IV
    D. I, II, III or IV

21. It was estimated in the early 21st century that child sexual abuse affects at least _____ children every year.   21.____

    A. 5,000   B. 10,000   C. 100,000   D. 1 million

22. Of the following, the child at greatest risk for becoming a victim of child abuse would be one who

    22.____

    A. is physically, emotionally, or mentally disabled
    B. remains silent when interacting with authority figures
    C. has a habit of talking back to authority figures
    D. is shy and introverted to begin with

23. Most-but certainly not all-children who are victims of abuse

    23.____

    A. refuse to talk about the situation with other adults
    B. are younger than three years of age
    C. exhibit no signs or symptoms
    D. have been abused by someone they know and trust

24. Looking at children 5 years after presentation for sexual abuse and comparing them to a similarly aged group of children who were not abused, one study found that the children who were sexually abused displayed

    24.____

    I.   increased tendency for depression
    II. lower self-esteem
    III. more disturbed behavior
    IV. increased tendency for anxiety disorder

    A. I only
    B. I and II
    C. I, II and IV
    D. I, II, III and IV

25. Which of the following is NOT a characteristic that is typically associated with the phenomenon known as child sexual abuse accommodation syndrome?

    25.____

    A. Helplessness
    B. Delay or retraction of disclosure
    C. Secrecy
    D. Regressive behavior

—————

KEY (CORRECT ANSWERS)

1.	D		11.	A
2.	A		12.	D
3.	A		13.	C
4.	D		14.	A
5.	D		15.	C
6.	A		16.	C
7.	C		17.	A
8.	C		18.	B
9.	C		19.	B
10.	C		20.	C

21.	C
22.	A
23.	D
24.	D
25.	D

TEST 2

DIRECTIONS: Each question or incomplete statement is followed by several suggested answers or completions. Select the one that BEST answers the question or completes the statement. *PRINT THE LETTER OF THE CORRECT ANSWER IN THE SPACE AT THE RIGHT.*

1. Of the following early interventional strategies, which can improve the outcome in a case of non-organic or psychosocial failure to thrive?
   I. Support groups for new mothers
   II. Education about how to recognize an infant's behavioral cues
   III. Counseling for parents who say they wanted a child of another gender
   IV. Breast-feeding/nutrition education

   A. I only
   B. I and II
   C. III only
   D. I, II, III and IV

1.____

2. While taking a medical history, a nurse may become alerted to possible warning signs regarding sexual abuse in the child's home environment. Of the following, the LEAST suspicious would be parents who

   A. know little about the child's health or have vague recollections of past medical history
   B. share intimate feelings and emotions in front of their children
   C. appear overly concerned with custody issues
   D. bicker or quarrel openly in front of the nurse

2.____

3. It would be considered "reasonable cause to suspect" abuse or maltreatment if a nurse

   A. feels it is possible that an injury was caused by neglect or nonaccidental means
   B. was told when reporting to the intake that the child's injury was most likely a case of abuse
   C. sees a case of recurrent fractures in a child
   D. has seen the child in the emergency department on several occasions

3.____

4. Physically abused children often have peer relationships characterized by

   A. withdrawal and shyness
   B. over-optimism
   C. anger and aggression
   D. over-dependence and "clinginess"

4.____

5. The risk that the sibling of a physically abused child will suffer abuse at the same time is about _____ percent.

   A. 20
   B. 40
   C. 60
   D. 80

5.____

6. When a child who is a suspected victim of physical or sexual abuse is transitioning from the intake history to the physical examination, the health care professional should

    I.   if a colposcope is used, describe it as a special camera that will not touch the child
    II.   assure the child that needles will not be used
    III. leave the room to allow the caretaker to help the child disrobe and put on a gown for the exam
    IV.   use a genital swab gently before the child is aware that one will be used

    A. I and III
    B. II, III and IV
    C. III and IV
    D. I, II, III and IV

    6._____

7. A child who is being sexually abused is more likely than others to

    I.   act out sexually explicit acts in play or depict sexual content in artwork
    II.   express that they have secrets they are unable to tell
    III. touch themselves in private parts more than normal
    IV.   use sexual words in appropriate to his or her age

    A. I and II
    B. I and IV
    C. II and III
    D. I, II, III and IV

    7._____

8. Guidelines to be considered in determining whether to hospitalize an abused child include:

    I.   It is not medically appropriate to hospitalize a child simply for the reason of guaranteeing his or her safety.
    II.   Most seriously injured children are best monitored in an inten sive care setting.
    III. Hospitalization may offer time to sort out difficult diagnostic and therapeutic decisions.
    IV.   The sole determining factor for hospitalization should be the seriousness of the child's injuries.

    A. I and II
    B. I, II and IV
    C. II and III
    D. I, II, III and IV

    8._____

9. The Muram diagnostic categorization system offers insight into how a variety of prepubertal genital examinations may assist in the diagnosis of child sexual abuse. In the Muram system, a finding of semen in the child's vagina would be classified as a Category _____ finding.

    A. I
    B. II
    C. III
    D. IV

    9._____

10. Child victims of Munchausen-by-proxy syndrome (MBPS) are usually   10.____

    A. of higher socioeconomic status
    B. from an ethnic minority
    C. boys
    D. about 3 years of age

11. Which of the following is true in most states?   11.____

    A. Child abuse cannot be reported anonymously.
    B. In nearly all cases, a person who reports child abuse cannot be sued.
    C. By law, abused children must be removed from their homes immediately.
    D. The person reported for abuse is entitled to know who made the report.

12. Common presentations for the abused, head-injured child include each of the following,   12.____
EXCEPT

    A. lethargy
    B. bradycardia
    C. irritability
    D. aphasia

13. Historical characteristics of abusive injuries include   13.____
    I. a significant an inexplicable delay in seeking treatment
    II. unexplained or vaguely explained injuries
    III. changing history
    IV. injuries incompatible with the stated history

    A. I only
    B. I, II and IV
    C. III and IV
    D. I, II, III and IV

14. For an 11-year-old child who is sexually abused, the most likely sign would be   14.____

    A. chest pains
    B. a fear of falling asleep
    C. an eating disorder
    D. regressive behaviors

15. The bruising pattern most frequently observed in cases of child abuse includes   15.____
    I. injuries on multiple edges of a child's body
    II. injuries confined to bony prominences
    III. multiple resolving injuries (i.e., those that occurred at different times and in different areas of the body)

    A. I only
    B. I and II
    C. I and III
    D. I, II and III

16. During the intake, the key to differentiating between accidental and nonaccidental injury   16.____
    lies primarily in the

    A. evidence of previous injuries
    B. appearance of bruises in unusual areas
    C. history and physical examination
    D. type of fracture

17. Health care providers are mandated reporters in all 50 states. The American Academy of   17.____
    Pediatrics recommends reporting a case of suspected sexual abuse when
    I.   the child presents with an STD
    II. the child shows more than one of the behavioral indicators of sexual abuse
    III. the child makes a clear disclosure of abusive sexual contact, with or without
         specific physical findings
    IV. physical examination findings are believed to be the result of abusive sexual
         contact

    A. I, II and III
    B. I, III and IV
    C. III and IV
    D. I, II, III and IV

18. One behavioral indicator of child abuse is a child that   18.____

    A. tends to avoid contact with adults
    B. exhibits an unusual fear of going to school
    C. exhibits unpredictable mood swings or extreme behaviors
    D. is overly critical of parents or caretakers

19. In addition to the genital area, an examination of a girl for whom sexual abuse is sus-   19.____
    pected should include the
    I.   conjunctiva
    II. oral pharynx
    III. extremities

    A. I and II
    B. II and III
    C. III only
    D. I, II and III

20. Ideally, the multidisciplinary team that handles the health care evaluation of suspected   20.____
    child physical or sexual abuse includes each of the following, EXCEPT a

    A. law enforcement officer
    B. physician
    C. social worker
    D. nurse

21. Among children who are younger than 1 year of age, about _____ percent of all serious   21.____
    intracranial injuries are caused by physical abuse.

    A. 35   B. 55   C. 75   D. 95

22. Demographic statistics suggest that incidents of child abuse and neglect 22.____

    A. occur mostly in urban areas
    B. occur mostly in rural areas
    C. occur mostly in ethnic inner-city areas
    D. are distributed among all areas and socioeconomic groups

23. Many of the acute signs of sexual abuse are likely to resemble a child's reaction to 23.____

    A. stress
    B. infection
    C. fatigue
    D. grief/mourning

24. As part of a history for an infant with pediatric growth failure and malnutrition, a nurse is 24.____
conducting a detailed history of food intake from infancy through the current period. This
part of the history should include
    I. a first-hand observation of the mother and infant during feeding
    II. the parents' or caretakers' perception of the problem
    III. a 72-hour diet diary
    IV. opinions from other family members about what might be the problem

    A. I only
    B. I, II and III
    C. II only
    D. I, II, III and IV

25. The term "emotional abuse" 25.____
    I. is not included in every state's definition of child abuse
    II. refers to the act of one person (a caretaker or parent) using his or her power
        or influence to adversely affect the mental well-being of a child
    III. may include rejection, corruption, and degradation
    IV. generally refers to a long-term situation

    A. I and II
    B. II and III
    C. II, III and IV
    D. I, II, III and IV

KEY (CORRECT ANSWERS)

1.	D	11.	B
2.	D	12.	D
3.	A	13.	D
4.	C	14.	B
5.	A	15.	C
6.	A	16.	C
7.	D	17.	B
8.	C	18.	C
9.	D	19.	B
10.	D	20.	A

21. D
22. D
23. A
24. B
25. D

———————

TEST 3

DIRECTIONS: Each question or incomplete statement is followed by several suggested answers or completions. Select the one that BEST answers the question or completes the statement. *PRINT THE LETTER OF THE CORRECT ANSWER IN THE SPACE AT THE RIGHT.*

1. Which of the following is viewed by the American Academy of Pediatrics to be "diagnostic," rather than "suggestive," of child abuse?   1._____

    A.   T. vaginalis   B.   Herpes
    C.   Condyloma acuminata   D.   Chlamydia

2. If a nurse mistrusts or doubts what he or she has observed or has been told about an injury, the nurse has   2._____

    A.   reasonable cause to suspect abuse
    B.   suspicion of abuse
    C.   testimonial evidence of abuse
    D.   documentary evidence of abuse

3. Most normal childhood injuries occur on the _____ and, by themselves, are probably not indicators of child abuse.   3._____

    A.   the backs of the arms   B.   front of the body
    C.   wrist and upper arm   D.   back of the body

4. Rapid laboratory tests, such as the rapid plasma reagin test, are generally not appropriate in the diagnosis of child sexual abuse because of their   4._____

    A.   requirement of caretaker consent
    B.   higher potential for false positives
    C.   higher potential for causing infection
    D.   inherent invasiveness

5. An accidental fall is LEAST likely to cause a bruise on the   5._____

    A.   cheekbone   B.   elbow
    C.   soft tissue of the cheek   D.   forehead

6. The best way for health professionals to improve the outcomes in child abuse cases is to   6._____

    A.   focus their diagnostic efforts on lower socioeconomic groups, in which most child abuse cases occur
    B.   recognize abusers as criminals from the beginning of the process, and view the problem as a law enforcement issue
    C.   participate in education and training programs that will help them to recognize child abuse
    D.   work with social service professionals to do everything possible to remove an abused child from the custody of the abuser

7. According to the American Psychiatric Association's Diagnostic and Statistical Manual of   7.____
Mental Disorders (DSM-IV), the most common conditions and symptoms that are cre-
ated or faked by parents or caretakers with Munchausen-by-proxy syndrome (MBPS)
include

    I.   diarrhea
    II. failure to thrive
    III. infections
    IV. asthma

  A. I and II
  B. I, II and III
  C. III and IV
  D. I, II, III and IV

8. Of the following, which should most clearly raise a nurse's suspicions about the possibil-   8.____
ity of child physical abuse?

  A. Inconsistent explanations about the sustained injuries
  B. Parents who are overindulgent and act as if the child can do no wrong
  C. A child who is irritable and frequently complains
  D. A child with skin abrasions all over her forearms, knees and elbows

9. As of 2007, physical discipline is permitted in all states, provided that it is reasonable and   9.____
not excessive. The standard for reasonableness is largely dependent on the

  A. child's age
  B. seriousness of the child's injury
  C. child's size
  D. culture in which the parent or caretaker was raised

10. Indicators of child emotional abuse typically include each of the following, EXCEPT   10.____

  A. fastidiousness about appearance
  B. severe anxiety
  C. avoidance of eye contact
  D. extreme dependence

11. Symptoms of abdominal trauma secondary to perforation, obstruction, or bleeding   11.____
include

    I.   sepsis
    II. vomiting
    III. pain
    IV. shock

  A. I and II
  B. I, III and IV
  C. II and III
  D. I, II, III and IV

12. Which of the following environmental variables generally constitutes the highest risk potential for child maltreatment?   12.____

    A. A child who is between 5 and 9 years of age
    B. A denial of water or electricity services to the home
    C. The family does not belong to a church or social group
    D. Recent changes in parental/caregiver marriage or relationship status

13. A child's reaction to physical or sexual abuse is influenced by   13.____
    I. their cognitive ability
    II. their treatment by medical personnel
    III. their social and family support system
    IV. how Child Protective Services handles the case

    A. I and III
    B. II and III
    C. II, III and IV
    D. I, II, III and IV

14. Which of the following warning signs for emotional abuse is LEAST common?   14.____

    A. Hostility
    B. Apathy
    C. Lack of concentration
    D. Depression

15. When a health care professional suspects child sexual abuse, the medical history should include questions regarding possible behavioral indicators of abuse. These typically include   15.____
    I. self-destructive behaviors such as drug abuse
    II. sexualized behavior inappropriate for the child's developmental level
    III. any abrupt behavioral changes
    IV. unreasonably high self-esteem

    A. I or II
    B. I, II and III
    C. II and IV
    D. I, II, III and IV3

16. Multiple bruises at various stages of healing can be associated with repetitive inflicted injuries in children, but are also symptomatic of   16.____

    A. achondroplasia
    B. melanoma
    C. eczema
    D. coagulopathy

17. Which of the following statements regarding environmental risk factors for abuse is TRUE?   17.____

    A. Children of single parents are at greater risk of abuse
    B. The risk for abuse is not affected by yearly household income
    C. Children from urban areas are at a greater risk of abuse
    D. Child abuse is most common among African American families

18. Children from _____ families are at significantly greater risk for both physical abuse and   18.____
    neglect.
        I.   poor
       II. single-parent
      III. large
      IV. racially mixed

    A. I and II
    B. I, II and III
    C. II, III and IV
    D. I, II, III and IV

19. Fractures that are "highly specific" for inflicted injury include each of the following,   19.____
    EXCEPT _____ fractures.

    A. posterior rib
    B. metaphyseal or "bucket handle"
    C. scapular
    D. ulnar

20. Children who allegedly have been exposed to HIV-positive perpetrators must begin HIV   20.____
    postexposure prophylaxis within _____ of exposure.

    A. 12 hours
    B. 36 hours
    C. 7-10 days
    D. 15-30 days

21. If called to court in a case of alleged child abuse, a nurse should generally adhere to   21.____
    each of the following guidelines, EXCEPT

    A. Be sure to check with the CPS caseworker or attorney to see if there will be a brief-
        ing before the court appearance
    B. Offer as many opinions as the court and the defense attorney will allow on the
        record.
    C. Speak slowly and offer concise answers.
    D. If you do not know the answer, don't guess; simply say you don't know.

22. Each of the following behaviors on the part of parents or caretakers is likely to be viewed   22.____
    suspiciously as suggestive of child abuse or molestation, EXCEPT

    A. insistence on personally driving/escorting the child to and from school
    B. constant attempts to be alone with the child
    C. the persistent habit of buying gifts for the child, for no apparent reason
    D. a pattern of wanting or attempting to take the child places

23. When a nurse makes a report to Child Protective Services, it is most important for the   23.____
    nurse to remember that in his role as a mandatory reporter,

    A. he has likely made the decision to bring criminal charges upon the child's caretaker
    B. the burden of proof is on him
    C. CPS has total responsibility for investigating and proving whether child maltreat-
        ment has occurred
    D. his name may be made available to the people he suspects of maltreatment

24. If child sexual abuse is suspected, general guidelines for the taking of the child's history include   24.____
    I.   formulating the interview in a way that allows the child to view it as a healing process in which they are able to gain some con trol over the situation
    II.   encouraging the child to use the medical term for all body parts, in order to make the details seem more clinical and less personal
    III. relying on non-leading questions as much as possible
    IV. asking direct questions and completing the interview in as brief a time as possible

    A. I only
    B. I and III
    C. I, II and III
    D. I, II, III and IV

25. In most states, mandatory reporters who failed to report child maltreatment   25.____
    I.   can be found guilty of a misdemeanor
    II.   can be found guilty of a felony
    III. can be held liable for civil damages for any subsequent injury to the child

    A. I and III
    B. II and III
    C. III only
    D. I, II and III

KEY (CORRECT ANSWERS)

1.	D		11.	D
2.	B		12.	D
3.	B		13.	D
4.	B		14.	A
5.	C		15.	B
6.	C		16.	D
7.	D		17.	A
8.	A		18.	B
9.	B		19.	D
10.	A		20.	B

21.	B
22.	A
23.	C
24.	B
25.	A

EXAMINATION SECTION
TEST 1

DIRECTIONS: Each question or incomplete statement is followed by several suggested
answers or completions. Select the one that BEST answers the question or
completes the statement. *PRINT THE LETTER OF THE CORRECT ANSWER
IN THE SPACE AT THE RIGHT.*

1. Child risk factors for abuse and neglect include   1._____
     I.   behavior problems
     II.   attention deficits
     III. internal locus of control
     IV.   anti-social peer group

     A.   I only
     B.   I, II and IV
     C.   II and III
     D.   I, II, III and IV

2. Bums account for about _____ percent of all cases of child physical abuse.   2._____

     A.   3-5
     B.   10-20
     C.   30-40
     D.   50-60

3. General somatic complaints that are often associated with child sexual abuse include   3._____
     each of the following, EXCEPT

     A.   encopresis
     B.   tinnitus
     C.   headaches
     D.   abdominal pain

4. Depending on their age at the time of maltreatment, children who are maltreated gener-   4._____
     ally have

     A.   a decreased ability to achieve important developmental milestones
     B.   hypochondriasis
     C.   a larger social network in adulthood because of the perceived need for stronger,
          stable relationships
     D.   average IQ scores

5. Excluding environmental and adult factors, the only child characteristic that has been   5._____
     associated with a higher risk of sexual abuse is

     A.   temperament
     B.   gender
     C.   conduct problems
     D.   age

6. A health care professional suspects that a child's injuries were caused by abuse. During   6.____
a medical history, if the health care professional offers an opinion about the etiology of
the child's injuries to the caretakers, the encounter could
     I.   serve as a warning to the caretakers to be more cautious in their handling
         of the child
     II.   cause unnecessary family distress in cases where the etiology ultimately is
         other than abuse
     III.   impede later law enforcement interrogation
     IV.   expose the health care professional to civil liability if the etiology is other
         than abuse

     A. I only   C. II or III
     B. I or IV   D. I, II, III or IV

7. Several studies suggest that among U.S. children who are abused and maltreated, about   7.____
percent exhibit symptoms of reactive attachment disorder.

     A. 10 to 30   C. 50 to 80
     B. 25 to 40   D. 75 to 95

8. Which of the following is LEAST likely to be a characteristic of an abusive parent or   8.____
household?

     A. A large number of children in a relatively confined space
     B. Emotional withdrawal from spouse and children
     C. Disorganized household
     D. Marital problems 3.

9. Most cases of suspected or substantiated sexual abuse of prepubertal girls have physical   9.____
examination findings that are

     A. normal
     B. in the anal area
     C. in the vaginal area
     D. distributed among several locations

10. Chronic findings attributable to ongoing sexual abuse may include each of the following,   10.____
EXCEPT

     A. open lacerations
     B. disrupted vascular patterns in translucent tissues
     C. remodeled hymenal tissue
     D. scarred mucous membranes

11. In cases of physical abuse, the most commonly encountered hand marks left on a child are   11.____

     A. grab marks: oval-shaped bruises resembling fingerprints
     B. pinch marks: two symmetrical crescent-shaped bruises
     C. linear marks: parallel bruises marking the edges of the fingers
     D. hand prints

12. Of the following child behaviors, which is most likely to be an indicator of possible physi-   12.____
cal abuse?

    A. Avoiding or withdrawing from physical contact
    B. Wearing lighter clothing than is appropriate for existing conditions
    C. Frequent hugging of other children
    D. Appearing anxious to return home after school

13. Of the following types of fractures, the one most strongly suggestive of physical abuse in   13.____
an infant who has learned to crawl would be a

    A. spiral fracture of the femur
    B. comminuted fracture of the fingertip
    C. chip fracture of the cheekbone
    D. transverse fracture of the ulna

14. If child sexual abuse is suspected, general guidelines for the medical intake include   14.____

    I. interviewing the child first
    II. interviewing the child and the caretaker(s) together before they are interviewed
       separately
    III. allowing the caretaker to join the child for the physical examination
    IV. to the extent possible, documenting specific quotes the child makes about
       how any injuries or conditions were caused
    A. I only
    B. I, II and IV
    C. III and IV
    D. I, II, III and IV

15. The examination position most often used for boys when diagnosing sexual abuse is the   15.____

    A. left lateral decubitus
    B. prone
    C. frog-leg supine
    D. knee-chest

16. Generally, about percent of child neglect cases involve parental/caretaker drug   16.___
or alcohol abuse.

    A. 10-30
    B. 30-50
    C. 50-70
    D. 70-80

17. Perpetrators of Munchausen-by-proxy syndrome (MB PS) are MOST likely to have a   17.____
background in

    A. law enforcement
    B. health care
    C. education
    D. child care

18. When a nonaccidental injury is caused by someone other than the child's parent or legal guardian, the health care professional should

    A. contact law enforcement, but not report to CPS
    B. contact law enforcement and report to CPS
    C. file a report to CPS, but leave law enforcement out of it
    D. leave the decision about contacting law enforcement or CPS up to the parent or legal guardian

18.____

19. Which of the following is a symptom of disinhibited reactive attachment disorder?

    A. excessive familiarity with unknown persons
    B. underdeveloped motor coordination
    C. an apparent lack of familiarity with normal body language
    D. avoidance of eye contact

19.____

20. What is the leading cause of death in abused children?

    A. Burns
    B. Blunt trauma
    C. Head trauma
    D. Blood loss

20.____

21. A child has disclosed the incidence of physical abuse to a nurse. The nurse should generally

    A. express a strongly negative opinion of the perpetrator
    B. express shock
    C. promise confidentiality
    D. reassure the child that he or she has done the right thing in reporting

21.____

22. In the year 2000, child abuse fatalities occurred at the rate of _____ in. the United States.

    A. 40 per day
    B. 4 per day
    C. 5 per week
    D. 50 per month

22.____

23. According to the U.S. Department of Health and Human Services, approximately _____ percent of young adults who have been abused will meet the diagnostic criteria for at least one psychiatric disorder by the age of 21.

    A. 33
    B. 60
    C. 80
    D. 99

23.____

24. Which of the following is MOST likely to be a sign that a baby has been violently shaken?

    A. Subdural hematoma
    B. Bruising at the base of the neck
    C. Bulging fontanel
    D. A skull fracture

24.____

25. In cases of suspected child maltreatment, the role of the nurse typically includes each of 25.____
the following, EXCEPT

    A. conducting the forensic interview
    B. reporting to Child Protective Services
    C. assisting in the treatment of any medical conditions
    D. securing the safety of the child

_____

KEY (CORRECT ANSWERS)

1.	B		11.	A
2.	B		12.	A
3.	B		13.	A
4.	A		14.	C
5.	B		15.	A
6.	C		16.	D
7.	C		17.	B
8.	B		18.	A
9.	A		19.	A
10.	A		20.	C

21.	D
22.	B
23.	C
24.	A
25.	A

_____

TEST 2

DIRECTIONS: Each question or incomplete statement is followed by several suggested answers or completions. Select the one that BEST answers the question or completes the statement. *PRINT THE LETTER OF THE CORRECT ANSWER IN THE SPACE AT THE RIGHT.*

1. Which of the following is a primary prevention activity?

    A. Parenting classes that are open to the community at large
    B. Assertiveness training for at-risk children
    C. Medical screenings for children in foster care
    D. Psychological screenings for low-income parents

1.____

2. The written report to CPS or a state central registry (SCR) in cases of suspected abuse typically contains

    A. a description of the nature and the extent of the child's injuries
    B. the home phone number of the person making the report
    C. an explanation of why abuse is suspected
    D. a list of previous incidents

2.____

3. Of the U.S. children who are abused each year, about _____ percent are under the age of four.

    A. 10
    B. 25
    C. 50
    D. 75

3.____

4. Child sexual abuse is most often committed by

    A. child care providers or people who work in educational settings
    B. fathers
    C. someone who is known and trusted by the child
    D. complete strangers

4.____

5. Early 21st-century estimates projected that 1 in _____ girls and 1 in _____ boys will have experienced an episode of sexual abuse while younger than 18 years.

    A. 2; 4
    B. 4; 6
    C. 5;10
    D. 10;40

5.____

6. Which of the following types of skeletal injuries is LEAST suspicious for child physical abuse?

    A. Long bone fractures at various stages of healing
    B. A compound fracture of the ulna
    C. Spiral, chip, or corner fractures of the metaphysis
    D. Unusual fractures of the ribs, scapula or lateral clavicle

6.____

7. The single leading cause of death for children aged four and younger in the United States is

    A. motor vehicle accidents
    B. falls
    C. child abuse and neglect
    D. residential fires

7.____

8. Child neglect would include the
    I. use of close confinement as a punishment
    II. failure to seek necessary medical care for a sick child
    III. failure to enroll a school-age child in an educational program
    IV. failure to seek periodic medical and dental examinations that may prevent disease

    A. I and II
    B. I, II and III
    C. II and III
    D. I, II, III and IV

8.____

9. Environmental risk factors for child sexual abuse include each of the following, EXCEPT

    A. caretaker or parent with multiple sexual partners
    B. caretaker or parent who was abused as a child
    C. being raised by a single male parent
    D. poverty

9.____

10. Of the following, the most likely warning sign of child physical abuse is

    A. Hyperactivity
    B. Chronic fatigue
    C. Suggesting harsh punishment for other children
    D. Confabulation or the telling of "tall tales"

10.____

11. Studies suggests that about _____ percent of abusive parents were themselves abused as children.

    A. 8
    B. 33
    C. 50
    D. 67

11.____

12. The Muram diagnostic categorization system offers insight into how a variety of prepubertal genital examinations may assist in the diagnosis of child sexual abuse. In the Muram system, a finding of T. vaginal is would be classified as a Category _____ finding.

    A. I
    B. II
    C. III
    D. IV

12.____

13. In a 4-year-old child who is being sexually abused, the most likely behavioral presenta-   13._____
tion would be

    A.   sleeping for extended periods
    B.   nightmares
    C.   thumb-sucking
    D.   eating disturbances

14. In cases of child physical or sexual abuse, the forensic interview   14._____
    I.   is mostly concerned with detailed answers to who, what, where, and when
         the abuse occurred
    II. can take the place of the medical history obtained by the health care provider
         for the child
    III. can be conducted by anyone who is qualified to take a medical history
    IV. for legal reasons, should be conducted in the presence of the child's caretak-
         ers

    A.   I and II
    B.   I, II and III
    C.   II and IV
    D.   I, II, III and IV

15. Of the following, a bruise on the _____ is LEAST likely to be accidental   15._____

    A.   thigh
    B.   knee
    C.   forehead
    D.   chin

16. Physical or behavioral indicators of child abuse should be considered to be   16._____

    A.   warning signals
    B.   forensic evidence
    C.   testimonial evidence
    D.   documented facts

17. Generally, the likelihood that a report of child maltreatment will be confirmed by a CPS   17._____
investigation is about _____ percent

    A.   5-15
    B.   10-30
    C.   40-60
    D.   60-80

18. When working with child who has recently divulged that he is being abused, an important   18._____
guideline is to

    A.   discuss the situation with colleagues to raise their awareness
    B.   offer some kind of physical comfort to the child, such as a warm hug
    C.   react immediately and negatively to the idea that the child has been abused
    D.   praise the child for his courage and reassure him that there are adults who care

19. Most jurisdictions hold that in order to be considered an "abused child," a child must be   19._____

    A. in a position of dependence on the parent or caretaker, regardless of age
    B. younger than 21 and the biological child of the abuser
    C. younger than 18
    D. younger than 18, or older than 18 with a disability that limits their autonomy

20. Caretakers of Munchausen-by-proxy syndrome (MBPS) victims usually appear to be   20._____

    A. suspicious of others, almost to the point of paranoia
    B. loving and overprotective
    C. angry and confrontational
    D. overbearing and aggressive

21. Among the following factors or events, shaken-baby syndrome is MOST likely to be precipitated by   21._____

    A. uncontrollable crying by the infant
    B. disciplinary problems
    C. parental/caretaker drug or alcohol abuse
    D. the refusal of an infant to feed

22. Which of the following is LEAST likely to be a behavioral sign of neglect in a school-age child?   22._____

    A. Unresponsiveness to the concept of caring
    B. Bullying
    C. Poor self-discipline
    D. Delayed language development

23. Reviews of physical examinations performed on evaluated for suspected child sexual abuse have revealed that about _____ percent of the girls who are victims of sexual abuse have abnormal physical findings.   23._____

    A. 5
    B. 25
    C. 50
    D. 75

24. The initial step of Child Protective Services' intake of a reported case of suspected abuse typically involves each of the following, EXCEPT a (n)   24._____

    A. assessment of the urgency of the response
    B. removal of the child from the environment in which the abuse is alleged to have occurred
    C. determination of whether the report meets statutory and agency guidelines
    D. decision whether to investigate

25. When called to court in a case of child abuse, the health care provider generally serves 25._____ in the role of

   I.   a lay fact witness to provide first-hand information about what occurred during he child's evaluation

   II.   an expert witness, if the provider has advanced training or considerable experience with child physical and/or sexual abuse, on the specifics of the evaluations that were performed as well as general interpretations of issues related to the case

   III. a character witness to offer impressions of the people involved in the case

   A. I only
   B. I and II
   C. II and III
   D. I, II and III

KEY (CORRECT ANSWERS)

1. A	11. B
2. A	12. C
3. D	13. C
4. C	14. A
5. B	15. A
6. B	16. A
7. C	17. C
8. C	18. D
9. C	19. D
10. C	20. B

21. A
22. A
23. A
24. B
25. B

_____

TEST 3

DIRECTIONS: Each question or incomplete statement is followed by several suggested answers or completions. Select the one that BEST answers the question or completes the statement. *PRINT THE LETTER OF THE CORRECT ANSWER IN THE SPACE AT THE RIGHT.*

1. Among children who have been abused, it is most accurate to say that they   1.____

    A. tend to develop attention deficit disorders
    B. exhibit a wide range of behaviors
    C. most often have some kind of physical finding that suggests abuse
    D. tend toward aggression in their behavioral responses

2. Which of the following signs most strongly suggests the forced feeding of a child?   2.____

    A. Bruises on the outside of the mouth
    B. Lacerations of the tongue or frenula
    C. Tearing or braising of the outer ear
    D. Bruising under the eyes

3. In order to report suspicions of child abuse to law enforcement and social service authorities, the person who reports must have   3.____

    A. reason to suspect that abuse has occurred
    B. the child's permission to report
    C. documented proof that abuse has occurred
    D. circumstantial evidence that abuse has occurred

4. For optimal visualization of the genital structures and a fair degree of comfort for the child, the best viewing position would be the   4.____

    A. right lateral
    B. knee-chest
    C. frog-leg supine
    D. Trendelenburg

5. Pre-school-aged children who have been sexually abused are likely to   5.____

    A. run away from home
    B. have nightmares
    C. exhibit clear physical signs of sexual abuse
    D. be hyperactive

6. When taking a medical history of a child in whom a health care professional suspects child abuse, guidelines include   6.____
    I. using open ended, nonleading questions particularly with younger children
    II. asking not only about physical abuse, but also about sexual abuse, domestic violence, and witnessed abuse
    III. obtaining all historical information from everyone separately, including children

    A. I only
    B. II and III
    C. III only
    D. I, II and III

7. When a person reports suspected child abuse, his or her name　　　　　　　7.____

    A. is told to the child
    B. is reported to the family
    C. remains anonymous only if the report is substantiated
    D. can remain anonymous regardless of the outcome

8. Which of the following is NOT an example of emotional abuse?　　　　　　　8.____

    A. Verbal assault
    B. Failure to provide essential care
    C. Close confinement
    D. Threatening physical harm

9. In prepubescent girls, the most common hymenal configuration is　　　　　　9.____

    A. crescent-shaped　　　　　　　C. annular
    B. septate　　　　　　　　　　　　D. imperforate

10. Each of the following is considered to be a key factor in the improvement of outcomes　　10.____
in the area of child maltreatment, EXCEPT the

    A. improvement of access to early intervention and primary prevention programs
    B. provision of social support programs to new parents
    C. focus on tertiary prevention
    D. education of health care professionals in recognizing and intervening appropriately
       in cases of maltreatment

11. Nationwide, CPS investigations reveal that about percent of the cases of child　　　11.____
maltreatment in the United States are cases of physical abuse.

    A. 10　　　　　　　B. 25　　　　　　　C. 50　　　　　　　D. 75

12. When conducting a child interview in the medical evaluation of suspected child sexual　　12.____
abuse, the full potential of the interview can be realized by a reliance on questions or
responses such as

    I.   "Tell me more."
    II.   "How did you feel when that was done to you?"
    III. "And then what happened?"
    IV. "Where was everyone else when this happened?"
    A. I only
    B. Iand III
    C. II and III
    D. I, II, III and IV

13. It is most accurate to say that _____ abused children go on to abuse their own children.　　13.____

    A. very few　　　　　B. some　　　　　C. about half　　　　　D. most3

14. Accidental bruises or cuts on the _____ are extremely rare and should almost always　　14.____
be regarded with suspicion

    A. back　　　　　　B. neck　　　　　　C. shoulder　　　　　D. legs

15. Which of the following is NOT a secondary prevention activity?   15.____
    A. Home visiting programs for new parents
    B. Parent education classes for parents with a history of alcohol and/or drug abuse
    C. Family counseling for families with a history of violence
    D. Respite care for parents with disabled children

16. For a 7-year-old child who has been sexually abused, the most likely behavioral presen-   16.____
tation would be

    A. a regression to baby talk
    B. separation anxiety
    C. extreme stranger anxiety
    D. a significant change in attitude or academic performance

17. Which of the following would NOT be a guideline for conducting a lab workup with a child   17.____
who is suspected to be a victim of sexual abuse?

    A. Place clothing in a plastic bag to preserve any forensic evidence
    B. Maintain and document a clear chain of custody
    C. Collect pubic hairs found on the child's body; if the child has pubic hair, sample
        510 hairs.
    D. Consider cultures to be the criterion standard for STD tests

18. Of the following types of maltreatment, the one most likely to cause a child fatality is   18.____

    A. physical abuse
    B. emotional abuse
    C. neglect
    D. sexual abuse

19. Which of the following is LEAST likely to be a behavioral indicator of child sexual abuse?   19.____

    A. encopresis or enuresis
    B. sleep disturbances
    C. withdrawal from friends or family
    D. excessive familiarity with strangers

20 In most situations, when a case of suspected abuse or neglect turns out to be unfounded,   20.____

    A. all the information identifying the subjects is expunged
    B. the health care institution is given written notice that it must be more careful about
        reporting
    C. the reporter cannot be prosecuted but is subject to civil liability
    D. the reporter is placed on administrative leave but is otherwise unpunished

21. Which of the following is a protective factor in a child (one that reduces the risk for abuse)?   21.____

    A. Good social skills
    B. External locus of control
    C. Passive coping style
    D. Bold, fiery temperament

22. Which of the following involves symptoms that approximate the appearance of a cigarette 22._____
    burn?
    A. Eczema   C. Keratosis pilaris
    B. Impetigo   D. Melanoma

23. In about _____ of the households where the mother is a victim of physical abuse,   23._____
    at least one child is a victim as well.
    A. 10   B. 30   C. 50   D. 70

24. Of the substantiated cases of child maltreatment in the United States, most victims suffer 24._____
    from
    A. physical abuse   C. emotional abuse
    B. sexual abuse   D. neglect

25. Children who are suspected of being sexually abused may need an examination   25._____
    emergently, urgently, or electively scheduled for a later time with their own physician.
    Generally, urgent examination may take place within of an incident of sexual abuse.
    A. 8-12 hours   C. 2-3 Days
    A. 12-24 hours   D. 7-10 days

KEY (CORRECT ANSWERS)

1.	B		11.	B
2.	B		12.	B
3.	A		13.	B
4.	C		14.	B
5.	B		15.	C
6.	D		16.	D
7.	D		17.	A
8.	B		18.	C
9.	A		19.	D
10.	C		20.	A

21.	A
22.	B
23.	C
24.	D
25.	C

EXAMINATION SECTION
TEST 1

DIRECTIONS: Each question or incomplete statement is followed by several suggested answers or completions. Select the one the BEST answers the question or completes the statement. *PRINT THE LETTER OF THE CORRECT ANSWER IN THE SPACE AT THE RIGHT.*

1. Each of the following is a risk factor that is associated with a greater likelihood for intimate partner violence, EXCEPT 1.____

    A. women aged 39 to 49
    B. stalking
    C. alcohol or drug abuse
    D. families with low incomes

2. In abusive domestic relationships, a woman's risk of homicide is typically greatest 2.____

    A. when she is living with the man
    B. when children are not present
    C. in the first two months of any separation
    D. immediately following an instance of acute battering

3. The historical standard of a sexual assault victim fighting her attacker and demonstrating the *utmost resistance* is an example of: 3.____

    A. victim precipitation
    B. victim provocation
    C. lack of victim consent
    D. offender *mens rea*

4. A woman is not yet ready to leave her abusive husband because she is unsure of how she will support her son, whom she intends to take with her when she does leave. The woman works with a domestic violence professional on a safety plan for her son to follow. This plan should include each of the following elements, EXCEPT 4.____

    A. find a safe place to retreat to during a battering episode.
    B. call 911 if you think somebody in the family might get hurt.
    C. if you don't approve of the abuser's behavior during an episode, tell him so.
    D. find a person you can trust to talk to about what is going on at home and how you feel about it

5. For a domestic violence professional, the process of assessment ends when 5.____

    A. the last assessment interview or form has been recorded
    B. a safety plan has been formulated
    C. the first set of behavioral and/or environmental goals are met
    D. the terminal phase of service is complete

6. *Victim precipitation* refers to the idea that the 6.____

    A. offender carefully selects victims with certain characteristics
    B. offender lacks a *mens rea,* or criminal intent
    C. victim somehow caused his or her own victimization
    D. victim should be the prime instigator of criminal prosecution

7. In cases of domestic violence, research suggests that criminal justice interventions are
   most effective at reducing the chances of reassault by perpetrators who

    7.____

   A. use the *loss of control* explanation for their attacks
   B. commit less severe violence
   C. are arrested as a result of a victim-initiated complaint
   D. commit sexual violence as part of their abusive behavior

8. *Permanency planning* refers to the policy of

    8.____

   A. developing a stable foster care plan for children removed from their homes
   B. assuring abused and neglected children a stable family situation throughout chid-
      hood
   C. using adoption for at-risk children
   D. interventions for children who are at risk of removal, or who have been removed
      from, their homes

9. The National Domestic Violence Hotline is a program of the U.S.

    9.____

   A. Department of Health and Human Services
   B. Department of Housing and Urban Development
   C. Department of Justice
   D. Occupational Health and Safety Administration

10. Which of the following is NOT a privileged relationship during the prosecution of child
    abuse?

    10.____

    A. Priest-penitent
    B. Lawyer client
    C. Psychologist-patient
    D. Doctor-patient

11. A domestic violence professional begins an investigation of a report by visiting the home
    of a family and observing that a child has several bruises on her back. arms, and legs. In
    order to maintain professional objectivity, the worker should describe the child as

    11.____

    A. self-destructive
    B. clumsy
    C. abused
    D. bruised

12. Generally, the odds of criminal victimization for the elderly are

    12.____

    A. about the same as other age groups
    B. slightly higher than other age groups
    C. lower than other age groups
    D. markedly higher than other age groups

13. The most prevalent form of elder maltreatment is   13.____

    A. physical abuse
    B. active neglect
    C. material abuse
    D. self-neglect

14. A domestic violence professional is unable to convince a victim of domestic violence to   14.____
leave her situation. The professional should advise the victim to
    I. fight back when the behavior begins, to make violence more difficult
    II. stay away from children during an abusive episode
    III. purchase a defensive device such as mace or a *stun gun* in case the vio-
        lence escalates to a level that is life-threatening
    IV. conceal the abuse as much as possible from family and friends

    A. I and III
    B. II only
    C. None of the above
    D. All of the above

15. Which of the following is LEAST likely to be a sign or symptom of elder abuse?   15.____

    A. bone fractures
    B. elder's sudden change in behavior
    C. elder reports of abuse
    D. untreated health problems

16. Physical discipline by a parent is permitted in all states, provided it is reasonable and not   16.____
excessive. The *reasonableness* standard is largely dependent on

    A. the size of the child
    B. whether the child is seriously hurt
    C. the culture in which the parent was raised
    D. the age of the child

17. The most common form of rape is described as_____ rape.   17.____

    A. stranger
    B. acquaintance
    C. sadistic
    D. spousal

18. Conflicts between two pieces of federal legislation, the Adoption Assistance and Child   18.____
Welfare Act of 1980 and the Child Abuse Prevention and Treatment Act of 1974, center
on the issue of

    A. what constitutes *abuse*
    B. whether details of a child's history of abuse should be revealed to parents who are
        candidates for adoption
    C. whether it's best for a child to remain in or be removed from an abusive situation
    D. what constitutes *neglect*

19. An order of protection is issued in New York, and afterwards the girlfriend of an abuser moves onto the Pine Ridge Indian Reservation in South Dakota. The abuser tracks her down, enters the reservation, and begins to harass the woman at her new home. Tribal law determines each of the following, EXCEPT

   A. the arrest authority of responding law enforcement
   B. how long the order is in effect
   C. detention and notification procedures
   D. penalties and sanctions for violations of the order

19.____

20. The_____ was instrumental in establishing policy guidelines for handling spouse abuse incidents

   A. Zimbardo experiment
   B. Minneapolis experiment
   C. President's Task Force on Family Violence
   D. President's Task Force on Victims of Crime

20.____

21. A woman has left her abusive boyfriend and wants to get her and her children's names legally changed, in order to make it more difficult to find them. The boyfriend is the father of the children. The main difficulty she will have in doing this is that

   A. the father must be notified of the children's name changes
   B. agencies and creditors are unlikely to recognize the children's new names along with her own
   C. the father will automatically be notified of the children's new names
   D. legally, the children's names cannot be changed

21.____

22. Women who have been beaten repeatedly over a period of many years often suffer from *battering syndrome* or *battered women's syndrome.*
Women who exhibit this syndrome share the essential characteristics of
   I. alcohol and/or substance abuse
   II. debilitating fear of physical aggression
   III. unpredictable displays of physical aggression
   IV. flashbacks

   A. I and II
   B. II and III
   C. III only
   D. I, II, III and IV

22.____

23. Battered women's shelters are typically funded through each of the following, EXCEPT

   A. grants from organizations like the United Way
   B. marriage license fees
   C. private donations
   D. victim compensation payouts

23.____

24. When a woman leaves an abuser, the abuser goes through a predictable process of emotions known as the *separation cycle*. The first phase of this process is usually

    24._____

    A. manipulative anger
    B. defaming the survivor to others
    C. indifference
    D. manipulative courting

25. Under the Violence Against Women Act, an order of protection is universally valid if it meets certain minimal requirements. These include

    25._____

       I. it cannot be issued *ex parte*
     II. the court that issued the order must have personal jurisdiction over the parties and subject matter jurisdiction over the case
    III. the respondent must have had notice and an opportunity to be heard
    IV. the order must be a criminal, rather than civil, order

    A. I only
    B. I and II
    C. II and III
    D. III and IV

KEY (CORRECT ANSWERS)

1.	A		11.	D
2.	C		12.	C
3.	C		13.	D
4.	C		14.	B
5.	D		15.	D
6.	C		16.	B
7.	B		17.	B
8.	B		18.	C
9.	A		19.	B
10.	D		20.	B

21.	A
22.	B
23.	D
24.	C
25.	C

TEST 2

DIRECTIONS: Each question or incomplete statement is followed by several suggested answers or completions. Select the one the BEST answers the question or completes the statement. *PRINT THE LETTER OF THE CORRECT ANSWER IN THE SPACE AT THE RIGHT.*

1. Professionals who are working with clients who are in an abusive relationship should try to communicate that

    A. leaving the abusive situation is always the safest solution
    B. usually, waiting to effect a mutual end to the relationship is the only lasting solution
    C. only the abused person can ultimately judge what will be the safest option
    D. ending an abusive relationship requires behavior changes from both partners

    1.____

2. Violence between_____ would typically NOT be covered under a domestic violence statute.

    A. two cohabiting homosexual lovers
    B. siblings
    C. grandfather and grandson
    D. two roommates

    2.____

3. Goals of advocacy for victims of domestic violence include
    I.   increasing victims' ability to make a successful transition to independence
    II.   empowering women to make significant changes and solve problems
    III. connecting the victim with community resources, both short-and long-term
    IV.   insuring the prosecution and punishment of the batterer

    A. II and III
    B. I, II, and III
    C. II, III, and IV
    D. All of the above

    3.____

4. Which of the following is NOT a theoretical explanation for elder abuse and neglect?

    A. Situational transaction
    B. Role reversal
    C. Violent subculture
    D. Social exchange

    4.____

5. The Wellstone/Murray amendment to the Personal Responsibility and Work Opportunity Reconciliation Act (PRWORA-commonly known as the Welfare Reform Act) means that victims of domestic violence

    A. may receive welfare benefits only if they take active steps to end an abusive situation, such as taking up residence at a shelter
    B. may not have to meet the work requirements and time limits that apply to other welfare recipients
    C. must receive psycho-educational group counseling in order to receive benefits
    D. are qualified for any state-funded intervention program

    5.____

6. Which of the following terms is synonymous with *repeat victimization*? 6.____

    A. Multiple offenders victimizing a single individual
    B. Offender recidivism
    C. Victim recidivism
    D. A single offender with multiple victims

7. Which of the following variables is a vulnerability factor for the elderly? 7.____

    A. Living alone or with someone
    B. Residential location
    C. Amount of fear of crime
    D. Degree of social support

8. A young wife visits a domestic violence professional and reports that she is extremely unhappy. She report numerous episodes of domestic violence, and asks the professional whether the marriage is worth saving. The professional should 8.____

    A. recommend divorce, given the domestic violence
    B. tell the woman that a divorce is their decision alone
    C. advise a trial separation
    D. contact the police about the domestic violence

9. In most states, professionals who are required to report the possibility of child maltreatment to the proper authority include 9.____
    I. police officers
    II. domestic violence professionals
    III. medical or hospital personnel
    IV. attorneys

    A. I and II
    B. I, II and III
    C. III only
    D. I, II, III and IV

10. In a family, which is a *low* risk factor for child abuse or neglect? 10.____

    A. Only child
    B. Limited physical and mental abilities of child
    C. Single parent
    D. Younger child

11. The government may intervene in cases of elder abuse if the 11.____
    I. older person requests it
    II. older person is found at a hearing to be incompetent
    III. abuse or neglect presents an unacceptable level of danger to the older person
    IV. abuse is properly reported and recorded by a visiting social services worker

    A. I only
    B. I and II
    C. I, II and III
    D. I, II, III and IV

12. For the survivor of abuse, the full faith and credit provisions of the Violence Against   12.____
Women Act mean that

    A. they can call on law enforcement officers anywhere in the United States to enforce
orders of protection across state or tribal lines

    B. they can apply for orders of protection in different and unlimited jurisdictions if they
decide to move across state lines

    C. if a victim's claim of domestic abuse has upheld by the law once, all subsequent
claims against the same perpetrator will be assumed to be factual unless proven
otherwise

    D. they will be eligible for certain services administered by the Department of Justice

13. Two months ago, not long after her husband assaulted her badly enough to break her   13.____
arm, a woman moved into a shelter for battered women. The husband is alcoholic and
has been abusive for as long as they've been married, about six years. The woman tells
a domestic violence professional that she has decided to return to her husband in an
attempt to save her marriage. The professional should

    A. discuss the possible consequences of returning to her spouse as compared to
remaining in the shelter, but let her make her own choice

    B. strongly advise the woman to remain in the shelter, using statistics that support the
contention that she will likely be abused again if she returns home

    C. tell the woman that if returning to her husband is her wish, then she should return
to her spouse.

    D. tell her that she should think of the welfare of her children before she decides to
return to an abusive household

14. Provisions of the Violence Against Women Act include each of the following, EXCEPT   14.____

    A. prioritization of home state jurisdictions over others in the enforcement of child cus-
tody orders

    B. prohibiting anyone facing a domestic violence protection order from possessing a
firearm

    C. establishment of crossing state lines to continue the abuse of a spouse or partner
as a federal crime

    D. requiring sexual offenders to pay restitution to their victims

15. Which of the following variables would MOST likely be classified as constituting a high   15.____
risk for either domestic violence or child abuse?

    A. A recent change in marital or relationship status
    B. Water and/or electricity inoperative
    C. A child between 5 and 9 years of age
    D. Family does not belong to a church or social group

16. As of 2003, there were seven U.S. states in which domestic violence protection orders   16.____
were explicitly unavailable for victims of same-sex abuse. Which of the following is one of
these states?

    A. Texas
    B. Illinois
    C. Wyoming
    D. New York

17. A battered wife has decided to take a case against her husband to Family Court. Which   17.____
of the following is a DISADVANTAGE associated with the prosecution of domestic violence offenses in Family Court?

    A. It is more difficult to receive a Temporary Order of Protection from Family Court.
    B. The only thing an Order of Protection issued by a Family Court can do is prevent
the abuser from causing physical harm.
    C. An Order of Protection issued by a Family Court cannot be automatically extended
once it expires.
    D. A Family Court judge cannot put an abuser in jail even if the abuser admits to doing
the things involved in the petition.

18. Which of the following is a guideline for domestic violence victim validation?   18.____

    A. Downplay the widespread prevalence of such crimes among all women
    B. Avoid speaking directly about the violence
    C. Stress the criminal nature of the violence and the fact that the victim is not to blame
    D. Seek verification of the victim's story from second parties

19. Child abuse generally does NOT refer to   19.____

    A. withholding of life's essentials
    B. nonaccidental infliction of injury
    C. fondling a child
    D. pornography

20. A woman is working with a domestic violence professional on a written personalized   20.____
safety plan. The FIRST element of such a plan should typically focus on

    A. the procedures for obtaining a protection order
    B. safety when preparing to leave
    C. a checklist of items to take when leaving
    D. safety during a violent incident

21. A woman fears that if she stays with her husband, the Child Protective Services agency   21.____
may attempt to take her children, who are also being abused, out of the home. The
domestic violence professional should be aware that such decisions are based on two
issues. These are
    I. the motivation, capacity for harm, and intent of the alleged abuser
    II. whether the domestic violence victim has a plan for leaving the abuser in
place and is ready to act on it
    III. the natural support network available to the mother and children.
    IV. the immediate danger or risk to the child

    A. I and IV
    B. II and III
    C. II and IV
    D. III and IV

22. An injunction in a spouse abuse situation may NOT be characterized by   22.____

    A. issuance on an *ex parte* basis
    B. having same effect as a trespass warning
    C. a filing fee waiver
    D. a status equivalent to that of divorce

23. Orders of protection against abusers often include terms that award custody of the minor   23.____
    children to the victim. Advocates for domestic violence victims should be aware that
    these custody provisions

    A. are not specifically enforceable if the victim takes the children across the state line
    B. are subject to the provisions of the Violence Against Women Act
    C. must be petitioned and filed separately for each child
    D. must be agreed to by the children's father

24. A woman comes to a domestic violence professional seeking help. She has been   24.____
    involved with a batterer for more than a year now, and the beatings are getting progres-
    sively worse-recently, blackening an eye so severely that she was forced to stay home
    from work. Strangely, this was not the event that drove the woman to seek help. What
    frightens the woman most is that she hardly recalls the last few episodes. She doesn't
    remember feeling any fear or pain while she was being assaulted, she says; she felt
    numb, mostly, and actually thought about the things she still had left to do on that day as
    she was being beaten. The professional should assume that the woman

    A. is using denial as a defense mechanism
    B. has entered the first phase of the separation cycle
    C. has begun to rely on dissociation as a defense mechanism
    D. has acquired a personality disorder

25. A certified copy of an order of protection generally contains a stamp, seal, or signature of   25.____
    the issuing judge or clerk of court, and a notation that the copy is an authentic duplicate
    of the original order of the court. Which of the following statements about certification is
    TRUE?
    I.   The Violence Against Women Act mandates that an order of protection be
         certified in order to be enforceable across state, territorial, or tribal lines
    II. Many jurisdictions require that a copy of a foreign order be certified for pur-
         poses of registration or filing.
    III. A copy of an order of protection is generally not considered valid by any
         applicable authority unless certified.

    A. I only
    B. I and II
    C. II only
    D. I, II and III

KEY (CORRECT ANSWERS)

1.	C	11.	B
2.	D	12.	A
3.	B	13.	A
4.	C	14.	A
5.	B	15.	A
6.	C	16.	D
7.	D	17.	D
8.	B	18.	C
9.	B	19.	A
10.	A	20.	D

21.	A
22.	D
23.	A
24.	C
25.	C

———

TEST 3

DIRECTIONS: Each question or incomplete statement is followed by several suggested answers or completions. Select the one the BEST answers the question or completes the statement. *PRINT THE LETTER OF THE CORRECT ANSWER IN THE SPACE AT THE RIGHT.*

1. When stalking takes place in conjunction with domestic violence, it is MOST likely to be associated with the

    A. the tension-building phase
    B. the battering episode
    C. the reconciliation period
    D. battered spouse's decision to end the cycle of violence

    1._____

2. The *cycle of violence* with respect to domestic violence means that:

    A. children who witness domestic violence between their parents do not grow up to become batterers themselves
    B. spousal violence grows over the years until one partner finally kills the other
    C. a battery takes place after a tension-building phase and is followed by a period of reconciliation
    D. eventually the woman will leave or divorce the husband

    2._____

3. The withholding of basic food, clothing and shelter from an aged victim by a caretaker is characterized as:

    A. abuse
    B. neglect
    C. aggravated elderly abuse
    D. third degree assault

    3._____

4. Batterers generally
    I.   deny responsibility for their actions
    II. take a long time to commit to a monogamous relationship
    III. have an excessive need for control
    IV. try to cut partners off from outside resources

    A. I and II
    B. I, III and IV
    C. III and IV
    D. I, II, III and IV

    4._____

5. A woman visits a domestic violence shelter and wants to talk with a worker there. The woman thinks she might be being abused by her boyfriend, but she is confused about what constitutes *abuse*. Questions the worker might ask include
    I.   After he has hit you, does he act sweet and loving?
    II. Has he forced you to have sex?
    III. What kind of situations precipitate his violent behavior?
    IV. Has he caused you to be late or to miss work?

    A. I and II
    B. I, II and IV
    C. II only
    D. I, II, III and IV

    5._____

6. Under the full faith and credit provisions of the Violence Against Women Act, a consent order

    A. does not require a finding of abuse in order to be enforceable
    B. is enforceable against the respondent, but not the petitioner, unless there has been a cross-filing
    C. is a criminal order of protection
    D. is not enforceable

6.____

7. Which of the following variables would most likely be classified as constituting no risk or a low risk for child abuse?

    A. Family is geographically isolated from community services
    B. A caretaker who is overly compliant with the investigator
    C. An injury on the child's torso
    D. One previous report of abuse

7.____

8. Which of the following is a major reason why domestic violence victims do not report abuse to the police?

    A. Apathy
    B. Language barriers
    C. Uncertainty about whether a crime was committed
    D. They don't think the police will do anything

8.____

9. Studies of domestic violence victims have suggested that about _____ percent of those who are employed experience some type of problem in the workplace as a direct result of the abuse or abuser.

    A. 25
    B. 45
    C. 75
    D. 95

9.____

10. Indian tribes recognize protection orders from other jurisdictions under the legal principle of

    A. comity
    B. double jeopardy
    C. full faith and credit
    D. vicarious liability

10.____

11. The phenomenon known as *secondary victimization* involves each of the following, EXCEPT

    A. the victim's family and friends
    B. the criminal justice system
    C. the offender
    D. victim compensation programs

11.____

12. The sibling of a physically abused child has approximately a _____ percent chance of being abused at the same time.

    A. 20
    B. 40
    C. 60
    D. 80

13. Mandates of the Victims of Child Abuse Act of 1990 include
      I. permitting testimony via two-way closed circuit television in certain circumstances
      II. limiting the scope of competency examinations for children unless ordered by a judge
      III. consultation with multi-disciplinary teams for information on professional evaluations
      IV. accompaniment throughout the trial by an adult attendant

    A. I only
    B. I and IV
    C. II, III, and IV
    D. I, II, III and IV

14. A woman is not yet ready to leave her abusive husband, but is willing to work with a domestic violence professional on a safety plan for minimizing risks and injuries during a battering episode. One of the strategies in such a plan is to identify safe areas of the house. Of the following, the safest area is probably the

    A. bedroom
    B. kitchen
    C. bathroom
    D. garage

15. Of the perpetrators of child maltreatment in the United States, approximately what percentage are parents?

    A. 25
    B. 50
    C. 75
    D. 95

16. Which of the following offenses would typically NOT be classified as a Family Offense Misdemeanor?

    A. An assault that breaks a bone
    B. Harassment over the phone
    C. An assault that causes substantial pain
    D. An assault that impairs the victims' physical condition

17. Infants who are born prematurely are proportionally over-represented in the population of physically abused infants and children. Each of the following is a likely factor in this situation, EXCEPT

    A. long initial separation from parents
    B. lower standard of *abuse* due to physical frailty

C. parental feelings of disappointment and guilt

D. infant difficulty in recognizing and responding to caregiving behaviors

18. It is estimated that approximately_____ percent of all battered women who seek help have diagnosable post-traumatic stress disorder (PTSD).   18.____

    A. 10

    B. 30

    C. 50

    D. 75

19. Which of the following is NOT a physiological explanation for rape?   19.____

    A. uncontrollable sex drive

    B. lack of available partners

    C. sublimation of repressed desires

    D. consequence of the natural selection process

20. Because many parents believe in and utilize corporal punishment as discipline, a professional must be able to differentiate physical abuse from ordinary spanking or corporal punishment. Which of the following is NOT a useful means of making this distinction?   20.____

    A. Parent striking the child in places that are easily injured

    B. Repeated episodes of corporal punishment

    C. Child's report that punishments are severe and painful

    D. Injury to child's body tissue

21. The decision to confirm a report of child abuse or neglect is likely to rely on each of the following, EXCEPT   21.____

    A. the intent of the perpetrator

    B. the availability of community resources that may help reduce the risk of abuse or neglect

    C. the degree to which the worker is certain that an injury was caused by willful or negligent acts of the caretaker or perpetrator

    D. information regarding past incidents or reports

22. According to the law in most states, a person arrested for domestic violence typically   22.____

    A. may be released on bail only if he or she promises not to return to the scene of the offense and commit another act of violence

    B. is eligible for release on his or her own recognizance (ROR) prior to first appearance before a judge or magistrate

    C. is not entitled to bail prior to first appearance

    D. has 30 days in which to vacate the domicile

23. Which of the following is a national child abuse prevention organization that relies on mutual support and parent leadership?   23.____

    A. Parents Anonymous

    B. The National Coalition Against Domestic Violence

    C. The Office of Juvenile Justice and Delinquency Prevention

    D. Childhelp USA

24. When leaving a violent domestic situation behind, a victim should generally do each of the following, EXCEPT

    A. provide relatives with relocation information
    B. avoid the use of credit cards
    C. take all important documents upon departure
    D. ask the police to supervise as belongings are removed, and to escort the departure

24.____

25. A woman has left her abusive husband and wants to get her name legally changed, in order to make it more difficult for her abuser to find her. State laws for name changes usually require publication. The woman wants to limit access to the knowledge of her new name, while still having the name recognized by the Social Security Administration and other parties. Usually, the options available to the woman include

    I. making a motion for her to notify each required party (creditors, agencies, the military) directly, without publication
    II. request publication of a notice that simply says she is changing her name, without saying what her new name will be, and indicating that anyone with questions can contact her lawyer.
    III. simply notifying each interested party (creditors, etc.) of the name change, without going through the courts
    IV. first applying for a new Social Security Number, under a different name, and then notify each interested party of the changes

    A. I and II
    B. II only
    C. II and III
    D. II, III and IV

25.____

KEY (CORRECT ANSWERS)

1.	D	11.	C
2.	C	12.	A
3.	B	13.	D
4.	B	14.	A
5.	A	15.	C
6.	A	16.	A
7.	C	17.	B
8.	D	18.	C
9.	D	19.	C
10.	A	20.	C

21.	B
22.	C
23.	A
24.	A
25.	A

EXAMINATION SECTION
TEST 1

DIRECTIONS: Each question or incomplete statement is followed by several suggested answers or completions. Select the one the BEST answers the question or completes the statement. *PRINT THE LETTER OF THE CORRECT ANSWER IN THE SPACE AT THE RIGHT.*

1. A woman who is not a U.S. citizen is being physically abused her husband, with whom she has two young children. The woman contacts a domestic violence professional about her legal options. The woman should know that the legal options available to her include   1.____
   - I.   a civil protection order
   - II.   a criminal protection order
   - III.   dissolution
   - IV.   a child custody order

   A.   I and II
   B.   II only
   C.   II, III and IV
   D.   I, II, III and IV

2. Approximately what percentage of female homicide victims are killed by their husbands or boyfriends?   2.____

   A.   15
   B.   30
   C.   60
   D.   90

3. Which of the following statements best expresses the idea of "learned helplessness"?   3.____

   A.   Victims in violent relationships report greater success over time in defusing their partner's anger
   B.   Victims in violent relationships learn how to become more contrite and more successful during the reconciliation phase
   C.   Victims are trying to learn how to control their offenders
   D.   Isolation and financial dependence are prime factors involved in victims' decisions to remain with their abusers

4. A model domestic violence response should include   4.____
   - I.   joint custody arrangements
   - II.   mediation between victims and offenders
   - III.   mutual restraining orders
   - IV.   couples therapy

   A.   I and IV
   B.   II an III
   C.   None of the above
   D.   At least one of the above

5. In an abusive relationship that involves one batterer and one victim, couples counseling   5.____
   is appropriate

   A.. for getting at the root of the batterer's anger and need to control the victim
   B. for determining whether the batterer might benefit from an intervention program
   C. before the first episode of physical assault occurs
   D. after the batterer completes an intervention program and is no longer violent

6. Of the following cases of child abuse, the most appropriate choice for a family preserva-   6.____
   tion effort would be a

   A. case involving a child older than 2 in which there is not a strong likelihood of further
      risk
   B. family who resists in-home services
   C. case of sexual abuse in which the perpetrator cannot be removed from access to
      the child victim
   D. family in which the parent is severely developmentally or psychiatrically disabled

7. The police have answered a second domestic violence call at the home of a husband   7.____
   and wife. The husband is identified as the primary aggressor. The wife does not want her
   husband arrested, and doesn't want any report made. In most jurisdictions, the police
   must make an arrest if

   A. the second call has taken place within 12 hours of the first
   B. there is evidence that a felony was committed
   C. they believe the husband is the primary aggressor
   D. they have probable cause to believe the husband struck the wife

8. The minimum required to trigger the mandatory reporting require ments of the Child   8.____
   Abuse Prevention and Treatment Act is

   A. reasonable suspicion
   B. suspicion shared by at least one other witness
   C. clear and convincing evidence
   D. a preponderance of evidence

9. Under the doctrine of _____, state-supported adult protective services programs pro-   9.____
   tect elderly people from abuse and neglect.

   A. *parens patriae*
   B. *habeas corpus*
   C. *in loco parentis*
   D. *volenti non fit injuri*

10. A battered wife has decided to press criminal charges against her husband. Advantages   10.____
    of criminal prosecution of domestic assault cases include
    I. the victim does not have to pay for legal representation
    II. possible probation for the offender, even if he is not convicted, which will
        ensure that his behavior is monitored
    III. the offender is forced to realize that his offenses against the victim are
         crimes, for which he will be held accountable
    IV. a lower burden of proof is placed on the victim

A. I and III
B. I, II and III
C. II and III
D. I, II, III and IV

11. Emergency room physicians contact the local police department after confirming diagnosis of physical abuse of a 12-year-old child. After the child receives medical treatment, police officers should

    11.____

A. arrest the adult who accompanied the child to the hospital
B. place the child in protective custody
C. get a search warrant to see whether there are other children in the house who might be at risk
D. initiate the adoption process

12. Behaviors that are common among battering personalities include each of the following, EXCEPT

    12.____

A. accusing the partner of flirting
B. expecting children to be capable of doing things beyond their ability
C. uniformly dispensing verbal abuse, without every complimenting the partner
D. blaming the partner for upsetting him/her

13. In most cases, a civil protection order may

    13.____

    I. evict an abuser from a shared household
    II. require the abuser to pay temporary monetary support
    III. prohibit the abuser from transferring, selling, or concealing property
    IV. be more complicated to file than a criminal protection order

A. I and II
B. I, II, and III
C. II and III
D. I, II, III and IV

14. In general, the BEST preventive support to families at risk for child abuse or neglect is provided by

    14.____

A. community natural helpers
B. self-help groups
C. individual caseworkers
D. formal interagency programs

15. About what percentage of adult protective service agencies' caseloads involve elder abuse?

    15.____

A. 10
B. 30
C. 50
D. 70

16. The most common type of child maltreatment in substantiated cases is

    16.____

A. neglect
B. physical abuse

C. sexual abuse

D. emotional abuse

17. A domestic violence professional is working with a victim who is planning to leave the state with her children. The professional and client are surprised when the victim's husband files for a mutual "no-contact" order. To make this order enforceable against the husband should he choose to harass or abuse the family in their new home state, the professional

    A. should forward a copy of the order to the appropriate law enforcement agency

    B. should insist that the victim file a cross petition

    C. should advise the victim to refuse the mutual consent agreement and file a unilateral petition for a consent order

    D. won't need to take any further additional steps, thanks to the full faith and credit provisions of the Violence Against Women Act

17.____

18. Among the general population, regardless of other factors, the chances that a person will exhibit abusive behavior is about _____ percent.

    A. 0-1

    B. 1-10

    C. 5-15

    D. 10-25

18.____

19. A "shield provision" in rape law means that:

    A. newspapers cannot publish the victim's name or address

    B. the person is entitled to assistance under the Witness Protection Act

    C. television news reporters may not display any pictures or videos showing the victim's face

    D. defense lawyers cannot bring up the victim's sexual history

19.____

20. In investigating a domestic violence incident in which both partners were involved, police must determine who was the primary aggressor. In order to determine this, they are required to do each of the following, EXCEPT

    A. consider whether one party acted in self defense

    B. assume that it was the husband unless there is strong evidence to the contrary

    C. compare the injuries inflicted on both parties

    D. determine whether any threats were made

20.____

21. The "fear-victimization paradox" means that

    A. the objective and subjective odds of victimization are balanced

    B. the objective odds of victimization are much higher than the subjective odds

    C. the objective odds of victimization are much lower than the subjective odds

    D. there is no difference between the objective and subjective odds of victimization

21.____

22. A "rape kit" is designed to help:

    A. police officers provide emotional first-aid to victims

    B. prosecutors maintain an up-to-date listing of relevant case law

    C. judges determine appropriate punishments under sentencing guidelines

    D. physicians during the forensic portion of the medical examination

22.____

23. Which of the following is MOST likely to be a physical indicator of child emotional abuse?   23.____

    A. Unexplained bruises
    B. Inappropriate clothing for weather conditions
    C. Below-average height and weight
    D. Speech disorders

24. Which of the following is NOT a type of stalker identified by researchers?   24.____

    A. Passer-by
    B. Psychopathic personality
    C. Celebrity
    D. Lust

25. A survivor of domestic abuse obtains a protection order against her same-sex partner in Hawaii. The order will still be enforceable if, several months later, she moves to   25.____

    I. New York
    II. Massachusetts
    III. Texas
    IV. California

    A. I only
    B. II and IV
    C. IV only
    D. I, II, III and IV

KEY (CORRECT ANSWERS)

1.	D		11.	B
2.	B		12.	C
3.	D		13.	B
4.	C		14.	A
5.	D		15.	D
6.	A		16.	A
7.	B		17.	B
8.	A		18.	B
9.	A		19.	D
10.	B		20.	B

21. C
22. D
23. D
24. A
25. D

TEST 2

DIRECTIONS: Each question or incomplete statement is followed by several suggested answers or completions. Select the one the BEST answers the question or completes the statement. *PRINT THE LETTER OF THE CORRECT ANSWER IN THE SPACE AT THE RIGHT*

1. Factors that place a man at risk as a potential batterer include
    I.   Drug or alcohol use
    II. 30-45 years of age
    III. Witnessing spousal abuse among parents
    IV. Poverty

    A. I and III
    B. I, II, and IV
    C. I, III, and IV
    D. All of the above

1._____

2. The U.S. Department of Justice has defined an abusive relationship as one in which the abuser uses a number of tactics in order to maintain power and control over his or her partner. These tactics include each of the following, EXCEPT

    A. Emotional and verbal abuse
    B. Learned helplessness
    C. Isolation
    D. Threats and intimidation

2._____

3. A woman is ready to leave her abusive boyfriend, and is working with a domestic violence professional on a safety plan for her departure. Part of the plan should be for the woman to pack an extra set of clothes to be kept elsewhere. The safest keeper of these clothes is generally a/an

    A. trusted next-door neighbor
    B. close family member
    C. trusted friend with whom the boyfriend is not familiar
    D. mutual friend

3._____

4. Non-stranger rapes account for more than_____percent of all rape victimization cases.
    A. 20
    B. 30
    C. 50
    D. 65

4._____

5. A family intervention modeled on the Child At Risk Field System (CARF) typically involves

    A. the abuser alone
    B. the abuser and the child or children who suffer the abuse
    C. both parents, assuming one is the abuser, and the abused child(ren)
    D. the entire family

5._____

6. During the _____ phase of the cycle of violence, one is most likely to encounter the idea of disinhibition.

    6._____

    A. battering episode
    B. tension-building
    C. arrest
    D. "honeymoon" or reconciliation

7. Which of the following takes place during the sentencing phase of a rape trial?

    7._____

    A. Consideration of the Victim Impact Statement
    B. Consideration of aggravating circumstances
    C. A re-invocation of shield provisions
    D. A relaxation of the privilege against self-incrimination

8. Which of the following items of information is most relevant to a domestic hearing?

    8._____

    A. Treatment plan for all members of household
    B. Statement of child
    C. Why safety of the child can't be insured in the home
    D. Comparison of parents

9. A woman who is not a U.S. citizen is being physically abused by her husband, who is a legal permanent resident. When the husband learns that the woman is planning to leave him, he threatens to take their children away from her and return to his home country. The FIRST step the woman should take would be to

    9._____

    A. notify the embassy of the husband's home country of the threat
    B. tell the children's schools not to release them to anyone but her
    C. collect recent photos, passports and birth certificates for the children
    D. apply for a custody order

10. If a respondent violates any provision of an injunction for protection against domestic violence, that act is considered to be a/an

    10._____

    A. rule infraction
    B. misdemeanor
    C. administrative violation
    D. violation of probation

11. The "victim precipitation" argument is characterized by the idea that

    11._____

    A. criminal acts can be explained by the behavior of the offender
    B. the victim becomes activated only when the offender emits certain signals
    C. the victim's behavior is necessary and sufficient to trigger the commission of a criminal act
    D. offenders plan their criminal acts in advance

12. A woman's partner has enrolled in a court-ordered intervention program for batterers. In discussing the likelihood of the program's success with a domestic violence professional, the woman wonders aloud: "How do I know he's really changing?" Positive signs that a batterer is really changing include each of the following, EXCEPT

    12._____

A. his acknowledgement that his behavior is wrong
B. the woman does not feel afraid when she is with him
C. he claims to be completely cured of his anger problem
D. the woman can express anger toward him without fear of intimidation or reprisal

13. Inflicted bruises on a child are so common at certain body sites that discovering them there is diagnostic of abuse. Which of the following is LEAST likely to be the site of an inflicted bruise?   13._____

    A. Forehead
    B. Neck
    C. Genitals
    D. Buttocks and lower back

14. "Elder abuse" includes each of the following behaviors, EXCEPT   14._____

    A. refusal to provide life necessities, such as food and water
    B. enforced social isolation
    C. force-feeding
    D. the inappropriate use of physical restraints

15. A major problem associated with mandatory reporting of elder abuse is that it   15._____

    A. exposes physicians to litigation
    B. places the blame on the offender
    C. allows intervention into unknown cases of abuse
    D. reinforces ageism by focusing on the victim rather than the offender

16. An order of protection is issued in Kansas. The wife of a batterer takes their three children and moves in with her mother in Washington State. Kansas state law determines each of the following, EXCEPT   16._____

    A. penalties and sanctions for violations of the order
    B. how long the order is in effect
    C. who is protected under the order
    D. the terms and conditions of the order

17. Which of the following is MOST likely to be a behavioral indicator of child physical abuse?   17._____

    A. Chronic fatigue
    B. Frequent tantrums
    C. Thumb sucking in older children
    D. Suggesting other children be punished harshly

18. Factors that may contribute to elder abuse include   18._____
    I. caregiver stress and isolation
    II. impairment of a dependent elder
    III. "cycle of violence" family history
    IV. personal problems of abusers

    A. I only
    B. I and III

C. II, III and IV
D. I, II, III and IV

19. "Twice-victimized", "double-insult", or "second-order trauma" refers to: 19.____

    A. the fact that a majority of victims are recidivists
    B. crime victims' enduring ordeal as the case winds through the criminal justice system
    C. the "hidden victimization" that exists throughout all social classes
    D. insurance companies failing to reimburse eligible victims

20. Generally, when a worker begins an investigation of an initial report of child abuse or neglect, the first question that must be investigated is: 20.____

    A. How serious is the current situation?
    B. What level of intervention in indicated?
    C. What has actually happened to the child or children in question?
    D. What is the risk of future harm to the child?

21. In order to change his/her Social Security number (SSN), a victim of domestic violence   21.____

    A. must be able to substantiate extreme abuse or life endangerment
    B. must establish that the abuser has either misused the victim's SSN or could be expected to misuse it to locate the victim
    C. furnish any evidence documenting harassment or abuse, such as police or medical reports or protection orders
    D. should apply electronically, rather than in person

22. Which of the following is NOT a public policy strategy for combating child maltreatment?   22.____

    A. Profiling of offenders and victims
    B. Victim compensation
    C. Parenting education
    D. Legal reform

23. The most common stalking behavior is   23.____

    A. following or spying on the partner
    B. making unwanted, harassing phone calls
    C. threatening to harm children or pets
    D. vandalizing property

24. It is a common assumption among domestic violence professionals that women stay with abusive partners because they fear the consequences of leaving. Research of the issue   24.____

    A. refutes the fear with the finding that incidents of abuse decrease substantially following separation
    B. refutes the fear with the finding that women are most likely to say they stay in an abusive relationship because they believe the abusive partner will change
    C. refutes this fear with the finding that women are most likely to say they stay in an abusive relationship because they feel they "deserve the abuse"
    D. confirms this fear, with the finding that incidents of abuse increase following separation

25. A survivor of domestic abuse is granted a lifetime order of protection by Indian tribal   25.____
    authorities. The order will still be enforceable if she moves to
    I.   a state where the maximum duration of an order is three years
    II. a reservation that is under the jurisdiction of a different tribe
    III. Mexico
    IV. Canada

    A. I and II
    B. I and IV
    C. I, II and III
    D. II, III and IV

KEY (CORRECT ANSWERS)

1.	C		11.	C
2.	B		12.	C
3.	C		13.	A
4.	C		14.	A
5.	D		15.	D
6.	A		16.	A
7.	B		17.	D
8.	D		18.	D
9.	D		19.	B
10.	B		20.	C

21.	C
22.	B
23.	A
24.	D
25.	A

TEST 3

DIRECTIONS: Each question or incomplete statement is followed by several suggested answers or completions. Select the one the BEST answers the question or completes the statement. *PRINT THE LETTER OF THE CORRECT ANSWER IN THE SPACE AT THE RIGHT.*

1. A woman is not yet ready to leave her abusive husband because she is unsure of how she will support her two children, whom she intends to take with her when she does leave. The woman is willing to work with a domestic violence professional on a safety plan for minimizing risks and injuries during a battering episode. Each of the following is a guideline to be followed in such a plan, EXCEPT

    A. never sharing details of the plan with the abuser
    B. never sharing details of the plan with the children
    C. making a habit of backing the car into the driveway and keeping it fueled
    D. tell trusted friends and neighbors know of the situation and devise a signal or code word for when help is needed

1.____

2. A victim of domestic violence is applying for benefits from the state department of social services, and wishes to invoke the waiver of certain requirements that is available to domestic violence victims. In order to receive the waiver, she will have to provide proof of the domestic violence. In most cases, the minimal proof required is comprised of
        I.   a sworn statement
        II. an order of protection
        III. hospital records
        IV. police reports

    A. I only
    B. II only
    C. I and II
    D. I, III and IV

2.____

3. Women who are involved in abusive relationships are generally LEAST likely to

    A. believe they can change the batterer's behavior
    B. exhibit consistent patterns of behavior
    C. feel shame or guilt
    D. express a fear of staying with the batterer

3.____

4. An *in camera* proceeding:

    A. allows child testimony to be videotaped outside the courtroom for later use
    B. violates the right to a public trial
    C. violates the defendant's right to cross-examination of all witnesses
    D. violates the hearsay rule regarding third-party testimony

4.____

5. Generally, the problem of elder victimization is becoming better known. Each of the following is a reason for this, EXCEPT

    A. increasing media exposure
    B. the growing elderly population

5.____

C. mandatory reporting regulations
D. increasing rates of offender apprehension

6. A jurisdiction that does not recognize marital rape under any condition is said to have: 6._____

    A. an absolute exemption
    B. a shield law
    C. spousal inclusion
    D. a consanguinity exemption

7. A woman's reasoning that it is all right for husbands to hit their wives is best explained by   7._____

    A. intrapsychic perspective
    B. learned helplessness
    C. socioculture
    D. PTSD

8. A domestic violence victim plans to leave with her children to live in another state. She   8._____
has received both an order of protection and a custody order. Once she moves, federal
laws that may be invoked to entitle the family to enforcement of the custody order under
full faith and credit include the
    I. Violence Against Women Act
    II. Uniform Child Custody Jurisdiction and Enforcement Act
    III. Parental Kidnapping Prevention Act
    IV. Indian Child Welfare Act

    A. I and II
    B. II and III
    C. II, III and IV
    D. I, II, III and IV

9. Several studies have been conducted on the personalities of battered women in order to   9._____
determine what makes them susceptible to abuse. The main problem with this approach
is that it

    A. places a certain amount of blame with the woman
    B. does not account for cultural differences
    C. hasn't revealed any personality traits that are shared consistently among battered
       women
    D. has no implications for prevention

10. Which of the following cases established tort liability for professionals who fail to report   10._____
suspected child abuse?

    A. *Canterbury v. Spence* (1972)
    B. *Landers v. Flood* (1976)
    C. *Krikorian v. Barry* (1987)
    D. *White v. North Carolina State Board of Examiners of Practicing Psychologists-*
       (1990)

11. In most stalking cases that also involve domestic violence, the most common reason why stalking behaviors cease is that the

    A. police warned the stalker
    B. victim moved to an undisclosed location
    C. stalker began another relationship
    D. stalker received professional help

11.____

12. During a first contact with a domestic violence professional, a woman discloses that she has been abused by her husband for many years and lives in constant fear. The professional should

    A. provide the client with a shelter referral
    B. insist that the client not return home
    C. report the husband to the police
    D. ask the client to bring her husband in for treatment

12.____

13. A child who is physically abused generally does NOT

    A. exhibit serious behavioral problems
    B. exhibit hypervigil ant or guarded behavior
    C. have bruises that are in different stages of healing
    D. show off injuries or bruises to other children

13.____

14. A woman's partner has enrolled in a court-ordered intervention program for batterers. The woman asks a domestic violence professional about the likelihood of the program's success. Without knowing the batterer personally, the professional knows that certain standards are common among programs that work better than others. These standards include

    I. strong encouragement of partner participation
    II. the use of "venting" exercises to channel physical displays of anger
    III. a curriculum that challenges the batterer's underlying belief system
    IV. a duration of 18 months or longer

    A. I only
    B. I, II and III
    C. II and III
    D. III and IV

14.____

15. Which of the following is NOT a key feature in a typical antistalking law?

    A. Whether the parties know each other
    B. Repeatedly following another person
    C. Placing the victim in fear for his or her well-being
    D. The criminal intent of the offender

15.____

16. A woman who is not a U.S. citizen is being physically abused by her husband, who is a U.S. citizen. Under the Violence Against Women Act, the woman can obtain lawful permanent residency through

    I. self-petitioning
    II. rehabilitative maintenance
    III. cancellation of removal
    IV. protective custody request

16.____

111

A. I only
B. I and III
C. II and III
D. III and IV

17. In most states, the _____ is the principal public agency responsible for both investigating reported cases of elder abuse and for providing victims and their families with treatment and protective services.

    17.____

A. Area Agency on Aging
B. Administration on Aging
C. Adult Protective Services
D. State Unit on Aging

18. What is the legal term for an individual who assumes parental obligations and status
without a formal, legal adoption?

    18.____

A. *Parens patriae*
B. *In loco parentis*
C. *Ad litem*
D. *In re*

19. Despite physical injury, which of the following expenses would NOT be compensable
under most state victim compensation statutes?

    19.____

A. Any attempt to prevent a crime
B. Aiding a crime victim
C. Apprehending a criminal
D. Assisting a law enforcement officer

20. Most intervention or education groups for men who batter report attrition rates in the
range of _____ percent.

    20.____

A. 15-30
B. 25-40
C. 50-75
D. 80-95

21. Victims of domestic violence who plan to leave an abusive situation should be advised to

    21.____

    I. contact a local shelter for information about rights, financial assistance, and
counseling
    II. maintain a journal of all violent incidents
    III. seek an alternative means of support for the abandoned spouse
    IV. practice an escape plan in case the need arises

A. I and IV
B. I, II and IV
C. I, III, and IV
D. All of the above

22. A counselor who works with a domestic violence victim views the battering episode as an
indicator of other underlying tensions in the relationship. The counselor has adopted the
_____ approach.

    22.____

A. family violence
B. spouse abuse
C. feminist
D. Freudian

23. Under the full faith and credit provisions of the Violence Against Woman Act, criminal orders of protection   23.____

    A. are not specifically enforceable in a jurisdiction that did not issue them
    B. are usually more difficult to enforce than civil orders
    C. have the same status as military orders of protection
    D. may or may not be enforceable in a jurisdiction that did not issue them, depending on statutes

24. Which of the following is LEAST likely to be included in the behavioral profile of an abused or neglected child?   24.____

    A. Excessive attention to physical appearance
    B. Immaturity
    C. Self-hatred
    D. Sexual sophistication (beyond age level)

25. Arguments against the idea of "victim precipitation" include attacks on each of the following assumptions, EXCEPT the idea that victims   25.____

    A. behave in ways that cause crime behavior causes crime
    B. give off signals to which offenders are prompted to respond
    C. demonstrate behaviors that are necessary and sufficient causal mechanisms
    D. often know their perpetrators

_____

KEY (CORRECT ANSWERS)

1.	B		11.	B
2.	A		12.	A
3.	B		13.	D
4.	A		14.	D
5.	D		15.	A
6.	A		16.	B
7.	C		17.	C
8.	C		18.	B
9.	A		19.	C
10.	B		20.	C

21.	B
22.	A
23.	B
24.	A
25.	D

_____

EXAMINATION SECTION
TEST 1

DIRECTIONS: Each question or incomplete statement is followed by several suggested answers or completions. Select the one the BEST answers the question or completes the statement. *PRINT THE LETTER OF THE CORRECT ANSWER IN THE SPACE AT THE RIGHT.*

1. A client and a professional meet to discuss the client's drinking problem and how it relates to the problems she's having in putting her life back together after leaving her abusive husband. During the interview, the worker asks the client: "You would be in a better position to hold down a job if you stopped drinking, wouldn't you?" This question will signal to the client that the professional

    1._____

    A. is more worried about whether the client can support herself than about whether she can stop drinking
    B. is not really asking a question, but already has an answer in mind
    C. does not understand the difficulties involved in alcoholism
    D. cares about whether the client remains employed

2. Typically—and unless the client is in crisis—the questioning process in a helping interview should progress

    2._____

    A. chronologically
    B. from general to specific
    C. from specific to general
    D. in a series of grouped topical units

3. When interviewing a client, a professional may sometimes make use of the questioning technique known as the "reaction probe." The purpose of the technique is to

    3._____

    A. point out inadequately covered content
    B. increase the emotional depth of the interview
    C. provoke an affective reaction from the client
    D. elicit a clearer explanation of personal situations

4. Of the following techniques or strategies that can be used by a professional during a client interview, which is most directive in nature?

    4._____

    A. Clarifying
    B. Reflecting
    C. Interpretation
    D. Paraphrasing

5. The primary effect of confrontation during a client interview is to

    5._____

    A. break down client defenses
    B. initiate reconsideration of behaviors
    C. force a client to face the facts
    D. introduce unpleasant content

6. During an interview with a battered young woman, the victim reaches the conclusion that she would like to return home. The professional has met with this woman several times previously, and has a strong personal feeling that she should leave the abusive situation. The BEST move on the part of the professional at this point would be to

    6._____

    A. try to help the client clarify the reasons behind her decision
    B. advise the client that her life may be in danger if she stays in this situation
    C. say nothing and leave the woman to make her own decisions
    D. tell the client that a room has been reserved for her at a local shelter, and that she should stay there for a while

7. During an interview, a professional sometimes utters minimal encouragements ("uh-huh," "I see," "hmm") while a client is speaking. Usually, the effect of these essentially meaningless sounds is to

    7._____

    A. distract the client from what she is trying to say
    B. assure the client that the professional is present and involved
    C. give the impression that the professinoal is only pretending to listen
    D. steer the client toward a particular topic or area of interest

8. During an interview with a client who has proven somewhat resistant the professional encounters a long silence from the client, who has just cut herself off in mid-sentence and is staring at the worker. The FIRST thing the worker should try to break the silence is to

    8._____

    A. summarize the client's last thoughts
    B. say something such as "uh-huh" or "I see," and then wait a moment
    C. say, "I wonder why you're silent."
    D. wait patiently for at least a minute before interjecting

9. During a client interview, the listening/intervention technique known as "reflection of feeling" is used to

    9._____

    A. intensify the depth of the interview
    B. encourage specific content for discussion
    C. respond to the client's verbalize thinking
    D. bring essential content to the surface of the discussion

10. During the assessment phase of an interview, checklists are most useful for identifying and selecting

    10._____

    A. problems for intervention
    B. specific objectives
    C. available resources
    D. general goals

11. Of the following, which should probably take place FIRST during an intake interview?

    11._____

    A. Developmental history
    B. Statement of presenting problem
    C. Initial intervention
    D. Cross-sectional history

12. In using the "reflection of meaning" technique in a client interview, a professional should   12.____
do each of the following, EXCEPT

    A. begin with a sentence stem such as "You mean..." or "Sounds like you believe..."
    B. offer an interpretation of the client's words.
    C. add paraphrasing of longer client statements.
    D. close with a "check-out" such as, "Am I hearing you right?"

13. In which of the following situations is the use of "small talk" in an opening interview   13.____
MOST likely to be contraindicated?

    A. Referral for ongoing marital problems
    B. Home visit to a general assistance client
    C. Domestic crisis intervention
    D. Court-ordered anger management counseling

14. During an interview with a family, a professional observes that the youngest son often   14.____
exhibits overly adaptive behavior – he strenuously attempts to comfort the father when the
father appears to be upset. Later, the practitioner learns that in school, the child often
becomes uneasy or upset whenever another child cries or acts out. The practitioner
should interpret these signs as suggestive of possible

    A. repressed memories of past trauma
    B. sexual abuse
    C. formation of a dysfunctional triad
    D. physical abuse

15. During an assessment interview, a professional and client explore the range of problems   15.____
that most concern the client. The NEXT step for the professional and client would be to

    A. rank the problems in their priority to the client
    B. determine how progress will be measured as these problems are addressed
    C. identify barriers to resolving each problem
    D. define each problem in explicit behavioral terms

16. When an interviewer considers what type of nonverbal behavior will be appropriate given   16.____
the interviewee's cultural background, the interviewer is making a decision about

    A. processing
    B. encoding
    C. decoding
    D. transmission

17. Questions that begin with the word "_____" are typically theones that clients find most   17.____
frustrating to answer in an interview.

    A. have
    B. why
    C. what
    D. how

18. During an interview, a client expresses feelings of being different or deviant. Which of the following techniques would be MOST appropriate for counteracting these feelings?   18.____

    A. Encouragement
    B. Reassurance
    C. Negative reinforcement
    D. Universal ization

19. During an assessment interview, a husband who has been convicted of physically abusing his wife states that the reason for the abuse was because "that's all she understands." In this case, the husband is practicing   19.____

    A. rationalization
    B. intellectualization
    C. a task-focused coping strategy
    D. an emotion-focused coping strategy

20. Accommodating is a skill in which domestic violence professionals communicate to the clients that they are being heard. This technique also assists professionals by ensuring that they have a clear understanding of the client's perceptions of the problems. Accommodating skills consist of   20.____
    I.   attending behaviors
    II. concreteness
    III. reflections
    IV. tracking

    A. I only
    B. I, II and III
    C. II and III
    D. I, II, III and IV

21. During an assessment interview, a professional and a client try to clarify and analyze the client's sense of self. If the worker wants to discover something about the client's self-acceptance, which of the following questions is MOST appropriate?   21.____

    A. To what extent do you worry about illness and physical incapacity?
    B. Is what you expect to happen mostly good or mostly bad?
    C. Do you enjoy the times when you are alone?
    D. Where do your other family members live?

22. Concreteness assists clients in focusing conversation or messages from vagueness to descriptive, specific, and operational language. Vagueness is often used unconsciously by clients to avoid addressing painful issues. Domestic professionals have the responsibility to assist clients in making concrete statements. Concreteness can be encouraged by: 22.____
    I.   examining perceptions and exploring the basis for the client's conclusions
    II. using concrete responses with clients
    III. clarifying unspecific or unfamiliar terms
    IV. drawing out details about experiences, interactions and behaviors

    A. I and II
    B. I, II and III

C. II and III
D. I, II, III and IV

23. Each of the following is a general guideline that should be used for effective listening dur-   23.____
ing the interview process, EXCEPT

    A. have a clear idea of the purpose of the interview before the session begins
    B. assume and accept a certain level of ignorance on the part of oneself
    C. develop a clear expectation about what the client will say during the interview
    D. listen for recurrent and dominant themes, rather than focus on detail

24. When interacting with clients from different cultures, domestic violence professionals   24.____
must

    I. recognize that discrepancies about time can be legitimate cultural differ-
      ences
    II. address clients as Mr., Ms., or Mrs. until given permission to use first names
    III. recognize that handshakes are intimate in some cultures and casual in oth-
      ers
    IV. be mindful that different cultures may assign different levels of authority and
      formality to the helping relationship

    A. I and II
    B. II only
    C. II, III and IV
    D. I, II, III and IV

25. During a client interview, a professional often repeats verbatim a key word or phrase from   25.____
the client's last response. The purpose of this repetition of content is to

    A. confront the client with contradictions or inaccuracies in his/her statements
    B. open the door for an interpretation of the client's statement
    C. encourage the client's choice of material to pursue
    D. distill client statements to their essential components

KEY (CORRECT ANSWERS)

1.	B		11.	B
2.	B		12.	B
3.	B		13.	C
4.	C		14.	D
5.	B		15.	D
6.	A		16.	B
7.	B		17.	B
8.	B		18.	D
9.	A		19.	A
10.	D		20.	B

21.	C
22.	D
23.	C
24.	D
25.	C

TEST 2

1. Helping professionals often make use of reframing to influence the direction of interviews. In the case of domestic violence, professionals should exercise extreme caution with this technique–if used improperly, it could

    A. suggest to the client that there is some positive intent behind the abuser's behavior
    B. alter the direction of information-gathering, from specific to general
    C. create a kind of victim/rescuer relationship between the client and the professional
    D. make the client to believe that he/she is not really being abused

1._____

2. In client interviews, "psychological attending" refers to how professionals

    A. congruently respond to the observed verbal and nonverbal behaviors of clients
    B. restate behaviors or beliefs in more positive ways
    C. convey a non-judgemental attitude
    D. restate of the person's multiple statements of feeling or content expressed over time

2._____

3. Tracking consists of a set of techniques that allows domestic violence professionals to influence the direction of interviews. Tracking skills include each of the following, EXCEPT

    A. summarization
    B. questions
    C. positive reframing
    D. springboarding

3._____

4. Which of the following questions or statements is MOST appropriate for a professional in initiating a helping relationship?

    A. "I understand you have a problem."
    B. "You came in here to see me about _____."
    C. "How can I help you today?"
    D. "I'm glad you came in to see me."

4._____

5. Which of the following is a guideline that should be observed in developing an assessment questionnaire for domestic violence victims?

    A. Develop several focused questionnaires rather than one all-purpose one.
    B. The most sensitive or probing questions should appear near the middle of the questionnaire.
    C. For complex ideas, form two-part questions.
    D. Include only open-ended questions.

5._____

6. General guidelines for cross-cultural interviews include   6._____
    - I. the use of summarizing in interviews
    - II. focusing on closed rather than open questions
    - III. remembering that not all cultures value openness and authen ticity
    - IV. extensive use of self-disclosure to increase client comfort

    A. I only
    B. I and II
    C. II, III and IV
    D. I, II, III and IV

7. In general, it is believed that interviewers who spend less than a minimum of _____ of   7._____
    an interview listening to the client are moreactive than they should be.

    A. one-fourth
    B. one-third
    C. one-half
    D. two thirds

8. In comparing a normal conversation and a helping interview, which of the following state-   8._____
    ments is generally TRUE?

    A. A conversation involves no subsequent accountability.
    B. A conversation involves a clear delineation of roles.
    C. An interview involves an equal distribution of power and authority.
    D. The interaction in an interview follows social expectations and norms.

9. In a client interview, a worker should typically use self-disclosure   9._____

    A. at a level that is tailored to client feedback
    B. intensely during the treatment phase in order to establish a bond
    C. as early as possible in the process to establish the expectation
    D. before other methods at client revelation have been attempted

10. During an intake interview, a professional makes the decision to severely curtail the gath-   10._____
    ering of past history between the client and her abuser, and instead focus on current
    interactions. Probably the greatest risk involved in this approach is that

    A. the heightened sense of emotional involvement might overwhelm the client
    B. the client may begin to doubt the competency of the therapist
    C. the client may become confused about the therapist's purpose
    D. there may be a lower degree of authenticity in client interactions

11. During an assessment interview, a professional should try as much as possible to get a   11._____
    client to arrange her description of the presenting problem

    A. narratively, in terms of how she sees it, no matter how incoherent
    B. chronologically, to facilitate the composition of a sociohistory
    C. thematically, in terms of recurring issues and problems in her life
    D. empirically, in terms only of what happened on particular dates or during particular
       periods

12. Which of the following is a guideline that should be used regarding the use of interpreta-   12._____
tion during a client interview?

    A. If a client rejects the interpretation, be prepared to defend it.
    B. Interpretations are most useful during intake and assessment interviews.
    C. Interpretations must be offered immediately after the statement that provokes
       them.
    D. Offer interpretations tentatively, as a hypothesis.

13. Which of the following is a disadvantage associated with the use of closed questions in   13._____
client interviews?

    A. May discourage reluctant or resistant clients from participating
    B. More difficult format for less experienced interviewers
    C. May encourage passive and restricted client participation
    D. Risks failure to obtain specific detailed content

14. Interviewing in the helping professions is often divided into four stages. Which of the fol-   14._____
lowing is MOST likely to be omitted during early interviews with domestic violence victims?

    A. Social
    B. Problem definition
    C. Focus
    D. Closure

15. Which of the following is NOT a guideline that should be used by a professional in sum-   15._____
marizing during an interview?

    A. Summarize when a transition to new content is desirable.
    B. The content of summaries should be ordered in the same way that the client
       ordered it, in order to avoid confusion.
    C. Wait to summarize until the content is sufficient to suggest a general theme.
    D. The client should participate in summarizing, either by summarizing him/herself, or
       by responding to the worker's summary.

16. In the helping interview, "facilitative genuineness" refers to   16._____

    A. an absence of mixed messages in communication with a person to affect change
    B. conveying the appropriate amount of authority for inspiring faith in the client
    C. tuning into a person's emotions and communicating understanding without losing
       objectivity
    D. the ability to maintain a non-judgmental attitude that conveys caring, concern, and
       acceptance of the other person as a unique human being

17. Which of the following should typically NOT be an objective of a worker's self-disclosure   17._____
during a client interview?

    A. Facilitating the client's willingness to communicate
    B. Modeling appropriate behavior for the client
    C. Pointing out an appropriate resolution or course of action
    D. Provoking a catharsis for the client

18. Usually, the purpose of opening an initial client interview with general conversation or   18._____
     "small talk" is to

    A. construct an unobtrusive opportunity for making and recording initial observations
    B. ease the client's transition from a familiar mode of speaking into a new and unfa-
        miliar role
    C. soften the client's defenses so that initial questioning will catch him/ her off guard
    D. downplay the seriousness of the interview

19. In client interviews, supportive statements by the professional are MOST likely to be   19._____
     effective if he or she can

    A. set aside feelings of disapproval for other client behaviors
    B. identify the client's feeling or the behavior for which the practitioner is expressing
        approval or encouragement
    C. use the statement to steer the client toward a specific course of action
    D. differentiate between the times when a client is genuinely hurting and when he/she
        is simply trying to gain sympathy

20. During a conversation, the wife of an abuser says to a domestic violence professional: "I   20._____
     just don't feel as if I have any friends out there who can help me deal with this".
     The domestic violence professional responds by saying: "It's important to you to have
     friends who help you through tough times".
     "Yes," the client says.
     The professional says: "Was there a time when you did - when there were friends you
     could turn to?"
     In this conversation, the professional is making use of the techniques

    A. reflecting and summarizing
    B. refraining and springboarding
    C. clarifying and attending
    D. problem definition and closure

21. Typically, the _____ stage of an interview is the one which is most powerful in determin-   21._____
     ing the interviewee's impression of the interview as a whole.

    A. opening
    B. questioning
    C. closing
    D. discussion

22. During an interview with a client, the professional says: "You remember a while ago,   22._____
     when we were talking about your wedding, you mentioned that that was the greatest day
     of your life. Can you tell me why you felt this way?" This is an example of the technique
     known as _____ transition.

    A. mutational
    B. cued
    C. reversional
    D. confrontational

23. During an interview, a client says, "He's changed completely. Sometimes it doesn't seem   23.____
as if he has any feelings left for me."
The professional responds by saying: "You seem to think he doesn't love you very much".
The client says, "So you think he loves me very much? What makes you say that?"
What has just occurred in this interview could be defined as a

    A. projection
    B. reaction formation
    C. displacement
    D. repression

24. Advantages of the use of open-ended questions in client interviews include   24.____
      I.   maximizing client freedom regarding content
      II.   providing client's cognitive and affective views of problem
      III.   easier format for inexperienced interviewers
      IV.   maximizing worker access to desirable data

    A. I and II
    B. I, II and III
    C. III only
    D. I, II, III and IV

25. During an assessment interview, a client tends to ramble through many digressions in   25.____
recounting her situation. In order to lend coherence to the session, the BEST approach
on the part of the professional would be to

    A. gently interrupting digressions with a reminder of the interview's purpose
    B. offer gentle reminders to the client after she has finished with a digression
    C. occasionally paraphrase client statements
    D. offer periodic summaries of the client's accounts

KEY (CORRECT ANSWERS)

1.	A	11.	A
2.	A	12.	D
3.	A	13.	C
4.	B	14.	A
5.	A	15.	B
6.	A	16.	A
7.	D	17.	C
8.	C	18.	B
9.	A	19.	B
10.	A	20.	B

21.	C
22.	C
23.	B
24.	A
25.	D

———

INTERVIEWING
EXAMINATION SECTION
TEST 1

DIRECTIONS: Each question or incomplete statement is followed by several suggested answers or completions. Select the one that BEST answers the question or completes the statement. *PRINT THE LETTER OF THE CORRECT ANSWER IN THE SPACE AT THE RIGHT.*

1. An interview is BEST conducted in private primarily because   1._____

    A.   the person interviewed will tend to be less self-conscious
    B.   the interviewer will be able to maintain his continuity of thought better
    C.   it will insure that the interview is "off the record"
    D.   people tend to "show off" before an audience

2. An interviewer can BEST establish a good relationship with the person being interviewed   2._____
    by

    A.   assuming casual interest in the statements made by the person being interviewed
    B.   taking the point of view of the person interviewed
    C.   controlling the interview to a major extent
    D.   showing a genuine interest in the person

3. An interviewer will be better able to understand the person interviewed and his problems   3._____
    if he recognizes that much of the person's behavior is due to motives

    A.   which are deliberate
    B.   of which he is unaware
    C.   which are inexplicable
    D.   which are kept under control

4. An interviewer's attention must be directed toward himself as well as toward the person   4._____
    interviewed. This statement means that the interviewer should

    A.   keep in mind the extent to which his own prejudices may influence his judgment
    B.   rationalize the statements made by the person interviewed
    C.   gain the respect and confidence of the person interviewed
    D.   avoid being too impersonal

5. More complete expression will be obtained from a person being interviewed if the inter-   5._____
    viewer can create the impression that

    A.   the data secured will become part of a permanent record
    B.   official information must be accurate in every detail
    C.   it is the duty of the person interviewed to give accurate data
    D.   the person interviewed is participating in a discussion of his own problems

6. The practice of asking leading questions should be avoided in an interview because the   6._____

    A.   interviewer risks revealing his attitudes to the person being interviewed
    B.   interviewer may be led to ignore the objective attitudes of the person interviewed
    C.   answers may be unwarrantedly influenced
    D.   person interviewed will resent the attempt to lead him and will be less cooperative

7. A good technique for the interviewer to use in an effort to secure reliable data and to reduce the possibility of misunderstanding is to

    A. use casual undirected conversation, enabling the person being interviewed to talk about himself, and thus secure the desired information
    B. adopt the procedure of using direct questions regularly
    C. extract the desired information from the person being interviewed by putting him on the defensive
    D. explain to the person being interviewed the information desired and the reason for needing it

7.____

8. You are interviewing a patient to determine whether she is eligible for medical assistance. Of the many questions that you have to ask her, some are routine questions that patients tend to answer willingly and easily. Other questions are more personal and some patients tend to resent being asked them and avoid answering them directly. For you to begin the interview with the more personal questions would be

    A. *desirable,* because the end of the interview will go smoothly and the patient will be left with a warm feeling
    B. *undesirable,* because the patient might not know the answers to the questions
    C. *desirable,* because you will be able to return to these questions later to verify the accuracy of the responses
    D. *undesirable,* because you might antagonize the patient before you have had a chance to establish rapport

8.____

9. While interviewing a patient about her family composition, the patient asks you whether you are married.
Of the following, the MOST appropriate way for you to handle this situation is to

    A. answer the question briefly and redirect her back to the topic under discussion
    B. refrain from answering the question and proceed with the interview
    C. advise the patient that it is more important that she answer your questions than that you answer hers, and proceed with the interview
    D. promise the patient that you will answer her question later, in the hope that she will forget, and redirect her back to the topic under discussion

9.____

10. In response to a question about his employment history, a patient you are interviewing rambles and talks about unrelated matters.
Of the following, the MOST appropriate course of action for you to take FIRST is to

    A. ask questions to direct the patient back to his employment history
    B. advise him to concentrate on your questions and not to discuss irrelevant information
    C. ask him why he is resisting a discussion of his employment history
    D. advise him that if you cannot get the information you need, he will not be eligible for medical assistance

10.____

11. Suppose that a person you are interviewing becomes angry at some of the questions   11.____
you have asked, calls you meddlesome and nosy, and states that she will not answer
those questions.
Of the following, which is the BEST action for you to take?

    A. Explain the reasons the questions are asked and the importance of the answers.
    B. Inform the interviewee that you are only doing your job and advise her that she
       should answer your questions or leave the office.
    C. Report to your supervisor what the interviewee called you and refuse to continue
       the interview.
    D. End the interview and tell the interviewee she will not be serviced by your depart-
       ment.

12. Suppose that during the course of an interview the interviewee demands in a very rude   12.____
way that she be permitted to talk to your supervisor or someone in charge.
Which of the following is probably the BEST way to handle this situation?

    A. Inform your supervisor of the demand and ask her to speak to the interviewee.
    B. Pay no attention to the demands of the interviewee and continue the interview.
    C. Report to your supervisor and tell her to get another interviewer for this inter-
       viewee.
    D. Tell her you are the one "in charge" and that she should talk to you.

13. Of the following, the outcome of an interview by an aide depends MOST heavily on the   13.____

    A. personality of the interviewee
    B. personality of the aide
    C. subject matter of the questions asked
    D. interaction between aide and interviewee

14. Some patients being interviewed are primarily interested in making a favorable impres-   14.____
sion. The aide should be aware of the fact that such patients are more likely than other
patients to

    A. try to anticipate the answers the interviewer is looking for
    B. answer all questions openly and frankly
    C. try to assume the role of interviewer
    D. be anxious to get the interview over as quickly as possible

15. The type of interview which an aide usually conducts is substantially different from most   15.____
interviewing situations in all of the following aspects EXCEPT the

    A. setting   B. kinds of clients
    C. techniques employed   D. kinds of problems

16. During an interview, an aide uses a "leading question." This type of question is so-called   16.____
because it generally

    A. starts a series of questions about one topic
    B. suggests the answer which the aide wants
    C. forms the basis for a following "trick" question
    D. sets, at the beginning, the tone of the interview

17. Casework interviewing is always directed to the client and his situation. The one of the following which is the MOST accurate statement with respect to the proper focus of an interview is that the

    A. caseworker limits the client to concentration on objective data
    B. client is generally permitted to talk about facts and feelings with no direction from the caseworker
    C. main focus in casework interviews is on feelings rather than facts
    D. caseworker is responsible for helping the client focus on any material which seems to be related to his problems or difficulties

18. Assume that you are conducting a training program for the caseworkers under your supervision. At one of the sessions, you discuss the problem of interviewing a dull and stupid client who gives a slow and disconnected case history. The BEST of the following interviewing methods for you to recommend in such a case in order to ascertain the facts is for the caseworker to

    A. ask the client leading questions requiring "yes" or "no" answers
    B. request the client to limit his narration to the essential facts so that the interview can be kept as brief as possible
    C. review the story with the client, patiently asking simple questions
    D. tell the client that unless he is more cooperative he cannot be helped to solve his problem

19. A recent development in casework interviewing procedure, known as multiple-client interviewing, consists of interviews of the entire family at the same time. However, this may not be an effective casework method in certain situations. Of the following, the situation in which the standard individual interview would be preferable is when

    A. family members derive consistent and major gratification from assisting each other in their destructive responses
    B. there is a crucial family conflict to which the members are reacting
    C. the family is overwhelmed by interpersonal anxieties which have not been explored
    D. the worker wants to determine the pattern of family interaction to further his diagnostic understanding

20. A follow-up interview was arranged for an applicant in order that he could furnish certain requested evidence. At this follow-up interview, the applicant still fails to furnish the necessary evidence. It would be MOST advisable for you to

    A. advise the applicant that he is now considered ineligible
    B. ask the applicant how soon he can get the necessary evidence and set a date for another interview
    C. question the applicant carefully and thoroughly to determine if he has misrepresented or falsified any information
    D. set a date for another interview and tell the applicant to get the necessary evidence by that time.

KEY (CORRECT ANSWERS)

1.	A		11.	A
2.	D		12.	A
3.	B		13.	D
4.	A		14.	A
5.	D		15.	C
6.	C		16.	B
7.	D		17.	D
8.	D		18.	C
9.	A		19.	A
10.	A		20.	B

TEST 2

DIRECTIONS: Each question or incomplete statement is followed by several suggested answers or completions. Select the one that BEST answers the question or completes the statement. *PRINT THE LETTER OF THE CORRECT ANSWER IN THE SPACE AT THE RIGHT.*

1. In interviewing, the practice of anticipating an applicant's answers to questions is gener-   1.____
    ally

    A. *desirable,* because it is effective and economical when it is necessary to interview
        large numbers of applicants
    B. *desirable,* because many applicants have language difficulties
    C. *undesirable,* because it is the inalienable right of every person to answer as he
        sees fit
    D. *undesirable,* because applicants may tend to agree with the answer proposed by
        the interviewer even when the answer is not entirely correct

2. When an initial interview is being conducted, one way of starting is to explain the pur-   2.____
    pose of the interview to the applicant. The practice of starting the interview with such an
    explanation is generally

    A. *desirable,* because the applicant can then understand why the interview is neces-
        sary and what will be accomplished by it
    B. *desirable,* because it creates the rapport which is necessary to successful inter-
        viewing
    C. *undesirable,* because time will be saved by starting directly with the questions
        which must be asked
    D. *undesirable,* because the interviewer should have the choice of starting an inter-
        view in any manner he prefers

3. For you to use responses such as "That's interesting," "Uh-huh" and "Good" during an   3.____
    interview with a patient is

    A. *desirable,* because they indicate that the investigator is attentive
    B. *undesirable,* because they are meaningless to the patient
    C. *desirable,* because the investigator is not supposed to talk excessively
    D. *undesirable,* because they tend to encourage the patient to speak freely

4. During the course of a routine interview, the BEST tone of voice for an interviewer to use   4.____
    is

    A. authoritative   B. uncertain
    C. formal   D. conversational

5. It is recommended that interviews which inquire into the personal background of an indi-   5.____
    vidual should be held in private. The BEST reason for this practice is that privacy

    A. allows the individual to talk freely about the details of his background
    B. induces contemplative thought on the part of the interviewed individual
    C. prevents any interruptions by departmental personnel during the interview
    D. most closely resembles the atmosphere of the individual's personal life

6. Assume that you are interviewing a patient to determine whether he has any savings accounts. To obtain this information, the MOST effective way to phrase your question would be:

    A. "You don't have any savings, do you?"
    B. "At which bank do you have a savings account?"
    C. "Do you have a savings account?"
    D. "May I assume that you have a savings account?"

6.____

7. You are interviewing a patient who is not cooperating to the extent necessary to get all required information. Therefore, you decide to be more forceful in your approach.
In this situation, such a course of action is

    A. *advisable,* because such a change in approach may help to increase the patient's participation
    B. *advisable,* because you will be using your authority more effectively
    C. *inadvisable,* because you will not be able to change this approach if it doesn't produce results
    D. *inadvisable,* because an aggressive approach generally reduces the validity of the interview

7.____

8. You have attempted to interview a patient on two separate occasions, and both attempts were unsuccessful. The patient has been totally uncooperative and you sense a personal hostility toward you.
Of the following, the BEST way to handle this type of situation would be to

    A. speak to the patient in a courteous manner and ask him to explain exactly what he dislikes about you
    B. inform the patient that you will not allow personality conflicts to disrupt the interview
    C. make no further attempt to interview the patient and recommend that he be billed in full
    D. discuss the problem with your supervisor and suggest that another investigator be assigned to try to interview the patient

8.____

9. At the beginning of an interview, a patient with normal vision tells you that he is reluctant to discuss his finances. You realize that it will be necessary in this case to ask detailed questions about his net income. When you begin this line of questioning, of the following, the LEAST important aspect you should consider is your

    A. precise wording of the question
    B. manner of questioning
    C. tone of voice
    D. facial expressions

9.____

10. A caseworker under your supervision has been assigned the task of interviewing a man who is applying for foster home placement for his two children. The caseworker seeks your advice as to how to question this man, stating that she finds the applicant to be a timid and self-conscious person who seems torn between the necessity of having to answer the worker's questions truthfully and the effect he thinks his answers will have on his application. Of the following, the BEST method for the caseworker to use in order to determine the essential facts in this case is to

10.____

A.   assure the applicant that he need not worry since the majority of applications for foster home placement are approved
B.   delay the applicant's narration of the facts important to the case until his embarrassment and fears have been overcome
C.   ignore the statements made by the applicant and obtain all the required information from his friends and relatives
D.   inform the applicant that all statements made by him will be verified and are subject to the law governing perjury

11.   Assume that a worker is interviewing a boy in his assigned group in order to help him find a job. At the BEGINNING of the interview, the worker should   11._____

A.   suggest a possible job for the youth
B.   refer the youth to an employment agency
C.   discuss the youth's work history and skills with him
D.   refer the youth to the manpower and career development agency

12.   As part of the investigation to locate an absent father, you make a field visit to interview one of the father's friends. Before beginning the interview, you identify yourself to the friend and show him your official identification.
For you to do this is, generally,   12._____

A.   *good practice,* because the friend will have proof that you are authorized to make such confidential investigations
B.   *poor practice,* because the friend may not answer your questions when he knows why you are interviewing him
C.   *good practice,* because your supervisor can confirm from the friend that you actually made the interview
D.   *poor practice,* because the friend may warn the absent father that your agency is looking for him

13.   You are interviewing a client in his home as part of your investigation of an anonymous complaint that he has been receiving Medicaid fraudulently. During the interview, the client frequently interrupts your questions to discuss the hardships of his life and the bitterness he feels about his medical condition.
Of the following, the BEST way for you to deal with these discussions is to   13._____

A.   cut them off abruptly, since the client is probably just trying to avoid answering your questions
B.   listen patiently, since these discussions may be helpful to the client and may give you information for your investigation
C.   remind the client that you are investigating a complaint against him and he must answer directly
D.   seek to gain the client's confidence by discussing any personal or medical problems which you yourself may have

14.   While interviewing an absent father to determine his ability to pay child support, you realize that his answers to some of your questions contradict his answers to other questions. Of the following, the BEST way for you to try to get accurate information from the father is to   14._____

A.   confront him with his contradictory answers and demand an explanation from him

B. use your best judgment as to which of his answers are accurate and question him accordingly
C. tell him that he has misunderstood your questions and that he must clarify his answers
D. ask him the same questions in different words and follow up his answers with related questions

15. Assume that an applicant, obviously under a great deal of stress, talks continuously and rambles, making it difficult for you to determine the exact problem and her need. In order to make the interview more successful, it would be BEST for you to

    15.____

A. interrupt the applicant and ask her specific questions in order to get the information you need
B. tell the applicant that her rambling may be a basic cause of her problem
C. let the applicant continue talking as long as she wishes
D. ask the applicant to get to the point because other people are waiting for you

16. A worker must be able to interview clients all day and still be able to listen and maintain interest.
Of the following, it is MOST important for you to show interest in the client because, if you appear interested,

    16.____

A. the client is more likely to appreciate your professional status
B. the client is more likely to disclose a greater amount of information
C. the client is less likely to tell lies
D. you are more likely to gain your supervisor's approval

17. When you are interviewing clients, it is important to notice and record how they say what they say — angrily, nervously, or with "body English" — because these signs may

    17.____

A. tell you that the client's words are the opposite of what the client feels and you may need to dig to find out what those feelings are
B. be the prelude to violent behavior which no aide is prepared to handle
C. show that the client does not really deserve serious consideration
D. be important later should you be asked to defend what you did for the client

18. The patient you are interviewing is reticent and guarded in responding to your questions. He is not providing the information needed to complete his application for medical assistance.
In this situation, the one of the following which is the most appropriate course of action for you to take FIRST is to

    18.____

A. end the interview and ask him to contact you when he is ready to answer your questions
B. advise the patient that you cannot end the interview until he has provided all the information you need to complete the application
C. emphasize to the patient the importance of the questions and the need to answer them in order to complete the application
D. advise the patient that if he answers your questions the interview will be easier for both of you

19. At the end of an interview with a patient, he describes a problem he is having with his teenage son, who is often truant and may be using narcotics. The patient asks you for advice in handling his son.
Of the following, the MOST appropriate action for you to take is to

    A. make an appointment to see the patient and his son together
    B. give the patient a list of drug counseling programs to which he may refer his son
    C. suggest to the patient that his immediate concern should be his own hospitalization rather than his son's problem
    D. tell the patient that you are not qualified to assist him but will attempt to find out who can

19.____

20. A MOST appropriate condition in the use of direct questions to obtain personal data in an interview is that, whenever possible,

    A. the direct questions be used only as a means of encouraging the person interviewed to talk about himself
    B. provision be made for recording the information
    C. the direct questions be used only after all other methods have failed
    D. the person being interviewed understands the reason for requesting the information

20.____

KEY (CORRECT ANSWERS)

1.	D		11.	C
2.	A		12.	A
3.	A		13.	B
4.	D		14.	D
5.	A		15.	A
6.	B		16.	B
7.	A		17.	A
8.	D		18.	C
9.	A		19.	D
10.	B		20.	D

READING COMPREHENSION
UNDERSTANDING AND INTERPRETING WRITTEN MATERIAL
EXAMINATION SECTION
TEST 1

DIRECTIONS: Each question or incomplete statement is followed by several suggested answers or completions. Select the one that BEST answers the question or completes the statement. *PRINT THE LETTER OF THE CORRECT ANSWER IN THE SPACE AT THE RIGHT.*

Questions 1-5.

DIRECTIONS: Questions 1 through 5 are to be answered SOLELY on the basis of the following paragraph.

There are several different schools of thought about the causes of juvenile delinquency. According to the *cultural-transmission* school of thought, delinquency is neither inborn nor developed independently. Children learn to become delinquents as members of groups in which delinquent conduct is already established and *the thing to do.* This school maintains that a child need not be different from other children or have any problems or defects of personality or intelligence in order to become a delinquent. On the other hand, the *psychogenic* school views delinquency as a method of coping with some underlying problem of adjustment. This school also holds that the tendency to become delinquent is not inherited. The delinquent, however, has frustrations, deprivations, insecurities, anxieties, guilt feelings, or mental conflicts which differ in kind or degree from those of non-delinquent children. Delinquency is thought of as a symptom of the underlying problem of adjustment in the same way as a fever is a symptom of an underlying infection. According to this school, if other children exhibit the same behavior, it is because they have independently found a similar solution to their problems.

1. Of the following, the MOST suitable title for the above paragraph would be

    A. PROBLEMS IN THE SCIENTIFIC STUDY OF JUVENILE DELINQUENCY
    B. THE EFFECT OF DISTURBED FAMILY SITUATION
    C. TWO THEORIES OF JUVENILE DELINQUENCY
    D. SOLUTIONS TO A MAJOR SOCIAL PROBLEM

1.____

2. According to the above paragraph, the *cultural-transmission* school of thought holds that there is a definite relationship between juvenile delinquency and the youths'

    A. intelligence   B. psychological problems
    C. family problems   D. choice of friends

2.____

3. According to the above paragraph, of the following, both schools of thought reject as a cause of juvenile delinquency the factor of

    A. guilt feelings   B. inherited traits
    C. repeated frustration   D. extreme insecurities

3.____

4. On the basis of the above paragraph, which of the following statements is CORRECT?   4.____

    A. The *cultural-transmission* school of thought maintains that a child independently develops delinquent behavior as a solution to his problems.
    B. The *psychogenic* school of thought holds that children become delinquents because it is *the thing to do.*
    C. The *cultural-transmission* school of thought maintains that delinquency is the visible symptom of an underlying personality problem.
    D. The *psychogenic* school of thought holds that delinquents have mental conflicts that differ in kind or degree from non-delinquents.

5. The author's attitude toward these schools of thought is that he   5.____

    A. describes them objectively without indicating partiality to either school of thought
    B. favors the *cultural-transmission* school of thought
    C. favors the *psychogenic* school of thought
    D. suggests that he thinks both schools of thought are incorrect

Questions 6-7.

DIRECTIONS: Questions 6 and 7 are to be answered SOLELY on the basis of the following paragraph.

    Behavior that seems strange to adults often is motivated by the child's desire to please his peers or to gain their attention. His feelings when ridiculed by his peers may range from grief to rage. It is difficult for the child to express such feelings and the reasons for them to adults for to do so he must admit to himself the bitter fact that persons whose friendship he wants really do not like him. Instead of directly expressing his feelings, he may reveal them through symptoms such as fault-finding, fighting back, and complaining. As a result, adults may not realize that when he is telling them how much he dislikes certain children, he may really be expressing how much he would like to be liked by these same children, or how deeply he feels contempt of himself.

6. This paragraph implies that a child's constant complaints about certain other children may be his way of expressing   6.____

    A. his desire to be accepted by them
    B. his dislike of the adults around him
    C. ridicule for those he does not like
    D. how many faults those other children have

7. According to the above paragraph, a child may find it difficult to express his grief at being rejected by his peer group because   7.____

    A. his rejection motivates him to behave strangely
    B. he knows that the adults around him would not understand his grief
    C. he may not be able to admit the fact of his rejection to himself
    D. his anger prevents him from expressing grief

Questions 8-9.

DIRECTIONS: Questions 8 and 9 are to be answered SOLELY on the basis of the following paragraph.

A very small child has no concept of right or wrong. However, as soon as he is sufficiently developed to be aware of forces outside himself, he will begin to see the advantage of behaving so as to win approval and avoid punishment. If the parents' standard of behavior is presented to the child in a consistent manner, the child will begin to incorporate that standard within himself so that he feels the urge to do what his parents want him to do, whether they are there or not. Furthermore, he will feel uncomfortable doing what he thinks is wrong even if there is no probability of discovery and punishment. If the parents' standard of behavior is NOT consistent, the child may grow up too confused to establish any ideal for himself. We then have a youngster who truly does not know right from wrong. He is in danger of having no firm standard of behavior, no conscience, and no feeling of guilt in defying the established community pattern.

8.   The author of the above passage implies that a child whose parents do NOT present him   8.____
with a consistent standard of behavior

    A.   will learn the difference between right and wrong when he is older
    B.   may feel no guilt when committing delinquent acts
    C.   will feel uncomfortable doing what he thinks is wrong
    D.   is likely to establish his own ideal standards

9.   The above paragraph implies that when a child feels the urge to do what his parents want   9.____
him to do, even if they are not present, it means that the child

    A.   sees the advantages of behaving so as to avoid punishment
    B.   has no concept of right and wrong
    C.   has begun to develop a conscience based on his parents' standard of behavior
    D.   is afraid that his parents will find out if he misbehaves

Questions 10-13.

DIRECTIONS: Questions 10 through 13 are to be answered SOLELY on the basis of the information in the following passage.

NEW YORK CITY GANGS

City social work agencies and the police have been meeting at City Hall to coordinate efforts to defuse the tensions among teenage groups that they fear could flare into warfare once summer vacations begin. Police intelligence units, with the help of the District Attorneys' offices, are gathering information to identify gangs and their territories. A list of 3,000 gang members has already been assembled, and 110 gangs have been identified. Social workers from various agencies like the Department of Social Services, Neighborhood Youth Corps, and the Youth Board, are out every day developing liaison with groups of juveniles through meetings at schools and recreation centers. Many street workers spend their days seeking to ease the intergang hostility, tracing potentially incendiary rumors, and trying to channel willing gang members into participation in established summer programs. The city's Youth Services Agency plans to spend a million dollars for special summer programs in ten main city areas where gang activity is most firmly entrenched. Five of the *gang neighborhoods* are clustered in an area forming most of southeastern Bronx, and it is here that most of the 110 identified gangs have formed. Special Youth Services programs will also be directed toward the Rockaway section of Queens, Chinatown, Washington Heights, and two neighborhoods in northern Staten Island noted for a lot of motorcycle gang activity. Some of these programs will emphasize sports and recreation, others vocational guidance or neighborhood improvement, but each program will be aimed at benefiting all youngsters in the area. Although none of the money will be spent specifically on gang members, the Youth Services Agency is consulting gang leaders, along with other teenagers, on the projects they would like developed in their area.

10. The above passage states that one of the steps taken by street workers in trying to defuse the tensions among teenage gangs is that of   10.____

    A. conducting summer school sessions that will benefit all neighborhood youth
    B. monitoring neighborhood sports competitions between rival gangs
    C. developing liaison with community school boards and parent associations
    D. tracing rumors that could intensify intergang hostilities

11. Based on the information given in the above passage on gangs and New York City's gang members, it is CORRECT to state that   11.____

    A. there are no teenage gangs located in Brooklyn
    B. most of the gangs identified by the Police are concentrated in one borough
    C. there is a total of 110 gangs in New York City
    D. only a small percentage of gangs in New York City is in Queens

12. According to the above passage, one IMPORTANT aspect of the program is that   12.____

    A. youth gang leaders and other teenagers are involved in the planning
    B. money will be given directly to gang members for use on their projects
    C. only gang members will be allowed to participate in the programs
    D. the parents of gang members will act as youth leaders

13. Various city agencies are cooperating in the attempt to keep the city's youth *cool* during the summer school vacation period.   13.____
The above passage does NOT specifically indicate participation in this project by the

    A. Police Department
    B. District Attorney's Office
    C. Board of Education
    D. Department of Social Services

Questions 14-16.

DIRECTIONS: Questions 14 through 16 are to be answered SOLELY on the basis of the following paragraph.

Drug abuse prevention efforts are only in their beginning stages. Far less is known about how to design programs that successfully counter the seductive effects which drugs have upon the young than about how to build clinics and programs to treat those who have become addicts. The latter can be done with enough dollars, managerial competence, and qualified personnel. The former depends upon such intangibles as community leadership, personal attitudes, and, in the final analysis, individual choices. Given this void in our society's understanding of what it is that makes us so vulnerable to addiction, government must build upon its growing experience to invest wisely in those efforts that offer positive alternatives to drug abuse.

14. The one of the following which is probably the BEST title for the above paragraph is   14._____

     A. THE YOUTHFUL DRUG ABUSER
     B. GOVERNMENT'S MANAGEMENT OF DRUG PROGRAMS
     C. A SCIENTIFIC ANALYSIS OF DRUG CURES
     D. THE DIFFICULTY OF DRUG ABUSE PREVENTION

15. According to the above paragraph, treating drug addicts as compared to preventing drug   15._____
addiction among the young is GENERALLY

     A. *easier,* mainly because there is more public interest in this method
     B. *harder,* mainly because qualified personnel are not readily available
     C. *easier,* mainly because there is more known about how to accomplish this objective
     D. *harder,* mainly because confirmed drug addicts do not give up the habit readily

16. According to the above paragraph, the role of government in dealing with the problem of   16._____
drug addiction and youth should be to

     A. build larger clinics and develop additional programs for treatment of offenders
     B. help attract youth to behavior which is more desirable than that provided by the drug culture
     C. provide the funds and personnel essential to successful enforcement programs
     D. establish centers for the study and analysis of those factors that make our citizens vulnerable to addiction

Questions 17-20.

DIRECTIONS: Questions 17 through 20 are to be answered SOLELY on the basis of the following paragraph.

Many of our city's most troubled drug addicts are not being reached by the existing treatment programs. They either refuse to enter treatment voluntarily or have dropped out of these programs. A substantial number of the city's heroin addicts, including some of the most crime-prone, are unlikely to be reached by the mere expansion of existing treatment programs.

17. According to the above paragraph, the drug addicts who have dropped out of existing   17._____
programs

     A. are habitual criminals beyond hope of chance
     B. could be reached by expanding existing programs
     C. include the seriously disturbed
     D. had been compelled to enroll in such programs

18. According to the above paragraph, some drug addicts are not being aided by current   18._____
treatment efforts because those addicts

     A. are serving excessively long prison sentences
     B. are unwilling to become involved in programs
     C. have been accepted by therapeutic communities
     D. have lost confidence in the city's programs

19. As used in the above paragraph, the underlined word prone means MOST NEARLY   19.____

    A. angered   B. bold   C. exclusive   D. inclined

20. As used in the above paragraph, the underlined word mere means MOST NEARLY   20.____

    A. formal   B. simple   C. remote   D. prompt

Questions 21-23.

DIRECTIONS: Questions 21 through 23 are to be answered SOLELY on the basis of the following passage.

A survey of the drinking behavior of 1,185 persons representing the adult population of Iowa in 2008 aged 21 years and older revealed that approximately 40 percent were abstainers. Of the nearly one million drinkers in the State, 47 percent were classed as light drinkers, 37 percent as moderate, and 16 percent as heavy drinkers. Twenty-two percent of the men drinkers were classed as heavy drinkers but only 8 percent of the women drinkers. The proportion of heavy drinkers increased with level of education among drinkers residing in the city - from 15 percent of the least educated to 22 percent of the most educated; but decreased among farm residents from 17 percent of the least educated to 4 percent of the most educated. Age differences in the extent of drinking were not pronounced. The age class of 36-45 had the lowest proportions of light drinkers, while the age class 61 and over had the lowest proportion of heavy drinkers.

21. According to the above passage, which one of the following statements concerning   21.____
heavy drinking would be CORRECT?

    A. Experts are in sharp conflict regarding the reason for heavy drinking.
    B. The amount of heavy drinking in the city is directly proportional to the amount of education.
    C. The degree of heavy drinking is directly proportional to the age class of the drinkers.
    D. The degree of heavy drinking is inversely to the number of light drinkers.

22. Of the total drinking population in Iowa, how many were moderate drinkers?   22.____

    A. 370,000   B. 438   C. 370   D. 438,150

23. What percent of the men drinkers surveyed were NOT heavy drinkers?   23.____

    A. 60%   B. 84%
    C. 78%   D. Cannot be determined

Questions 24-25.

DIRECTIONS: Questions 24 and 25 are to be answered SOLELY on the basis of the following paragraph.

A drug-user does not completely retreat from society. While a new user, he must begin participation in some group of old users in order to secure access to a steady supply of drugs. In the process, his readiness to engage in drug use, which stems from his personality and the social structure, is reinforced by new patterns of associations and values. The more the individual is caught in this web of associations, the more likely it is that he will persist in drug use, for he has become incorporated into a subculture that exerts control over his behavior. However, it is also true that the resulting tics among addicts are not as strong as those among participants in criminal and conflict subcultures. Addiction is in many ways an individualistic adaptation for the *kick* is essentially a private experience. The compelling need for the drug is also a divisive force for it leads to intense competition among addicts for money. Forces of this kind thus limit the relative cohesion which can develop among users.

24. According to the above paragraph, the MAIN reason why new drug users associate with old users is a   24.____

    A. fear of the police
    B. common hatred of society
    C. need to get drugs
    D. dislike of being alone

25. According to the above paragraph, which of the following statements is INCORRECT?   25.____

    A. Drug users encourage each other to continue taking drugs.
    B. Gangs that use drugs are more cohesive than other delinquent gangs.
    C. A youth's desire to use drugs stems from his personality as well as the social structure.
    D. Addicts get no more of a *kick* from using drugs in a group than alone.

KEY (CORRECT ANSWERS)

1.	C		11.	B
2.	D		12.	A
3.	B		13.	C
4.	D		14.	D
5.	A		15.	C
6.	A		16.	B
7.	C		17.	C
8.	B		18.	B
9.	C		19.	D
10.	D		20.	B

21.	B
22.	A
23.	C
24.	C
25.	B

143

TEST 2

DIRECTIONS: Each question or incomplete statement is followed by several suggested answers or completions. Select the one that BEST answers the question or completes the statement. *PRINT THE LETTER OF THE CORRECT ANSWER IN THE SPACE AT THE RIGHT.*

Questions 1-5.

DIRECTIONS: Questions 1 through 5 are to be answered SOLELY on the basis of the following passage.

In an attempt to describe what is meant by a delinquent subculture, let us look at some delinquent activities. We usually assume that when people steal things, they steal because they want them to eat or wear or otherwise use them; or because they can sell them; or even –if we are given to a psychoanalytic turn of mind – because on some deep symbolic level the things stolen substitute or stand for something unconsciously desired but forbidden. However, most delinquent gang stealing has no such utilitarian motivation at all. Even where the value of the object stolen is itself a motivating consideration, the stolen sweets are often sweeter than those acquired by more legitimate and prosaic means. In homelier language, stealing *for the hell of it* and apart from considerations of gain and profit is a valued activity to which attaches glory, prowess, and profound satisfaction.

Similarly, many other delinquent activities are motivated mainly by an enjoyment in the distress of others and by a hostility toward non-gang peers as well as adults. Apart from the more dramatic manifestations in the form of gang wars, there is keen delight in terrorizing *good* children and in driving them from playgrounds and gyms for which the gang itself may have little use. The same spirit is evident in playing hooky and in misbehavior in school. The teacher and her rules are not merely to be evaded. They are to be flouted.

All this suggests that the delinquent subculture is not only a set of rules, a design for living which is different from or indifferent to or even in conflict with the norms of the *respectable* adult society. It actually takes its norms from the larger culture but turns them upside down. The delinquent's conduct is right, by the standards of his subculture, precisely BECAUSE it is wrong by the standards of the larger culture.

1. Of the following, the MOST suitable title for the above passage is   1.____

    A. DIFFERENT KINDS OF DELINQUENT SUBCULTURES
    B. DELINQUENT HOSTILITY TOWARD NON-GANG PEERS
    C. METHODS OF DELINQUENT STEALING
    D. DELINQUENT STANDARDS AS REVEALED BY THEIR ACTIVITIES

2. It may be inferred from the above passage that MOST delinquent stealing is motivated by a   2.____

    A. need for food and clothing
    B. need for money to buy drugs
    C. desire for peer-approval
    D. symbolic identification of the thing stolen with hidden desires

3. The passage IMPLIES that an important reason why delinquents play hooky and misbe-   3.____
   have in school is that the teachers

    A. represent *respectable* society
    B. are boring
    C. have not taught them the values of the adult society
    D. are too demanding

4. In the above passage, the author's attitude toward delinquents is   4.____

    A. critical   B. objective
    C. overly sympathetic   D. confused

5. According to the above passage, which of the following statements is CORRECT?   5.____

    A. Delinquents derive no satisfaction from stealing.
    B. Delinquents are not hostile toward someone without a reason.
    C. The common motive of many delinquent activities is a desire to frustrate others.
    D. The delinquent subculture shares its standards with the *respectable* adult culture.

Questions 6-8.

DIRECTIONS: Questions 6 through 8 are to be answered SOLELY on the basis of the follow-
                  ing paragraph.

A fundamental part of the youth worker's role is changing the interaction patterns which
already exist between the delinquent group and the representatives of key institutions in the
community; e.g., the policeman, teacher, social worker, employer, parent, and storekeeper.
This relationship, particularly its definitional character, is a two-way proposition. The offending
youth or group will usually respond by fulfilling this prophecy. In the same way, the delinquent
expects punishment or antagonistic treatment from officials and other representatives of middle class society. In turn, the adult concerned may act to fulfill the prophecy of the delinquent.
Stereotyped patterns of expectation, both of the delinquents and those in contact with them,
must be changed. The worker can be instrumental in changing these patterns.

6. Of the following, the MOST suitable title for the above paragraph is   6.____

    A. WAYS TO PREDICT JUVENILE DELINQUENCY
    B. THE YOUTH WORKER'S ROLE IN CREATING STEREOTYPES
    C. THE YOUTH WORKER'S ROLE IN CHANGING STEREOTYPED PATTERNS OF
        EXPECTATION
    D. THE DESIRABILITY OF INTERACTION PATTERNS

7. According to the above paragraph, a youth who misbehaves and is told by an agency   7.____
   worker that *his group is a menace to the community* would PROBABLY eventually
   respond by

    A. withdrawing into himself
    B. continuing to misbehave
    C. making a greater attempt to please
    D. acting indifferent

8. In the above paragraph, the author's opinion about stereotypes is that they are   8.____

A.   *useful,* primarily because they are usually accurate
B.   *useful,* primarily because they make a quick response easier
C.   *harmful,* primarily because the adult community will be less aware of delinquents as a group
D.   *harmful,* primarily because they influence behavior

Questions 9-15.

DIRECTIONS: Questions 9 through 15 are to be answered SOLELY on the basis of the information in the following passage.

Laws concerning juveniles make it clear that the function of the courts is to treat delinquents, not to punish them. Many years ago, children were detained in jails or police lockups along with adult offenders. Today, however, it is recognized that separate detention is important for the protection of the children. Detention is now regarded as part of the treatment process.

Detention is not an ordinary child care job. On the one hand, it must be distinguished from mere shelter care, which is a custodial program for children whose families cannot care for them adequately. On the other hand, it must be distinguished from treatment in mental health institutions, which is meant for children who have very serious mental or psychological problems. The children in a detention facility are there because they have run into trouble with the law and because they must be kept in safe custody for a short period until the court decides the final action to be taken in each child's case.

The Advisory Committee on Detention and Shelter Care has outlined several basic objectives for a good detention service. One objective is secure custody. Like adults who are being detained until their cases come up before the court, children too will often want to escape from detention. Security measures must be adequate to prevent ordinary escape attempts, although at the same time a jail-like atmosphere should be avoided. Another objective is to provide constructive activities for the children and to give individual guidance through casework and group sessions. A final objective is to study each child individually so that useful information can be provided for court action and so that the mental, emotional, or other problems that have contributed to the child's difficulties can be identified.

9.   According to the above passage, laws concerning juveniles make it clear that the MAIN aim of the courts in handling young offenders is to _____ juvenile delinquents.   9.____

A.   punish
B.   provide treatment for
C.   relieve the families of
D.   counsel families which have

10.   The above passage IMPLIES that the former practice of locking up juveniles along with adults was   10.____

A.   *good* because it was more efficient than providing separate facilities
B.   *good* because children could then be protected by the adults
C.   *bad* because the children were not safe
D.   *bad* because delinquents need mental health treatment

11. The above passage says that a detention center differs from a shelter care facility in that the children in a detention center   11.____

    A. have been placed there permanently by their families or by the courts
    B. come from families who cannot or will not care for them
    C. have serious mental or psychological problems
    D. are in trouble with the law and must be kept in safe custody temporarily

12. The above passage mentions one specific way in which detained juveniles are like detained adults.   12.____
This similarity is that both detained juveniles and detained adults

    A. may try to escape from the detention facility
    B. have been convicted of serious crimes
    C. usually come from bad family backgrounds
    D. have mental or emotional problems

13. The above passage lists several basic objectives that were outlined by the Advisory Committee on Detention and Child Care.   13.____
Which one of the following aims is NOT given in the list of Advisory Committee objectives?

    A. Separating juvenile offenders from adult offenders
    B. Providing secure custody
    C. Giving individual guidance
    D. Providing useful information for court action

14. The above passage mentions a *custodial program*. This means MOST NEARLY   14.____

    A. janitor services
    B. a program to prevent jail escapes
    C. caretaking services for dependent children
    D. welfare payments to families with children

15. The above passage says that *security measures* are needed in a detention center PRIMARILY in order to   15.____

    A. prevent unauthorized persons from entering
    B. prevent juveniles from escaping
    C. ensure that records are safeguarded for court action
    D. create a jail-like atmosphere

Questions 16-22.

DIRECTIONS: Questions 16 through 22 are to be answered SOLELY on the basis of the following passage.

    Adolescents are among the last social groups in the world to be given the full nineteenth-century colonial treatment. Our colonial administrators, at least at the higher policymaking levels, are usually of the enlightened sort who decry the punitive expedition except as an instrument of last resort, though they are inclined to tolerate a shade more brutality in the actual school or police station than the law allows. They prefer, however, to study the young with a view to understanding them, not for their own sake but in order to learn how to induce them to abandon their barbarism and assimilate the folkways of normal adult life. The model emissary to the world of youth is no longer the tough disciplinarian but the trained youth worker, who works like a psychoanalytically oriented anthropologist. Like the best of mission-aries, he is sent to work with, and is aware and critical of the larger society he represents. But fundamentally, he accepts it and often does not really question its basic value or its right to send him to wean the young from savagery.

The economic position of *the adolescent society,* like that of other colonies, is highly ambiguous. It is simultaneously a costly drain on the commonwealth and a vested interest of those members of the commonwealth who earn their living and their social role by exploiting it. Juvenile delinquency is destructive and wasteful, and efforts to control and combat it are expensive. Schooling is even more expensive. Both undertakings are justified on the assump-tion that youth must be drawn into the social order if the social order is to continue, and this is self-evident. But both act as agents of society as it now is, propagating social values and assumptions among a youth often cynical and distrustful but ignorant of the language or the moral judgments in terms of which social complaints might be couched. Neither the youth agency nor the school is usually competent or sufficiently independent to help adolescents examine the sources of their pain and conflict and think its meaning through, using their con-tinuing experience of life to help them build better social arrangements in their turn. This, in a democracy, ought clearly to be among the most fundamental functions of citizenship educa-tion; in a public school system geared and responsive to local political demands and inter-ests, it may well be impossible. Official agencies dealing with youth vary enormously in the pretexts and techniques with which they approach their clientele, from those of the young worker attached to a conflict gang to those of the citizenship education teacher in the aca-demic track of a suburban high school. But they all begin, like a Colonial Office, with the assumption that the long-term interests of their clientele are consistent with the present inter-ests of their sponsor.

16. The clientele and sponsor of official agencies dealing with youth are the   16._____

   A. young and the adult   B. young and the educators
   C. educators and the young   D. adult and the middle class

17. The author believes that the adolescent society is   17._____

   A. a drain on the commonwealth from which almost no one benefits
   B. the mainstay of the economy
   C. mercilessly exploited by certain adults
   D. costly to the government but a financial boon to certain adults

18. The author feels that society's present attempts to assimilate youth are motivated by   18._____

   A. greed
   B. a desire to end juvenile delinquency
   C. a desire to maintain the status quo
   D. a desire to induce the young to abandon their barbarism

19. The author is _____ society and _____ of youth.   19._____

   A. *approving* of present day; disapproving
   B. *approving* of present day; approving
   C. *disapproving* of adult; disapproving
   D. *disapproving* of adult; approving

20. According to the above passage, the BASIC function of citizenship education in a   20.____
    democracy ought to be to

    A. help adolescents examine the source of their pain and conflict
    B. help adolescents think the meaning of their problems through
    C. enable adolescents to perceive the meaning of experience
    D. enable adolescents to improve society through an understanding of their problems

21. The author is LEAST critical of   21.____

    A. nineteenth-century Colonialists
    B. the trained youth worker
    C. the members of the commonwealth who earn their living exploiting youth
    D. official agencies dealing with youth

22. It is implied in the above passage that   22.____

    A. colonialism is beneficial to the colonies
    B. society should not be stagnant but needs change
    C. society should have more effective ways of disciplining recidivists
    D. youth is more interested in track than citizenship education

Question 23.

DIRECTIONS: Question 23 is to be answered SOLELY on the basis of the following passage.

    Some adolescents find it very difficult to take the first step toward independence. Instead
of experimenting as his friends do, a teenager may stay close to home, conforming to his parents' wishes. Sometimes parents and school authorities regard this untroublesome youngster
with satisfaction and admiration, but they are wrong to do so. A too-conforming adolescent
will not develop into an independent adult.

23. The above passage implies that a teenager who always conforms to his parents' wishes   23.____

    A. should be admired by his teachers
    B. will develop into a troublesome person
    C. will become very independent
    D. should be encouraged to act more independently

Questions 24-25.

DIRECTIONS: Questions 24 and 25 are to be answered SOLELY on the basis of the following
              paragraph.

    The skilled children's counselor can encourage the handicapped child to make a maxi-
mum adjustment to the demands of learning and socialization. She will be aware that the
child's needs are basically the same as those of other children and yet she will be sensitive to
his special needs and the ways in which these are met. She will understand the frustration
the child may experience when he cannot participate in the simple activities of childhood. She
will also be aware of the need to help him to avoid repeated failures by encouraging him to
engage in projects in which he can generally succeed and perhaps excel.

24. According to the above paragraph, it is important for the children's counselor to realize that the handicapped child   24._____

    A. should not participate in ordinary activities
    B. must not be treated in any special way
    C. is sensitive to the counselor's problems
    D. has needs similar to those of other children

25. According to the above paragraph, the counselor can BEST help the handicapped child to avoid frustrating situations by encouraging him to   25._____

    A. participate in the same activities as *normal* children
    B. participate in activities which are not too difficult for him
    C. engage in projects which are interesting
    D. excel in difficult games

KEY (CORRECT ANSWERS)

1.	D		11.	D
2.	C		12.	A
3.	A		13.	A
4.	B		14.	C
5.	C		15.	B
6.	C		16.	A
7.	B		17.	D
8.	D		18.	C
9.	B		19.	D
10.	C		20.	D

21.	B
22.	B
23.	D
24.	D
25.	B

PREPARING WRITTEN MATERIAL

PARAGRAPH REARRANGEMENT
COMMENTARY

The sentences which follow are in scrambled order. You are to rearrange them in proper order and indicate the letter choice containing the correct answer at the space at the right.

Each group of sentences in this section is actually a paragraph presented in scrambled order. Each sentence in the group has a place in that paragraph; no sentence is to be left out. You are to read each group of sentences and decide upon the best order in which to put the sentences so as to form as well-organized paragraph.

The questions in this section measure the ability to solve a problem when all the facts relevant to its solution are not given.

More specifically, certain positions of responsibility and authority require the employee to discover connections between events sometimes, apparently, unrelated. In order to do this, the employee will find it necessary to correctly infer that unspecified events have probably occurred or are likely to occur. This ability becomes especially important when action must be taken on incomplete information.

Accordingly, these questions require competitors to choose among several suggested alternatives, each of which presents a different sequential arrangement of the events. Competitors must choose the MOST logical of the suggested sequences.

In order to do so, they may be required to draw on general knowledge to infer missing concepts or events that are essential to sequencing the given events. Competitors should be careful to infer only what is essential to the sequence. The plausibility of the wrong alternatives will always require the inclusion of unlikely events or of additional chains of events which are NOT essential to sequencing the given events.

It's very important to remember that you are looking for the best of the four possible choices, and that the best choice of all may not even be one of the answers you're given to choose from.

There is no one right way to solve these problems. Many people have found it helpful to first write out the order of the sentences, as they would have arranged them, on their scrap paper before looking at the possible answers. If their optimum answer is there, this can save them some time. If it isn't, this method can still give insight into solving the problem. Others find it most helpful to just go through each of the possible choices, contrasting each as they go along. You should use whatever method feels comfortable, and works, for you.

While most of these types of questions are not that difficult, we've added a higher percentage of the difficult type, just to give you more practice. Usually there are only one or two questions on this section that contain such subtle distinctions that you're unable to answer confidently, and you then may find yourself stuck deciding between two possible choices, neither of which you're sure about.

EXAMINATION SECTION
TEST 1

DIRECTIONS: The sentences that follow are in scrambled order. You are to rearrange them in proper order and indicate the letter choice containing the correct answer. *PRINT THE LETTER OF THE CORRECT ANSWER IN THE SPACE AT THE RIGHT.*

1. Below are four statements labeled W., X., Y., and Z.   1._____
   W.   He was a strict and fanatic drillmaster.
   X.   The word is always used in a derogatory sense and generally shows resent-ment and anger on the part of the user.
   Y.   It is from the name of this Frenchman that we derive our English word, martinet.
   Z.   Jean Martinet was the Inspector-General of Infantry during the reign of King Louis XIV.

   The *PROPER* order in which these sentences should be placed in a paragraph is:

   A. X, Z, W, Y   B. X, Z, Y, W   C. Z, W, Y, X   D. Z, Y, W, X

2. In the following paragraph, the sentences which are numbered, have been jumbled.   2._____
   1.   Since then it has undergone changes.
   2.   It was incorporated in 1955 under the laws of the State of New York.
   3.   Its primary purpose, a cleaner city, has, however, remained the same.
   4.   The Citizens Committee works in cooperation with the Mayor's Inter-departmen-tal Committee for a Clean City.

   The order in which these sentences should be arranged to form a well-organized para-graph is:

   A. 2, 4, 1, 3   B. 3, 4, 1, 2   C. 4, 2, 1, 3   D. 4, 3, 2, 1

Questions 3-5.

DIRECTIONS: The sentences listed below are part of a meaningful paragraph but they are not given in their proper order. You are to decide what would be the *best order* in which to put the sentences so as to form a well-organized paragraph. Each sentence has a place in the paragraph; there are no extra sentences. You are then to answer questions 3 to 5 inclusive on the basis of your rearrangements of these scrambled sentences into a properly organized paragraph.

In 1887 some insurance companies organized an Inspection Department to advise their clients on all phases of fire prevention and protection. Probably this has been due to the smaller annual fire losses in Great Britain than in the United States. It tests various fire prevention devices and appliances and determines manufacturing hazards and their safeguards. Fire research began earlier in the United States and is more advanced than in Great Britain. Later they established a laboratory specializing in electrical, mechanical, hydraulic, and chemical fields.

3. When the five sentences are arranged in proper order, the paragraph starts with the sentence which begins

    A. "In 1887..."   B. "Probably this ..."   C. "It tests ..."
    D. "Fire research ..."   E. "Later they ..."

3._____

4. In the last sentence listed above, "they" refers to

    A. insurance companies
    B. the United States and Great Britain
    C. the Inspection Department
    D. clients
    E. technicians

4._____

5. When the above paragraph is properly arranged, it ends with the words

    A. "... and protection."   B. "... the United States."
    C. "... their safeguards."   D. "... in Great Britain."
    E. "... chemical fields."

5._____

KEY (CORRECT ANSWERS)

    1. C
    2. C
    3. D
    4. A
    5. C

TEST 2

DIRECTIONS: In each of the questions numbered 1 through 5, several sentences are given. For each question, choose as your answer the group of numbers that represents the *most logical* order of these sentences if they were arranged in paragraph form. *PRINT THE LETTER OF THE CORRECT ANSWER IN THE SPACE AT THE RIGHT.*

1.   1.   It is established when one shows that the landlord has prevented the tenant's enjoyment of his interest in the property leased.
      2.   Constructive eviction is the result of a breach of the covenant of quiet enjoyment implied in all leases.
      3.   In some parts of the United States, it is not complete until the tenant vacates within a reasonable time.
      4.   Generally, the acts must be of such serious and permanent character as to deny the tenant the enjoyment of his possessing rights.
      5.   In this event, upon abandonment of the premises, the tenant's liability for that ceases.
      The CORRECT answer is:

      A.   2, 1, 4, 3, 5   B.   5, 2, 3, 1, 4   C.   4, 3, 1, 2, 5
      D.   1, 3, 5, 4, 2

1.____

2.   1.   The powerlessness before private and public authorities that is the typical experience of the slum tenant is reminiscent of the situation of blue-collar workers all through the nineteenth century.
      2.   Similarly, in recent years, this chapter of history has been reopened by anti-poverty groups which have attempted to organize slum tenants to enable them to bargain collectively with their landlords about the conditions of their tenancies.
      3.   It is familiar history that many of the workers remedied their condition by joining together and presenting their demands collectively.
      4.   Like the workers, tenants are forced by the conditions of modern life into substantial dependence on these who possess great political arid economic power.
      5.   What's more, the very fact of dependence coupled with an absence of education and self-confidence makes them hesitant and unable to stand up for what they need from those in power.
      The CORRECT answer is:

      A.   5, 4, 1, 2, 3   B.   2, 3, 1, 5, 4   C.   3, 1, 5, 4, 2
      D.   1, 4, 5, 3, 2

2.____

3.   1.   A railroad, for example, when not acting as a common carrier may contract away responsibility for its own negligence.
      2.   As to a landlord, however, no decision has been found relating to the legal effect of a clause shifting the statutory duty of repair to the tenant.
      3.   The courts have not passed on the validity of clauses relieving the landlord of this duty and liability.
      4.   They have, however, upheld the validity of exculpatory clauses in other types of contracts.
      5.   Housing regulations impose a duty upon the landlord to maintain leased premises in safe condition.

3.____

6. As another example, a bailee may limit his liability except for gross negligence, willful acts, or fraud.

The CORRECT answer is:

A. 2, 1, 6, 4, 3, 5
B. 1, 3, 4, 5, 6, 2
C. 3, 5, 1, 4, 2, 6
D. 5, 3, 4, 1, 6, 2

4.
1. Since there are only samples in the building, retail or consumer sales are generally eschewed by mart occupants, and in some instances, rigid controls are maintained to limit entrance to the mart only to those persons engaged in retailing.
2. Since World War I, in many larger cities, there has developed a new type of property, called the mart building.
3. It can, therefore, be used by wholesalers and jobbers for the display of sample merchandise.
4. This type of building is most frequently a multi-storied, finished interior property which is a cross between a retail arcade and a loft building.
5. This limitation enables the mart occupants to ship the orders from another location after the retailer or dealer makes his selection from the samples.

The CORRECT answer is:

A. 2, 4, 3, 1, 5
B. 4, 3, 5, 1, 2
C. 1, 3, 2, 4, 5
D. 1, 4, 2, 3, 5

4._____

5.
1. In general, staff-line friction reduces the distinctive contribution of staff personnel.
2. The conflicts, however, introduce an uncontrolled element into the managerial system.
3. On the other hand, the natural resistance of the line to staff innovations probably usefully restrains over-eager efforts to apply untested procedures on a large scale.
4. Under such conditions, it is difficult to know when valuable ideas are being sacrificed.
5. The relatively weak position of staff, requiring accommodation to the line, tends to restrict their ability to engage in free, experimental innovation.

The CORRECT answer is:

A. 4, 2, 3, 1, 3
B. 1, 5, 3, 2, 4
C. 5, 3, 1, 2, 4
D. 2, 1, 4, 5, 3

5._____

KEY (CORRECT ANSWERS)

1. A
2. D
3. D
4. A
5. B

TEST 3

DIRECTIONS: Questions 1 through 4 consist of six sentences which can be arranged in a logical sequence. For each question, select the choice which places the numbered sentences in the *most logical* sequence. *PRINT THE LETTER OF THE CORRECT ANSWER IN THE SPACE AT THE RIGHT.*

1.   1. The burden of proof as to each issue is determined before trial and remains upon the same party throughout the trial.   1.____
     2. The jury is at liberty to believe one witness' testimony as against a number of contradictory witnesses.
     3. In a civil case, the party bearing the burden of proof is required to prove his contention by a fair preponderance of the evidence.
     4. However, it must be noted that a fair preponderance of evidence does not necessarily mean a greater number of witnesses.
     5. The burden of proof is the burden which rests upon one of the parties to an action to persuade the trier of the facts, generally the jury, that a proposition he asserts is true.
     6. If the evidence is equally balanced, or if it leaves the jury in such doubt as to be unable to decide the controversy either way, judgment must be given against the party upon whom the burden of proof rests.

The CORRECT answer is:

A. 3, 2, 5, 4, 1, 6   B. 1, 2, 6, 5, 3, 4   C. 3, 4, 5, 1, 2, 6
D. 5, 1, 3, 6, 4, 2

2.   1. If a parent is without assets and is unemployed, he cannot be convicted of the crime of non-support of a child.   2.____
     2. The term "sufficient ability" has been held to mean sufficient financial ability.
     3. It does not matter if his unemployment is by choice or unavoidable circumstances.
     4. If he fails to take any steps at all, he may be liable to prosecution for endangering the welfare of a child.
     5. Under the penal law, a parent is responsible for the support of his minor child only if the parent is "of sufficient ability."
     6. An indigent parent may meet his obligation by borrowing money or by seeking aid under the provisions of the Social Welfare Law.

The CORRECT answer is:

A. 6, 1, 5, 3, 2, 4   B. 1, 3, 5, 2, 4, 6   C. 5, 2, 1, 3, 6, 4
D. 1, 6, 4, 5, 2, 3

3.　1.　Consider, for example, the case of a rabble rouser who urges a group of twenty people to go out and break the windows of a nearby factory.

3.＿＿＿

　　2.　Therefore, the law fills the indicated gap with the crime of inciting to riot.

　　3.　A person is considered guilty of inciting to riot when he urges ten or more persons to engage in tumultuous and violent conduct of a kind likely to create public alarm.

　　4.　However, if he has not obtained the cooperation of at least four people, he cannot be charged with unlawful assembly.

　　5.　The charge of inciting to riot was added to the law to cover types of conduct which cannot be classified as either the crime of "riot" or the crime of "unlawful assembly."

　　6.　If he acquires the acquiescence of at least four of them, he is guilty of unlawful assembly even if the project does not materialize.

The CORRECT answer is:

A.　3, 5, 1, 6, 4, 2　　　B.　5, 1, 4, 6, 2, 3　　　C.　3, 4, 1, 5, 2, 6
D.　5, 1, 4, 6, 3, 2

4.　1.　If, however, the rebuttal evidence presents an issue of credibility, it is for the jury to determine whether the presumption has, in fact, been destroyed.

4.＿＿＿

　　2.　Once sufficient evidence to the contrary is introduced, the presumption disappears from the trial.

　　3.　The effect of a presumption is to place the burden upon the adversary to come forward with evidence to rebut the presumption.

　　4.　When a presumption is overcome and ceases to exist in the case, the fact or facts which gave rise to the presumption still remain.

　　5.　Whether a presumption has been overcome is ordinarily a question for the court.

　　6.　Such information may furnish a basis for a logical inference.

The CORRECT answer is:

A.　4, 6, 2, 5, 1, 3　　　B.　3, 2, 5, 1, 4, 6　　　C.　5, 3, 6, 4, 2, 1
D.　5, 4, 1, 2, 6, 3

KEY (CORRECT ANSWERS)

1.　D
2.　C
3.　A
4.　B

PREPARING WRITTEN MATERIALS

EXAMINATION SECTION
TEST 1

DIRECTIONS: Each question or incomplete statement is followed by several suggested answers or completions. Select the one that BEST answers the question or completes the statement. *PRINT THE LETTER OF THE CORRECT ANSWER IN THE SPACE AT THE RIGHT.*

Questions 1-25.

DIRECTIONS: Questions 1 through 25 consist of sentences which may or may not be examples of good English usage. Consider grammar, punctuation, spelling, capitalization, awkwardness, etc. Examine each sentence, and then choose the correct statement about it from the four choices below it. If the English usage in the sentence given is better than it would be with any of the changes suggested in options B, C, and D, choose option A. Do not choose an option that will change the meaning of the sentence.

1. According to Judge Frank, the grocer's sons found guilty of assault and sentenced last Thursday.

    A. This is an example of acceptable writing.
    B. A comma should be placed after the word *sentenced.*
    C. The word *were* should be placed after *sons.*
    D. The apostrophe in *grocer's* should be placed after the *s.*

1.____

2. The department heads assistant said that the stenographers should type duplicate copies of all contracts, leases, and bills.

    A. This is an example of acceptable writing.
    B. A comma should be placed before the word *contracts.*
    C. An apostrophe should be placed before the *s* in *heads.*
    D. Quotation marks should be placed before *the stenographers* and after *bills.*

2.____

3. The lawyers questioned the men to determine who was the true property owner?

    A. This is an example of acceptable writing.
    B. The phrase *questioned the men* should be changed to *asked the men questions.*
    C. The word *was* should be changed to *were.*
    D. The question mark should be changed to a period.

3.____

4. The terms stated in the present contract are more specific than those stated in the previous contract.

    A. This is an example of acceptable writing.
    B. The word *are* should be changed to *is.*
    C. The word *than* should be changed to *then.*
    D. The word *specific* should be changed to *specified.*

4.____

5. Of the few lawyers considered, the one who argued more skillful was chosen for the job.   5.____

    A. This is an example of acceptable writing.
    B. The word *more* should be replaced by the word *most*.
    C. The word *skillful* should be replaced by the word *skillfully*.
    D. The word *chosen* should be replaced by the word *selected*.

6. Each of the states has a court of appeals; some states have circuit courts.   6.____

    A. This is an example of acceptable writing.
    B. The semi-colon should be changed to a comma.
    C. The word *has* should be changed to *have*.
    D. The word *some* should be capitalized.

7. The court trial has greatly effected the child's mental condition.   7.____

    A. This is an example of acceptable writing.
    B. The word *effected* should be changed to *affected*.
    C. The word *greatly* should be placed after *effected*.
    D. The apostrophe in *child's* should be placed after the *s*.

8. Last week, the petition signed by all the officers was sent to the Better Business Bureau.   8.____

    A. This is an example of acceptable writing.
    B. The phrase *last week* should be placed after *officers*.
    C. A comma should be placed after *petition*.
    D. The word *was* should be changed to *were*.

9. Mr. Farrell claims that he requested form A-12, and three booklets describing court procedures.   9.____

    A. This is an example of acceptable writing.
    B. The word *that* should be eliminated.
    C. A colon should be placed after *requested*.
    D. The comma after *A-12* should be eliminated.

10. We attended a staff conference on Wednesday the new safety and fire rules were discussed.   10.____

    A. This is an example of acceptable writing.
    B. The words *safety, fire,* and *rules* should begin with capital letters.
    C. There should be a comma after the word *Wednesday*.
    D. There should be a period after the word *Wednesday,* and the word *the* should begin with a capital letter.

11. Neither the dictionary or the telephone directory could be found in the office library.   11.____

    A. This is an example of acceptable writing.
    B. The word *or* should be changed to *nor*.
    C. The word *library* should be spelled *libery*.
    D. The word *neither* should be changed to *either*.

12. The report would have been typed correctly if the typist could read the draft.

12._____

    A. This is an example of acceptable writing.
    B. The word *would* should be removed.
    C. The word *have* should be inserted after the word *could.*
    D. The word *correctly* should be changed to *correct.*

13. The supervisor brought the reports and forms to an employees desk.

13._____

    A. This is an example of acceptable writing.
    B. The word *brought* should be changed to *took.*
    C. There should be a comma after the word *reports* and a comma after the word *forms.*
    D. The word *employees* should be spelled *employee's.*

14. It's important for all the office personnel to submit their vacation schedules on time.

14._____

    A. This is an example of acceptable writing.
    B. The word *It's* should be spelled *Its.*
    C. The word *their* should be spelled *they're.*
    D. The word *personnel* should be spelled *personal.*

15. The supervisor wants that all staff members report to the office at 9:00 A.M.

15._____

    A. This is an example of acceptable writing.
    B. The word *that* should be removed and the word *to* should be inserted after the word *members.*
    C. There should be a comma after the word *wants* and a comma after the word *office.*
    D. The word *wants* should be changed to *want,* and the word *shall* should be inserted after the word *members.*

16. Every morning the clerk opens the office mail and distributes it.

16._____

    A. This is an example of acceptable writing.
    B. The word *opens* should be changed to *open.*
    C. The word *mail* should be changed to *letters.*
    D. The word *it* should be changed to *them.*

17. The secretary typed more fast on a desktop computer than on a tablet.

17._____

    A. This is an example of acceptable writing.
    B. The words *more fast* should be changed to *faster.*
    C. There should be a comma after the words *desktop computer.*
    D. The word *than* should be changed to *then.*

18. The typist used an extention cord in order to connect her typewriter to the outlet nearest to her desk.

18._____

    A. This is an example of acceptable writing.
    B. A period should be placed after the word *cord,* and the word *in* should have a capital *I.*
    C. A comma should be placed after the word *typewriter.*
    D. The word *extention* should be spelled *extension.*

19. He would have went to the conference if he had received an invitation.

19._____

    A.   This is an example of acceptable writing.
    B.   The word *went* should be replaced by the word *gone*.
    C.   The word *had* should be replaced by *would have*.
    D.   The word *conference* should be spelled *conferance*.

20. In order to make the report neater, he spent many hours rewriting it.

20._____

    A.   This is an example of acceptable writing.
    B.   The word *more* should be inserted before the word *neater*.
    C.   There should be a colon after the word *neater*.
    D.   The word *spent* should be changed to *have spent*.

21. His supervisor told him that he should of read the memorandum more carefully.

21._____

    A.   This is an example of acceptable writing.
    B.   The word *memorandum* should be spelled *memorandom*.
    C.   The word *of* should be replaced by the word *have*.
    D.   The word *carefully* should be replaced by the word *careful*.

22. It was decided that two separate reports should be written.

22._____

    A.   This is an example of acceptable writing.
    B.   A comma should be inserted after the word *decided*.
    C.   The word *be* should be replaced by the word *been*.
    D.   A colon should be inserted after the word *that*.

23. She don't seem to understand that the work must be done as soon as possible.

23._____

    A.   This is an example of acceptable writing.
    B.   The word *doesn't* should replace the word *don't*.
    C.   The word *why* should replace the word *that*.
    D.   The word *as* before the word *soon* should be eliminated.

24. He excepted praise from his supervisor for a job well done.

24._____

    A.   This is an example of acceptable writing.
    B.   The word *excepted* should be spelled *accepted*.
    C.   The order of the words *well done* should be changed to *done well*.
    D.   There should be a comma after the word *supervisor*.

25. What appears to be intentional errors in grammar occur several times in the passage.

25._____

    A.   This is an example of acceptable writing.
    B.   The word *occur* should be spelled *occurr*.
    C.   The word *appears* should be changed to *appear*.
    D.   The phrase *several times* should be changed to *from time to time*.

KEY (CORRECT ANSWERS)

1.	C		11.	B
2.	C		12.	C
3.	D		13.	D
4.	A		14.	A
5.	C		15.	B
6.	A		16.	A
7.	B		17.	B
8.	A		18.	D
9.	D		19.	B
10.	D		20.	A

21.	C
22.	A
23.	B
24.	B
25.	C

TEST 2

DIRECTIONS: Each question consists of a sentence which may or may not be an example of good formal English usage. Examine each sentence, considering grammar, punctuation, spelling, capitalization, and awkwardness. Then choose the CORRECT statement about it from the four options below it. If the English usage in the sentence given is better than any of the changes suggested in options B, C, or D, pick option A. Do not pick an option that will change the meaning of the sentence. *PRINT THE LETTER OF THE CORRECT ANSWER IN THE SPACE AT THE RIGHT.*

1. I don't know who could possibly of broken it.   1._____

    A.   This is an example of acceptable writing.
    B.   The word *who* should be replaced by the word *whom*.
    C.   The word *of* should be replaced by the word *have*.
    D.   The word *broken* should be replaced by the word *broke*.

2. Telephoning is easier than to write.   2._____

    A.   This is an example of acceptable writing.
    B.   The word *telephoning* should be spelled *telephoneing*.
    C.   The word *than* should be replaced by the word *then*.
    D.   The words *to write* should be replaced by the word *writing*.

3. The two operators who have been assigned to these consoles are on vacation.   3._____

    A.   This is an example of acceptable writing.
    B.   A comma should be placed after the word *operators*.
    C.   The word *who* should be replaced by the word *whom*
    D.   The word *are* should be replaced by the word *is*.

4. You were suppose to teach me how to operate a plugboard.   4._____

    A.   This is an example of acceptable writing.
    B.   The word *were* should be replaced by the word *was*.
    C.   The word *suppose* should be replaced by the word *supposed*.
    D.   The word *teach* should be replaced by the word *learn*.

5. If you had taken my advice; you would have spoken with him.   5._____

    A.   This is an example of acceptable writing.
    B.   The word *advice* should be spelled *advise*.
    C.   The words *had taken* should be replaced by the word *take*.
    D.   The semicolon should be changed to a comma.

6. The clerk could have completed the assignment on time if he knows where these materials were located.   6._____

    A.   This is an example of acceptable writing.
    B.   The word *knows* should be replaced by *had known*.
    C.   The word *were* should be replaced by *had been*.
    D.   The words *where these materials were located* should be replaced by *the location of these materials*.

7. All employees should be given safety training. Not just those who have accidents.   7.____

    A. This is an example of acceptable writing.
    B. The period after the word *training* should be changed to a colon.
    C. The period after the word *training* should be changed to a semicolon, and the first letter of the word *Not* should be changed to a small *n*.
    D. The period after the word *training* should be changed to a comma, and the first letter of the word *Not* should be changed to a small *n*.

8. This proposal is designed to promote employee awareness of the suggestion program,   8.____
to encourage employee participation in the program, and to increase the number of suggestions submitted.

    A. This is an example of acceptable writing.
    B. The word *proposal* should be spelled *preposal*.
    C. The words *to increase the number of suggestions submitted* should be changed to *an increase in the number of suggestions is expected*.
    D. The word *promote* should be changed to *enhance,* and the word *increase* should be changed to *add to*.

9. The introduction of inovative managerial techniques should be preceded by careful analysis of the specific circumstances and conditions in each department.   9.____

    A. This is an example of acceptable writing.
    B. The word *techniques* should be spelled *techneques*.
    C. The word *inovative* should be spelled *innovative*.
    D. A comma should be placed after the word *circumstances* and after the word *conditions*.

10. This occurrence indicates that such criticism embarrasses him.   10.____

    A. This is an example of acceptable writing.
    B. The word *occurrence* should be spelled *occurence*.
    C. The word *criticism* should be spelled *criticism*.
    D. The word *embarrasses* should be spelled *embarasses*.

11. He can recommend a mechanic whose work is reliable.   11.____

    A. This is an example of acceptable writing.
    B. The word *reliable* should be spelled *relyable*.
    C. The word *whose* should be spelled *who's*.
    D. The word *mechanic* should be spelled *mecanic*.

12. She typed quickly; like someone who had not a moment to lose.   12.____

    A. This is an example of acceptable writing.
    B. The word *not* should be removed.
    C. The semicolon should be changed to a comma.
    D. The word *quickly* should be placed before instead of after the word *typed*.

13. She insisted that she had to much work to do.   13.____

    A. This is an example of acceptable writing.
    B. The word *insisted* should be spelled *insisted*.

165

    C.   The word *to* used in front of *much* should be spelled *too*.
    D.   The word *do* should be changed to *be done*.

14.   The report, along with the accompanying documents, were submitted for review.   14.____

    A.   This is an example of acceptable writing.
    B.   The words *were submitted* should be changed to *was submitted*.
    C.   The word *accompanying* should be spelled *accompaning*.
    D.   The comma after the word *report* should be taken out.

15.   If others must use your files, be certain that they understand how the system works, but   15.____
    insist that you do all the filing and refiling.

    A.   This is an example of acceptable writing.
    B.   There should be a period after the word *works,* and the word *but* should start a new
        sentence.
    C.   The words *filing* and *refiling* should be spelled *fileing* and *refileing*.
    D.   There should be a comma after the word *but*.

16.   The appeal was not considered because of its late arrival.   16.____

    A.   This is an example of acceptable writing.
    B.   The word *its* should be changed to *it's*.
    C.   The word *its* should be changed to *the*.
    D.   The words *late arrival* should be changed to *arrival late*.

17.   The letter must be read carefuly to determine under which subject it should be filed.   17.____

    A.   This is an example of acceptable writing.
    B.   The word *under* should be changed to *at*.
    C.   The word *determine* should be spelled *determin*.
    D.   The word *carefuly* should be spelled *carefully*.

18.   He showed potential as an office manager, but he lacked skill in delegating work.   18.____

    A.   This is an example of acceptable writing.
    B.   The word *delegating* should be spelled *delagating*.
    C.   The word *potential* should be spelled *potencial*.
    D.   The words *he lacked* should be changed to *was lacking*.

19.   His supervisor told him that it would be all right to receive personal mail at the office.   19.____

    A.   This is an example of acceptable writing.
    B.   The words *all right* should be changed to *alright*.
    C.   The word *personal* should be spelled *personel*.
    D.   The word *mail* should be changed to *letters*.

20.   The report, along with the accompanying documents, were submitted for review.   20.____

    A.   This is an example of acceptable writing.
    B.   The words *were submitted* should be changed to *was submitted*.
    C.   The word *accompanying* should be spelled *accompaning*.
    D.   The comma after the word *report* should be taken out.

KEY (CORRECT ANSWERS)

1.	C		11.	A
2.	D		12.	C
3.	A		13.	C
4.	C		14.	B
5.	D		15.	A
6.	B		16.	A
7.	D		17.	D
8.	A		18.	A
9.	C		19.	A
10.	A		20.	B

DOMESTIC VIOLENCE

More women are injured in domestic incidents than by car accidents, muggings, and rapes combined. In fact, every 15 seconds a woman in this country is beaten by her current or former partner. According to the Public Safety Institute of the University of North Florida, domestic violence is the number one cause of birth defects in infants. Billions of dollars are spent annually researching disease prevention and cure, while domestic violence is allowed to spread uncontrolled.

Even though domestic violence has finally surfaced as a national problem, there is still much to be done. Most states have developed strict enforcement and prosecution policies but have done little in the area of prevention. Domestic violence begins with pre-conceived notions as to what individual roles are within a relationship, and these notions exist at a very early age. Energy and resources must be focused on attacking this problem at the root causes. That is, educating youth as to the non-acceptance of violence within relationships. For too long, young women have believed that sudden outbreaks of violence by their boyfriends or mates is an acceptable occurrence for any of the following reasons:

- "Men are like that."
- "He's been under a lot of pressure lately."
- "He only acts like that when he drinks."
- "I started it."
- "I drove him to it."
- "He's very jealous because he loves me so much."

The truth is, there is NO excuse for abuse.

Another misnomer is that unless a woman is physically abused, then she is not abused at all. Emotional abuse, psychological abuse, sexual abuse, financial abuse, and verbal abuse can be just as devastating as physical abuse. Children learn from their parents and peers. If abusive relationships are allowed to continue, then the children interpret this as a sign of normalcy in the relationship. This, in turn, becomes a model for their own personal relationships.

The history of domestic abuse is a sorry saga for humanity. Since the "caveman" dragged his mate into the cave by her hair, people have been assigning roles to men and women based on dominance or submission. Laws, religions, and society mores have all played a part in developing our attitudes toward women. Considering that this country prides itself on human rights and equality, the fact is that the right to vote for women was adopted only within the 20th century. The nation is still struggling with women's rights and the rights of all minorities. Until the walls of the status quo are torn down, very little progress can be made. If the youth are educated and attitudes toward abuse in relationships are successfully changed, domestic violence prevention can move forward for the next generation.

WHAT IS DOMESTIC VIOLENCE?

Domestic violence is a pattern of coercive tactics which can include physical, psychological, sexual, economic, and emotional abuse, perpetrated by one person against another within the confines of a particular relationship, with the goal of establishing and maintaining power and control over the victim. This may happen in a variety of relationships: between husband and wife, divorced or separated couples, parents and children, grandparents and children, between cousins or siblings, or people with children in common.

Some examples of the different types of abuse are:

Physical: hitting, biting, hair pulling, pushing, kicking

Psychological and Emotional: putting them down, mind games, telling secrets, giving the silent treatment, jealousy

Verbal: name calling, criticizing, publicly humiliating

Sexual: forced sex, continued advances after being told "no," making partner do things that make them uncomfortable

Financial: holding back money, buying everything including personal items, keeping bank books and other financial records from the partner

INDICATORS OF ABUSE

Does your partner:
- Hit, punch, slap, kick, shove or bite you?
- Threaten to hurt you and/or your children?
- Threaten to hurt friends or family members?
- Have sudden outbursts of anger or rage?
- Behave in an overprotective manner?
- Become jealous without reason?
- Prevent you from seeing family or friends?
- Prevent you from going where you want?
- Prevent you from working or attending school?
- Destroy personal property or sentimental items?
- Deny you access to family assets, such as bank accounts?
- Control all finances?
- Force you to have sex against your will?
- Force you to engage in sex acts that you don't enjoy?
- Insult you or call you derogatory names?
- Use intimidation or manipulation to control you?
- Humiliate you in front of others?
- Turn minor incidents into major arguments?
- Abuse or threaten to abuse pets?

If you answered yes to any of these questions, you may be a victim of domestic violence. You are not to blame and you are not alone—millions of women are abused by their partners every year. Not all acts of domestic violence are violations of the law. In any case, you need not face domestic violence alone. You deserve help, and help is available.

YOUR RIGHTS UNDER THE LAW

As per the Criminal Procedure Law and the Family Court Act, victims of domestic violence shall be advised of their following rights:

- If you are the victim of domestic violence, you may request that the police assist in providing for your safety and that of your children, including providing information on how to obtain a temporary order of protection.
- You may also request that the police assist you in obtaining your essential personal effects and locating and taking you to, or assist you in making arrangements to take you and your children to a safe place within the police department's jurisdiction, including but not limited to a domestic violence shelter, a family member's or a friend's home, or a similar place of safety.
- If you or your children are in need of medical treatment, you have the right to request that the police assist you in obtaining such medical treatment.
- You may request a copy of any incident reports from the police department, at no cost to you.
- You may ask the police department or the district attorney to file a criminal complaint.
- You also have the right to file a petition in the family court when a family offense has been committed against you.
- You have the right to have your petition and request for an order of protection filed on the same day you appear in court, and such request must be heard that same day or the next day the court is in session.

Either court may issue an order of protection from conduct constituting a family offense which could include, among other provisions, an order for the respondent or defendant to stay away from you and your children. If the family court is not in session, you may seek immediate assistance from the criminal court in obtaining an order of protection, even if you choose to have the case proceed in only the family court. The forms you need to obtain an order of protection are available from the family court and local criminal court. Filing a criminal complaint or a family court petition containing allegations that are knowingly false is a crime.

WHY DON'T DOMESTIC VIOLENCE VICTIMS LEAVE THE RELATIONSHIP?

There are many reasons that victims of domestic violence remain in the abusive relationship. Some of these reasons are stated below. Remember, whether or not these reasons seem sound to others, they are powerful factors in the lives of the victims:

- Fear that leaving will precipitate more violence
- Emotional dependency on the marriage
- Lack of financial resources
- Concern about the effects on the children
- Loss of economic security
- Feeling of love toward the abuser
- Denial of the abuse
- Fear of social isolation
- Strong cultural or religious beliefs
- Feelings of shame
- Acceptance of the violence as normal
- Lack of protection from abuser
- Lack of information regarding rights
- Prior unsuccessful attempts

WHAT TO DO IF YOU ARE A VICTIM

- If you are in immediate danger, call 911.
- When calling the police, inform the dispatcher if you already have an order of protection. Violating an order of protection is a crime.
- If there are witnesses to the abuse, ask them to speak with the police. It is important that this be done as soon as possible.
- If you are hurt, get medical attention. If you call the police, they will assist you in getting medical treatment for you and your children. The police may also ask to take pictures of your injuries. This will help the criminal and/or family court in deciding the case.
- Ask the police to stay with you and your children until your safety is assured. If you need transportation to a safe place within the jurisdiction of the police department, the police will either transport you or arrange for such transportation.

WHICH COURT SHOULD YOU GO TO?

In certain circumstances, you can choose to go to either criminal court, family court, or both. The police officer who arrives at the scene will inform you of the various court options available to you. You can also call the police department for help with information regarding court options.

Criminal Court

Criminal court's purpose is to prosecute the offender, which may result in a criminal conviction. That does not necessarily mean that the offender will be sent to jail. Sentencing is determined by the judge and there are many possible sentences that do not involve jail. For example, a criminal court judge may order the defendant to complete a batterer's prevention program or drug and alcohol treatment programs. Alternatively, the judge may sentence the abuser to probation, a conditional discharge, community service, or a fine. A jail sentence may be imposed where the judge feels there is no other reasonable alternative for a particular defendant or where he or she feels that such a sentence is necessary to protect the victim from further danger. An order of protection can be obtained in criminal court if criminal charges have been filed. The District Attorney's Officer prosecutes all cases filed in criminal court.

Family Court

Family court is a civil court and its proceedings are closed to the general public. However, you are entitled to bring a friend, relative, or victim's advocate with you to court. Family court's purpose is to attempt to stop the violence. A family court judge may sentence the respondent to probation and to complete a batterer's prevention program or treatment programs for drug and alcohol abuse. Family court also decides matters involving child custody and visitation, child support, and spousal support.

In order for a case to be heard in family court, the parties involved must be related to each other in one of the following ways:

- Married to each other

- Were formally married to each other
- Have a child in common
- Related by blood
- Related by marriage

HOW YOU CAN ASSIST DOMESTIC ABUSE VICTIMS

- Educate yourself about the myths and facts of abuse
- Express your concern and support for them
- Practice active listening techniques
- Let them make their own decisions and accept them
- Don't judge their decisions
- Be calm when discussing the issue
- Recognize and praise their good qualities
- Tell them it's not their fault
- Encourage them to be who they want to be
- Help them clarify their feelings
- Never condone the abuse
- Don't be a mediator
- Encourage them to confide in someone they trust
- Be aware that violence escalates in frequency and severity
- Recommend professional help if the situation is serious
- Remember, you can't help unless they are ready to be helped
- Understand that getting out takes time
- Never put yourself in a dangerous situation
- Tell them that assault is against the law regardless of relationship

---

GLOSSARY OF
LEGAL, MEDICAL, SOCIAL WORK TERMS

TABLE OF CONTENTS

Page

TABLE OF CONTENTS
(Continued)

GLOSSARY OF

Legal, Medical, Social Work Terms

ABANDONMENT

Act of a parent or caretaker leaving a child without adequate supervision or provision for his/her needs for an excessive period of time. State laws vary in defining adequacy of supervision and the length of time a child may be left alone or in the care of another before abandonment is determined. The age of the child also is an important factor. In legal terminology, "abandonment cases" are suits calling for the termination of parental rights.

ABDOMINAL DISTENTION

Swelling of the stomach area. The distention may be caused by internal injury or obstruction or by malnutrition.

ABRASION

Wound in which an area of the body surface is scraped of skin or mucous membrane.

ABUSE (See CHILD ABUSE AND NEGLECT)

ABUSED CHILD (See INDICATORS OF CHILD ABUSE AND NEGLECT)

ABUSED PARENT

Parent who has been abused as a child and who therefore may be more likely to abuse his/her own child.

ABUSER, PASSIVE (See PASSIVE ABUSER)

ACADEMY OF CERTIFIED SOCIAL WORKERS (ACSW)

Professional category identifying experienced social workers. Eligibility is determined by written examination following two years' full-time or 3,000 hours part-time paid post-Master's degree experience and continuous National Association of Social Workers (NASW) membership.

ACTING OUT

1) Behavior of an abusive parent who may be unconsciously and indirectly expressing anger toward his/her own parents or other significant person.
2) Aggressive or sexual behavior explained by some psychoanalytic theorists as carrying out fantasies or expressing unconscious feelings and conflicts.
3) Children's play or play therapy activities used as a means of expressing hitherto repressed feelings.

ACUTE CARE CAPACITY

Capacity of a community to respond quickly and responsibly to a report of a child abuse or neglect. It involves receiving the report and providing a diagnostic assessment including both a medical assessment and an evaluation of family dynamics. It also involves rapid intervention, including immediate protection of the child when needed and referral for long term care or service to the child and his/her family.

ADJUDICATION HEARING

Court hearing in which it is decided whether or not charges against a parent or caretaker are substantiated by admissible evidence. Also known as jurisdictional or evidentiary hearing.

ADMISSIBLE EVIDENCE

Evidence which may be legally and properly used in court. (See also EVIDENCE, EVIDENTIARY STANDARDS, EXPERT TESTIMONY)

ADVOCACY

Interventive strategy in which a helping person assumes an active role in assisting or supporting a specific child and /or family or a cause on behalf of children and/or families. This could involve finding and facilitating services for specific cases or developing new services or promoting program coordination. The advocate uses his/her power to meet client needs or to promote causes.

AFFIDAVIT
Written statement signed in the presence of a Notary Public who "swears in" the signer. The contents of the affidavit are stated under penalty of perjury. Affidavits are frequently used in the initiation of juvenile court cases and are, at times, presented to the court as evidence.

AGAINST MEDICAL ADVICE (AMA)
Going against the orders of a physician. In cases of child abuse or neglect, this usually means the removal of a child from a hospital without the physician's consent.

AID TO FAMILIES WITH DEPENDENT CHILDREN (AFDC) (See SOCIAL SECURITY ACT)

ALLEGATION
An assertion, declaration, or statement of a party to a legal action, which sets out what he or she expects to prove. In a child abuse or neglect case, the allegation forms the basis of the petition or accusation containing charges of specific acts of maltreatment which the petitioner hopes to prove at the trial.

ALOPECIA
Absence of hair from skin areas where it normally appears; baldness.

AMERICAN ACADEMY OF PEDIATRICS (AAP)
P.O. Box 1034
Evanston, Illinois 60204
AAP is the pan-American association of physicians certified in the care of infants, children, and adolescents. It was founded in 1930 for the primary purpose of ensuring "the attainment of all children of the Americas of their full potential for physical, emotional, and social health." Services and activities of AAP include standards-setting for pediatric residencies, scholarships, continuing education,

standards-setting for child health care, community health services, consultation, publications, and research.

AMERICAN HUMANE ASSOCIATION, CHILDREN'S DIVISION (AHA)
5351 S. Roslyn St.
Englewood, Colorado 80110
National association of individuals and agencies working to prevent neglect, abuse, and exploitation of children. Its objectives are to inform the public of the problem, to promote understanding of its causes, to advise on the identification and protection of abused and neglected children, and to assist in organizing new and improving existing child protection programs and services. Some of the programs and services of CDAHA include research, consultation and surveys, legislative guidance, staff development training and workshops, and publications. AHA includes an Animal Division in addition to the Children's Division.

AMERICAN PUBLIC WELFARE ASSOCIATION (APWA)
1125 Fifteenth St. N.W. Suite 300
Washington, D.C. 20005
APWA was founded in 1930 and has, from its inception, been a voluntary membership organization composed of individuals and agencies interested in issues of public welfare. National in scope, its dual purpose is to: 1) exert a positive influence on the shaping of national social policy, and 2) promote professional development of persons working in the area of public welfare. APWA sponsors an extensive program of policy analysis and research, testimony and consultation, publications, conferences, and workshops. It works for policies which are more equitable, less complex, and easier to administer in order that public welfare personnel can respond efficiently and effectively to the needs of persons they serve.

ANNUAL REVIEW OF DEPENDENCY CASES
Annual or other periodic reviews of dependency cases to determine whether continued

child placement or court supervision of a child is necessary. Increasingly required by state law, such reviews by the court also provide some judicial supervision of probation or casework services.

ANOMIE
A state of anomie is characterized by attitudes of aimlessness, futility, and lack of motivation and results from the breakdown or failure of standards, rules, norms, and values that ordinarily bind people together in some socially organized way.

ANOREXIA
Lack or loss of appetite for food.

APATHY-FUTILITY SYNDROME
Immature personality type often associated with child neglect and characterized by an inability to feel and to find any significant meaning in life. This syndrome, often arising from early deprivations in childhood, is frequently perpetuated from generation to generation within a family system. (Polansky)

APPEAL
Resort to a higher court in an attempt to have a decision or ruling of the lower court corrected or reversed because of some claimed error or injustice. Appeals follow several different formats. Occasionally, appeals will result in a rehearing of the entire case. Usually, however, appeals are limited to consideration of questions of whether the lower court judge correctly applied the law to the facts of the case.

ASSESSMENT
1) Determination of the validity of a reported case of suspected child abuse or neglect through investigatory interviews with persons involved. This could include interviews with the family, the child, school, and neighbors, as well as with other professionals and para-professionals having direct contact with the child or family.
2) Determination of the treatment potential and treatment plan for confirmed cases.

ASSAULT
Intentional or reckless threat of physical injury to a person. Aggravated assault is committed with the intention of carrying out the threat or other crimes. Simple assault is committed without the intention of carrying out the threat or if the attempt at injury is not completed. (See also BATTERY, SEXUAL ASSAULT)

ATROPHY
Wasting away of flesh, tissue, cell, or organ.

AVITAMINOSIS
Condition due to complete lack of one or more essential vitamins. (See also HYPOVITAMINOSIS)

BATTERED CHILD SYNDROME
Term introduced in 1962 by C. Henry Kempe, M.D., in the *Journal of the American Medical Association* in an article describing a combination of physical and other signs indicating that a child's internal and/or external injuries result from acts committed by a parent or caretaker. In some states, the battered child syndrome has been judicially recognized as an accepted medical diagnosis. Frequently this term is misused or misunderstood as the only type of child abuse and neglect. (See also CHILD ABUSE AND NEGLECT)

BATTERED WOMEN
Women who are victims of non-accidental physical and/or psychological injury inflected by a spouse or mate. There seems to be a relationship between child abuse and battered women, with both often occurring in the same family. (See also SPOUSE ABUSE)

BATTERY
Offensive contact or physical violence with a person without his/her consent, and which may or may not be preceded by a threat of assault. Because a minor cannot legally give consent, any such contact or violence against a child is considered battery. The action may be aggravated, meaning intentional, or it may be simple, meaning that the action was not intentional or did not cause

severe harm. Assault is occasionally used to mean attempted battery. (See also ASSAULT)

BEST INTERESTS OF THE CHILD
Standard for deciding among alternative plans for abused or neglected children. This is also known as the least detrimental alternative principle. Usually it is assumed that it is in the child's best interest and least detrimental if the child remains in the home, provided that the parents can respond to treatment. However, the parents' potential for treatment may be difficult to assess and it may not be known whether the necessary resources are available. A few authorities believe that except where the child's life is in danger, it is always in the child's best interest to remain in the home. This view reflects the position that in evaluating the least detrimental alternative and the child's best interest, the child's psychological as well as physical well-being must be considered. In developing a plan, the best interest of the child may not be served because of parents' legal rights or because agency policy and practice focuses on foster care. The best interest of the child and least detrimental alternative principles were articulated as a reaction to the overuse of child placement in cases of abuse and neglect. Whereas "best interest of the child" suggests that some placement may be justified, "least detrimental alternative" is stronger in suggesting that any placement or alternative can have some negative consequences and should be monitored.

BEYOND A REASONABLE DOUBT (See EVIDENTIARY STANDARDS)

BONDING
The psychological attachment of mother to child which develops during and immediately following childbirth. Bonding, which appears to be crucial to the development of a health parent/child relationship, may be studied during and immediately following delivery to help identify potential families-at-risk. Bonding is normally a natural occurrence but it may be disrupted by separation of mother and baby

or by situational or psychological factors causing the mother to reject the baby at birth.

BRUISE (See INTRADERMAL HEMORRHAGE)

BURDEN OF PROOF
The duty, usually falling on the state as petitioner in a child maltreatment case, of producing evidence at a trial so as to establish the truth of the allegations against the parent. At the commencement of a trial, it is always up to the petitioner to first present evidence which proves their case. (See also EVIDENCE, EVIDENTIARY STANDARDS)

BURN
Wound resulting from the application of too much heat. Burns are classified by the degree of damage caused.
  1st degree: Scorching or painful redness of the skin.
  2nd degree: Formation of blisters.
  3rd degree: Destruction of outer layers of the skin.

BURN OUT (See staff burn out.)

CALCIFICATION
Formation of bone. The amount of calcium deposited can indicate via X-ray the degree of healing of a broken bone or the location of previous fractures which have healed prior to the X-ray.

CALLUS
New bone formed during the healing process of a fracture.

CALVARIUM
Dome-like portion of the skull.

CARETAKER
A person responsible for a child's health or welfare, including the child's parent, guardian, or other person within the child's own home; or a person responsible for a child's health or welfare in a relative's home, foster care home, or residential institution. A caretaker is responsible for meeting a child's

basic physical and psychological needs and for providing protection and supervision.

CARTILAGE
The hard connective tissue that is not bone but, in the unborn and growing child, may be the forerunner of bone before calcium is deposited in it.

CASE MANAGEMENT
Coordination of the multiplicity of services required by a child abuse and neglect client. Some of these services may be purchased from an agency other than the mandated agency. In general, the role of the case manager is not the provision of direct services but the monitoring of those services to assure that they are relevant to the client, delivered in a useful way, and appropriately used by the client. To do this, a case manager assumes the following responsibilities.
1) Ascertains that all mandated reports have been properly filed.
2) Informs all professionals involved with the family that
   reports of suspected child abuse or neglect have been made.
3) Keeps all involved workers apprised of new information.
4) Calls and chairs the intial case conference for assessment, disposition, and treatment plans; conference may include parents, physician, probation worker, police, public health nurse, private therapist, parent aide, protective service and welfare workers, or others.
5) Coordinates interagency follow-up.
6) Calls further case conferences as needed. (See also PURCHASE OF SERVICE)

CASEWORK
A method of social work intervention which helps an individual or family improve their functioning in society by changing both internal attitudes and feelings and external circumstances directly affecting the individual or family. This contrasts with community organization and other methods of social work intervention which focuses on changing institutions or society. Social casework relies on a relationship between the worker and client as the primary tool for effecting change.

CATEGORICAL AID
Government financial assistance given to individuals who are aged or disabled or to families with dependent children. The eligibility requirements and financial assistance vary for different categories of persons, according to the guidelines of the Social Security Act. (See also SOCIAL SECURITY ACT)

CENTRAL REGISTER
Records of child abuse reports collected centrally from various agencies under state law or voluntary agreement. Agencies receiving reports of suspected abuse check with the central register to determine whether prior reports have been received by other agencies concerning the same child or parents. The purposes of central registers may be to alert authorities to families with a prior history of abuse, to assist agencies in planning for abusive families, and to provide data for statistical analysis of child abuse. Due to variance in state laws for reporting child abuse and neglect, there are diverse methods of compiling these records and of access to them. Although access to register records is usually restricted, critics warn of confidentiality problems and the importance of expunging unverified reports. (See also EXPUNGEMENT)

CHILD
A person, also known as minor, from birth to legal age of maturity for whom a parent and/or caretaker, foster parent, public or private home, institution, or agency is legally responsible. The 1974 Child Abuse Prevention and Treatment Act defines a child as a person under 18. In some states, a person of any age with a developmental disability is defined as a child.

CHILD ABUSE (See CHILD ABUSE AND NEGLECT)

CHILD ABUSE AND NEGLECT (CAN)
All-inclusive term, as defined in the Child Abuse Prevention and Treatment Act, for "the physical or mental injury, sexual abuse, negligent treatment or maltreatment of a child under the age of eighteen by a person who is responsible for the child's welfare. There is agreement that some parental care and supervision is essential, there is disagreement as to how much is necessary for a minimally acceptable environment.

Child Abuse refers specifically to an act of commission by a parent or caretaker which is not accidental and harms or threatens to harm a child's physical or mental health or welfare. All 50 States have a child abuse reporting law with varying definitions of child abuse and varying provisions as to who must and may report, penalties for not reporting, and required agency action following the report. Factors such as the age of the child and the severity of injury are important in determining abuse.

Physical Abuse
Child abuse which results in physical injury, including fractures, burns, bruises, welts, cuts, and/or internal injuries. Physical abuse often occurs in the name of discipline or punishment, and ranges from a slap of the hand to use of objects such as straps, belts, kitchen utensils, pipes, etc. (See also BATTERED CHILD SYNDROME)

Psychological/Emotional Abuse
Child abuse which results in impaired psychological growth and development. Frequently occurs as verbal abuse or excessive demands on a child's performance and results in a negative self-image on the part of the child and disturbed child behavior. May occur with or without physical abuse.

Sexual Abuse
Child abuse which results in any act of a sexual nature upon or with a child. Most states define any sexual involvement of a parent or caretaker with a child as a sexual act and therefore abuse. The most common form is incest between fathers and daughters.

Verbal Abuse
A particular form of psychological/emotional abuse characterized by constant verbal harassment and denigration of a child. Many persons abused as children report feeling more permanently damaged by verbal abuse than by isolated or repeated experiences of physical abuse.

Child Neglect refers to an act of omission, specifically the failure of a parent or other person legally responsible for a child's welfare to provide for the child's basic needs and proper level of care with respect to food, clothing, shelter, hygiene, medical attention, or supervision. Most states have neglect and/or dependency statutes; however, not all states require the reporting of neglect. While there is agreement that some parental care and supervision is essential, there is disagreement as to how much is necessary for a minimally acceptable environment. Severe neglect sometimes occurs because a parent is apathetic, impulse-ridden, mentally retarded, depressed, or psychotic.

Educational Neglect
Failure to provide for a child's cognitive development. This may include failure to conform to state legal requirements regarding school attendance.

Medical Neglect
Failure to seek medical or dental treatment for a health problem or condition which, if untreated, could become severe enough to represent a danger to the child. Except among religious sects prohibiting medical treatment, medical neglect is usually only one part of a larger family problem.

Moral Neglect
Failure to give a child adequate guidance in developing positive social values, such as parents who allow or teach their children to steal.

Physical Neglect
Failure to provide for a child's basic survival needs, such as food, clothing, shelter, and supervision, to the extent that the failure represents a hazard to the child's health or safety. Determining neglect for lack of supervision depends upon the child's age and competence, the amount of unsupervised time, the time of day when the child is unsupervised, and the degree of parental planning for the unsupervised period. For a particular kind of physical neglect involving failure to feed a baby or small child sufficiently, see FAILURE TO THRIVE SYNDROME.

Psychological /Emotional Neglect
Failure to provide the psychological nurturance necessary for a child's psychological growth and development. It is usually very difficult to prove the cause and effect relationship between the parent's unresponsiveness and lack of nurturance and the child's symptoms, and many states do not include psychological or emotional neglect in their reporting laws.

CHILD ABUSE PREVENTION AND TREATMENT ACT (PUBLIC LAW 93-247)

Act introduced and promoted in Congress by then U.S. Senator Walter Mondale and signed into law on January 31, 1974. The act established the National Center on Child Abuse and Neglect in the HEW Children's Bureau and authorized annual appropriations of between $15 million and $25 million through Fiscal Year 1977, but it is anticipated that Congress will extend the act for several years. Actual appropriations have been less than authorized. The purpose of the National Center is to conduct and compile research, provide an information clearinghouse, compile and publish training materials, provide technical assistance, investigate national incidence, and fund demonstration projects related to prevention, identification, and treatment of child abuse and neglect. In the 1974 act, not more than 20% of the appropriated funds may be used for direct assistance to states, which must be in compliance with specific legislative requirements including, among others, reporting and investigation of suspected neglect as well as abuse, provision of multidisciplinary programs, and appointment of a *guardian ad litem* to represent the child in all judicial proceedings. The act emphasizes multidisciplinary approaches. It also provides for funding for parent self-help projects.

Many persons do not understand that this act is primarily to support research and demonstration projects. Much larger amounts of funding for the ongoing provisions of child abuse and neglect services are provided to states through Title IV-B and Title XX of the Social Security Act.

CHILD DEVELOPMENT

Pattern of sequential stages of interrelated physical, psychological, and social development in the process of maturation from infancy and total dependence to adulthood and relative independence. Parents need to understand the level of maturity consistent with each stage of development and should not expect a child to display a level of maturity of which the child is incapable at a particular stage. Abusive or neglectful parents frequently impair a child's healthy growth and development because they do not understand child development or are otherwise unable to meet the child's physical, social, and psychological needs at a given stage or stages of development.

CHILD HEALTH VISITOR

Professional or paraprofessional who visits a home shortly after the birth of a baby and periodically thereafter to identify current and potential child health and development and family stress problems and to facilitate use of needed community services. While currently operating in many European countries, child health visitor programs are rare in the U.S. because they are perceived as contrary to the right to privacy and parental rights. A universal mandatory child health visitor program has, however, been recommended by several authorities as the most effective way to assure children's rights and prevent child abuse and neglect. Also known as Home Health Visitor.

CHILD IN NEED OF SUPERVISION
Juvenile who has committed a delinquent act and has been found by a children's court judge to require further court supervision, such as 1) probation, or 2) the transfer of custody of the child to a relative or public or private welfare agency for a period of time, usually not to exceed one year. Also known as Person in Need of Supervision (PINS) or Minor in Need of Supervision (MINS).

CHILD NEGLECT (See CHILD ABUSE AND NEGLECT)

CHILD PORNOGRAPHY
The obscene or pornographic photography, filming, or depiction of children for commercial purposes. Recent campaigns have begun to increase public awareness of this problem. Also as a result of public pressure against these materials, the federal government and some states are currently implementing special legislation to outlaw the sale and interstate transportation of pornographic materials that portray children engaged in explicit sexual acts.

CHILD PROSTITUTION
Legislation prohibiting the use of children as prostitutes is currently being implemented by the federal government and many states. The use of or participation by children in sexual acts with adults for reward or financial gain when no force is present.

CHILD PROTECTIVE SERVICES or CHILD PROTECTION SERVICES (CPS)
A specialized child welfare service, usually part of a county department of public welfare, legally responsible in most states for investigating suspected cases of child abuse and neglect and intervening in confirmed cases. Qualifications of CPS workers vary, with some counties employing CPS workers without prior human services training and others requiring at least a , Bachelor's degree in social work. With over 3,000 counties in the U.S., there are many kinds of CPS programs of varying quality. Common to most is the problem of insufficient staff overburdened with excessive caseloads. This plus the pressure of CPS work creates stress for many CPS staff. (See also STAFF BURNOUT, STAFF FLIGHT, and STAFF SATISFACTION)

CHILD WELFARE AGENCY
A public or voluntary agency providing service to children in their own homes and/or in day care, and which may be licensed to place children in foster homes, group homes, or institutions or into permanent adoptive homes. The number of children served annually by child welfare agencies in the U.S. is estimated to be over one million, the majority being served by public agencies. Payments for foster care represent well over half the total of child welfare agencies' expenditures.

Child welfare agencies which meet certain standards, including Standards for Protective Services, are accredited by the Child Welfare League of America. It is estimated that the majority of social workers employed by these accredited agencies hold a Master's degree. In public child welfare agencies, Master's degree social workers are a minority, with specific educational requirements varying from state to state. However, unlike many other fields of social work which share responsibility with other professions, child welfare is a domain for which social work has been accorded major responsibility. Believing that child protection is a public child welfare agency responsibility, few private agencies provide it.

CHILD WELFARE LEAGUE OF AMERICA (CWLA)
67 Irving Place
New York,
N.Y. 10003
Founded in 1920, the Child Welfare League of America is a privately supported, non-sectarian organization which is dedicated to the improvement of care and services for

deprived, neglected, and dependent children and their families. Its program is directed toward helping agencies and communities in the U.S. and Canada to provide essential social services to promote the well-being of children. CWLA is an advocate for children and families, a clearinghouse and forum for knowledge and experience of persons in the field, and a coordinating facility through which all concerned with child welfare can share their efforts. Programs of the League and its membership of over 300 affiliated public and private agencies include: accreditation of agencies, adoption services, conferences, consultation, training, library/information services, publications, personnel services, public affairs and legislative programs, standards development, and surveys.

CHILD WELFARE RESOURCE INFORMATION EXCHANGE

A project of the Children's Bureau of the Administration for Children, Youth and Families, HEW. It is a source for materials on exemplary programs, curricula, technologies, and methods which ahve brought more effective and efficient services to children. Its purpose is to improve the delivery of child welfare services by identifying successful programs, methods, research, and materials, and by assisting agencies in adapting them for their own use. The Exchange disseminates information it has gathered through abstracts, a bimonthly bulletin, regional workshops, and colloquia.

CHILDHOOD LEVEL OF LIVING SCALE (CLL)

Instrument used to measure the level of physical and emotional/cognitive care a child is receiving in his/her home. Rated are adequacy of food, clothing, furniture, etc., as well as evidence of affection, type of discipline, and cultural stimulation. The scale is designed to be used as a guide to assessing nurturance levels rather than as objective evidence of neglect.

CHILDREN-AT-RISK

May refer to the possibility that children in the custody of a state or county will get lost in a series of placements or for other reasons not be returned to their natural homes when these homes are no longer threatening to the children's welfare. May also refer to children in potentially abusive institutions, but usually refer to children in families-at-risk. (See also FAMILIES-AT-RISK)

CHILDREN'S DEFENSE FUND (CDF) 1520 New Hampshire Ave., N.W. Washington, D.C. 20036

A non-profit organization founded in 1973. Staff includes researchers, lawyers, and others dedicated to long-range and systematic advocacy on behalf of children. CDF works at federal, state, and local levels to reform policies and practices which harmfully affect large numbers of children. Activities include investigation and public information, litigation, monitoring of federal agencies, and technical assistance to local organizations. Program priorities are to assure the rights of children to proper education, adequate health care, comprehensive child care and family support services, fair and humane treatment in the juvenile justice system, and the avoidance of institutionalization.

CHILDREN'S RIGHTS

Rights of children as individuals to the protections provided in the Constitution as well as to the care and protection necessary for normal growth and development. Children's rights are actually exercised through adult representatives and advocates. The extent to which children's rights are protected varies according to the individual state laws providing for the identification and treatment of child abuse and neglect. An unresolved issue is the conflict between children's rights and parents' rights or rights to privacy. (See also PARENTS' RIGHTS)

CHIP FRACTURE (See FRACTURE)

CIRCUMSTANTIAL EVIDENCE (See EVIDENCE)

CIVIL PROCEEDING
Any lawsuit other than criminal prosecutions. Juvenile and family court cases are civil proceedings. Also called a civil action.

CLEAR AND CONVINCING EVIDENCE
(See EVIDENTIARY STANDARDS)

CLOTTING FACTOR
Material in the blood that causes it to coagulate. Deficiencies in clotting factors can cause profuse internal or external bleeding and/or bruising, as in the disease hemophilia. Bruises or bleeding caused by such a disease may be mistaken as resulting from abuse.

COLON
The large intestine.

COMMINUTED FRACTURE (See FRACTURE)

COMMISSION, ACTS OF
Overt acts by a parent or caretaker toward a child resulting in physical or mental injury, including but not limited to beatings, excessive disciplining, or exploitation. (See also CHILD ABUSE AND NEGLECT)

COMMISSIONER (See HEARING OFFICER)

COMMUNITY AWARENESS
A community's level of understanding of child abuse and neglect. Ideally, this should include knowledge about the extent and nature of the problem and how to use the local resources. In reality, community awareness tends to focus on reporting rather than treatment and prevention.

COMMUNITY COUNCIL FOR CHILD ABUSE AND NEGLECT
Community group, including both professionals and citizens, which attempts to develop and coordinate resources and/or legislation for the prevention, identification, and treatment of child abuse and neglect. It is often the name given to the program coordination

component of the community team (see COMMUNITY TEAM).

COMMUNITY EDUCATION
Developed for public audiences, this type of local level education provides understanding about a problem or issue of community and/or societal relevance, and information about appropriate community resources and services available to deal with the problem or issue. Sponsored by a professional agency or citizens' group, community education is usually provided through an ongoing speaker's bureau, through periodic lecture and discussion meetings open to the general public or offered to special groups, and/or through the local media and other publicity devices.

With reference to child abuse and neglect, it is important to combine community education with public awareness. Generally, public awareness is geared only to reporting child abuse and neglect, and may communicate a punitive image toward parents who abuse or neglect their children without communicating an understanding of the problem.

COMMUNITY NEGLECT
Failure of a community to provide adequate support and social services for families and children, or lack of community control over illegal or discriminatory activities with respect to families and children.

COMMUNITY ORGANIZATION
A social work method of achieving change in human service organizations or service delivery and utilization through social planning and/or social action. This kind of intervention rests explicitly or implicitly on understanding the nature of the community or service system which is the target of change and on organizing members of the community or system to participate in the change process. Professional community organizers assist, but do not direct, community groups in developing community organization strategies of confrontation, collaboration, coalition,

etc. Since child abuse and neglect is a multi-disciplinary, multiagency problem, community organization for coordination of services is imperative.

COMMUNITY SUPPORT SYSTEMS
Community resources such as schools, public health services, day care centers, welfare advocacy, whose utilization can aid in preventing family dysfunction and child abuse and neglect, and aid in treating identified cases of abuse and neglect.

COMMUNITY TEAM
Often used incorrectly to refer to a multidisciplinary professional group which only diagnoses and plans treatment for specific cases of child abuse and neglect. More accurately, a community team separates the diagnosis and treatment functions and provides a third component for education, training, and public relations. The community tream also includes a community task force or council, including citizens as well as professionals from various disciplines, which coordinates the three community team components and advocates for resources and legislation. Citizens on the community team also monitor the professionals and agency participants. For effective child abuse and neglect management, a community team should be established for every geographic area of 400,000 to 500,000 population, and should consist of the following components:

Identification/Diagnostic Team Component
The identification/diagnostic team component has primary responsibility for diagnosing actual cases of child abuse and neglect among those which are reported or otherwise come to their attention, providing acute care or crisis intervention for the child in immediate danger, and developing long-term treatment recommendations. This team should be multidisciplinary and should probably include a public health nurse,

pediatrician, psychologist or psychiatrist, lawyer, law enforcement person, case aides, and a number of child protective services workers. The protective services workers on the diagnostic team undergo unusual physical and emotional fatigue, and they should have a two or three week break from this activity every several months. However, to further relieve this stress, the diagnostic team, and not the protective services workers alone, should make and be accountable for all decisions. To function effectively, this team must establish protocol, define roles of each team member, establish policies and procedures, and establish a network of coordination with acute care service agencies.

Long Term Treatment Component
The long term treatment component has responsibility to review treatment needs and progress of specific cases periodically, to establish treatment goals, to coordinate existing treatment services, and to develop new treatment programs. This component should include supervisors and workers from supportive and advocacy services as well as from adult, children, and family treatment programs. The community team must assure provision and use of this component.

Education, Training, and Public Relations Component
The education, training, and public relations component has responsibility for community and professional awareness and education. Professional education includes implementation and/or evaluation of ongoing training programs for professionals and paraprofessionals.

The interrelationship among these various components is diagrammed below:

A - Identification and Diagnosis	1 - Case Coordination
B - Long-Term Treatment	2 - Professional Training and Recruitment
C - Education, Training, Public Relations	3 - Public and Professional ducation, Professional Training
	4 - Program Coordination

COMPLIANCE

1) The behavior of children who readily yield to demands in an attempt to please abusive or neglectful parents or caretakers.
2) A state child abuse and neglect law which conforms to requirements outlined in the Child Abuse Prevention and Treatment Act and further HEW regulations, and which therefore permits funding under this act for child abuse and neglect activities in the state. (See also CHILD ABUSE PREVENTION AND TREATMENT ACT)

COMPLAINT

1) An oral statement, usually made to the police, charging criminal, abusive, or neglectful conduct.
2) A district attorney's document which starts a criminal prosecution.
3) A petitioner's document which starts a civil proceeding. In juvenile or family court, the complaint is usually called a petition.
4) In some states, term used for a report of suspected abuse or neglect.

COMPOUND FRACTURE (See FRACTURE)

COMPREHENSIVE EMERGENCY SERVICES(CES)

A community system of coordinated services available on a 24-hour basis to meet emergency needs of children and/or families in crisis. Components of a CES system can include 24-hour protective services, homemaker services, crisis nurseries, family shelters, emergency foster care, outreach, and follow-up services.

CONCILIATION COURT (See COURTS)

CONCUSSION

An injury of a soft structure resulting from violent shaking or jarring; usually refers to a brain concussion.

CONFIDENTIALITY

Professional practice of not sharing with others information entrusted by a client or patient. Sometimes communications from parent to physician or social worker are made with this expectation but are later used in court, and many physicians and social workers are torn between legal vs. professional obligations. Confidentiality which is protected by statute is known as privileged communications. Confidentiality need not obstruct information sharing with a multidisciplinary team provided that the client is advised of the sharing and the team has articulated its own policy and guidelines on confidentiality. (See also PRIVILEGED COMMUNICATIONS)

CONGENITAL

Refers to any physical condition present at birth, regardless of its cause.

CONJUNCTIVA

Transparent lining covering the white of the eye and eyelids. Bleeding beneath the conjunctiva can occur spontaneously or from accidental or non-accidental injury.

CONTRAINDICATION

Reason for not giving a particular drug or prescribing a particular treatment, as it may do more harm than good.

CONTUSION

A wound producing injury to soft tissue without a break in the skin, causing bleeding into surrounding tissues.

CORPORAL PUNISHMENT

Physical punishment inflected directly upon the body. Some abusive parents mistakenly believe that corporal punishment is the only way to discipline children, and some child development specialists believe that almost all parents must occasionally resort to corporal punishment to discipline or train children. Other professionals believe that corporal punishment is never advisable. In a Supreme Court ruling (Ingraham vs. Wright, April 19, 1977), corporal punishment in the schools was upheld. The Supreme Court ruled that the cruel and unusual punishment clause of the Eighth Amendment does not apply to corporal punishment in the schools. (See also DISCIPLINE).

CORTEX
Outer layer of an organ or other body structure.

COURTS
Places where judicial proceedings occur. There is an array of courts involved with child abuse and neglect cases, partly because different states divide responsibility for certain proceedings among different courts, and also because tradition has established a variety of names for courts which perform similar functions. Child abuse reports can result in proceedings in any of the following courts:

Criminal Court
Usually divided into superior court, which handles felony cases, and municipal court, which handles misdemeanors and the beginning stages of most felony cases.

Domestic Relations Court
A civil court in which divorces and divorce custody hearings are held.

Family Court
A civil court which, in some states, combines the functions of domestic relations, juvenile, and probate courts. Establishment of family courts is often urged to reform the presently wasteful and poorly-coordinated civil court system. Under some proposals, family courts would also deal with criminal cases involving family relations, thus improving coordination in child abuse litigation.

Court of Conciliation
A branch of domestic relations courts in some states, usually staffed by counselors and social workers rather than by lawyers or judges, and designed to explore and promote reconciliation in divorce cases.

Juvenile Court
Juvenile court, which has jurisdiction over minors, usually handles cases of suspected delinquency as well as cases of suspected abuse or neglect. In many states, terminations of parental rights occur in juvenile court proceedings, but that is generally the limit of juvenile court's power over adults.

Probate Court
Probate court may handle cases of guardianship and adoption in addition to estates of deceased persons.

CRANIUM
The skull.

CRIMINAL PROSECUTION
The process involving the filing of charges of a crime, followed by arraignment and trial of the defendant. Criminal prosecution may result in fines, imprisonment, and/or probation. Criminal defendants are entitled to acquittal unless charges against them are proven beyond a reasonable doubt. Technical rules of evidence exclude many kinds of proof in criminal trials, even though that proof might be admissible in civil proceedings. Criminal defendants are entitled to a jury trial; in many civil proceedings concerning children, there is no right to a jury trial.

CRISIS INTERVENTION
Action to relieve a specific stressful situation or series of problems which are immediately threatening to a child's health and/or welfare. This involves alleviation of parental stress through provision of emergency services in the home and/or removal of the child from the home. (See also EMERGENCY SERVICES and COMPREHENSIVE EMERGENCY SERVICES)

CRISIS NURSERY
Facility offering short-term relief of several hours to several days' duration to parents temporarily unable or unwilling to care for their children. The primary purpose are child protection, stabilization of the home, and prevention of child abuse and neglect.

CUSTODY
The right to care and control of a child and the duty to provide food, clothing, shelter, ordinary medical care, education, and discipline for a child. Permanent legal custody

may be taken from a parent or given up by a parent by a court action (see TERMINATION OF PARENTAL RIGHTS). Temporary custody of a child may be granted for a limited time only, usually pending further action or review by the court. Temporary custody may be granted for a period of months or, in the case of protective or emergency custody, for a period of hours or several days.

Emergency Custody

The ability of a law enforcement officer, pursuant to the criminal code, to take temporary custody of a child who is in immediate danger and place him/her in the control of child protective services. A custody hearing must usually be held within 48 hours of such action. Also known as police custody.

Protective Custody

Emergency measure taken to detain a child, often in a hospital, until a written detention request can be filed. In some states, telephone communication with a judge is required to authorize protective custody. In other states, police, social workers, or doctors have statutory authority to detain minors who are in imminent danger. (See also DETENTION)

CUSTODY HEARING

Hearing, usually held in children's court, to determine who has the rights of legal custody of a minor. It may involve one parent against the other or the parents vs. a social service agency.

CYCLE OF CHILD ABUSE OR NEGLECT

(See
WORLD OF ABNORMAL REARING)

DAUGHTERS UNITED

Organization name sometimes used for self-help groups of daughters who have been sexually abused. Daughters United is one component of a model Child Sexual Abuse Treatment Program in Santa Clara County, California. (See also PARENTS UNITED)

DAY CARE

A structured, supervised place for children to go more or less regularly while parents work or attend school. Experts believe that family stress can be relieved by more extensive provision of day care services, and day care providers are increasingly concerned with identification and prevention of child abuse and neglect.

DAY TREATMENT

1) Program providing treatment as well as structured supervision for children with identified behavioral problems, including abused and neglected children, while they remain in their own, foster, or group homes. Day treatment services usually include counseling with families or caretakers with whom the children reside.
2) Treatment and structured activities for parents or entire families in a treatment setting from which they return to their own homes evenings and weekends.

DELINQUENCY

Behavior of a minor which would, in the case of an adult, constitute criminal conduct. In some states, delinquency also includes "waywardness" or disobedient behavior on the part of the child. In contrast to dependency cases, where the parent(s) rather than the minor is assumed responsible, delinquency cases assume that the minor has some responsibility for his/her behavior.

DENVER MODEL

A multidisciplinary hospital-community coalition which originated in Denver, Colorado, and which has become a model replicated by many other programs. The following diagram outlines the components:

TIME	PLACE	FUNCTION
	Community	Child is identified as suspected abuse or neglect.
24 hours	Hospital	Child is admitted to hospital.
	Hospital	Telephone report is made to protective services.
	Community	Home is evaluated by protective services.
72 hours	Both	Dispositional conference is held.
	Community	Court is involved if needed.
2 weeks	Both	Implement dispositional plan.
6-9 months	Community	Maintain case.
	Both	Long-term Treatment program is followed.
	Both	Child is returned home when home has been made safe.

DEPENDENCY

A child's need for care and supervision from a parent or caretaker. Often a legal term referring to cases of children whose natural parent(s) cannot or will not properly care for them or supervise them so that the state must assume this responsibility. Many states distinguish findings of dependency, for which the juvenile is assumed to have little or no responsibility, from findings of delinquency, in which the juvenile is deemed to be at least partially responsible for his/her behavior.

DETENTION

The temporary confinement of a person by a public authority. In a case of child abuse or neglect, a child may be detained pending a trial when a detention hearing indicates that it is unsafe for the child to remain in his/her own home. This is often called protective custody or emergency custody. The child may be detained in a foster home, group home, hospital, or other facility.

DETENTION HEARING

A court hearing held to determine whether a child should be kept away from his/her parents until a full trial of neglect, abuse, or delinquency allegations can take place. Detention hearings must usually be held within 24 hours of the filing of a detention request. (See also CUSTODY)

DETENTION REQUEST

A document filed by a probation officer, social worker, or prosecutor with the clerk of a juvenile or family court, asking that a detention hearing be held, and that a child be detained until the detention hearing has taken place. Detention requests must usually be filed within 48 hours of the time protective custody of the child begins. (See also CUSTODY)

DIAGNOSTIC TEAM (See COMMUNITY TEAM)

DIAPHYSIS

The shaft of a long bone.

DIFFERENTIAL DIAGNOSIS

The determination of which of two or more diseases or conditions a patient may be suffering from by systematically comparing and contrasting the clinical findings.

DIRECT EVIDENCE (See EVIDENCE)

DIRECT SERVICE PROVIDERS

Those groups and individuals who directly interact with clients and patients in the delivery of health, education, and welfare services, or those agencies which employs them. It includes, among others, policemen, social workers, physicians, psychiatrists, and clinical psychologists who see clients or patients.

DISCIPLINE

1) A branch of knowledge or learning or a particular profession, such as law, medicine, or social work.
2) Training that develops self-control, self-sufficiency, orderly conduct. Discipline is

often confused with punishment, particularly by abusive parents who resort to corporal punishment. Although interpretations of both "discipline" and "punishment" tend to be vague and often overlapping, there is some consensus that discipline has positive connotations and punishment is considered negatively. Some general comparisons between the terms are:

a) Discipline can occur before, during, and/or after an event; punishment occurs only after an event.
b) Discipline is based on respect for a child and his/her capabilities; punishment is based on behavior or events precipitating behavior.
c) Discipline implies that there is an authority figure; punishment implies power and dominance vs. submissiveness.
d) The purpose of discipline is educational and rational; the purpose of punishment is to inflict pain, often in an attempt to vent frustration or anger.
e) Discipline focuses on deterring future behavior by encouraging development of internal controls; punishment is a method of external control which may or may not alter future behavior.
f) Discipline can lead to extrapolation and generalized learning patterns; punishment may relate only to a specific event.
g) Discipline can strengthen interpersonal bonds and recognizes individual means and worth; punishment usually causes deterioration of relationships and is usually a dehumanizing experience.
h) Both discipline and punishment behavior patterns may be transmitted to the next generation.

According to legal definitions applying to most schools and school districts, to accomplish the purposes of education, a schoolteacher stands in the place of a parent and may exercise powers of control, restraint, discipline, and correction as necessary, provided that the discipline is reasonable. The Supreme Court has ruled that under certain circumstances, the schools may also employ corporal punishment. (See also CORPORAL PUNISHMENT)

DISLOCATION
The displacement of a bone, usually disrupting a joint, which may accompany a fracture or may occur alone.

DISPOSITION
The order of a juvenile or family court issued at a dispositional hearing which determines whether a minor, already found to be a dependent or delinquent child, should continue in or return to the parental home, and under what kind of supervision, or whether the minor should be placed out-of-home, and in what kind of setting: a relative's home, foster home, or institution. Disposition in a civil case parallels sentencing in a criminal case.

DISPOSITIONAL CONFERENCE
A conference, preferably multidisciplinary, in which the child, parent, family, and home diagnostic assessments are evaluated and decisions are made as to court involvement, steps needed to protect the child, and type of long-term treatment. This conference should be held within the first 72 hours after hospital admission or reporting of the case.

DISPOSITIONAL HEARING (See DISPOSITION)

DISTAL
Far; farther from any point of reference. Opposite of proximal.

DOMESTIC RELATIONS COURT (See COURTS)

DUE PROCESS
The rights of persons involved in legal proceedings to be treated with fairness. These rights include the right to adequate notice in advance of hearings, the right to notice of allegations of misconduct, the right to assis-

tance of a lawyer, the right to confront and cross-examine witnesses, and the right to refuse to give self-incriminating testimony. In child abuse or neglect cases, courts are granting more and more due process to parents in recognition of the fact that loss of parental rights, temporarily or permanently, is as serious as loss of liberty. However, jury trials and presumptions of innocence are still afforded in very few juvenile or family court cases.

DUODENUM
The first portion of the small intestine which connects it to the stomach.

EARLY AND PERIODIC SCREENING, DIAGNOSIS, AND TREATMENT (EPSDT)
Program enacted in 1967 under Medicaid (Title 19 of the Social Security Act), with early detection of potentially crippling or disabling conditions among poor children as its goal. The establishment of EPSDT was a result of studies indicating that physical and mental defects were high among poor children and that early detection of the problems and prompt receipt of health care could reduce the consequences and the need for remedial'services in later life. Although a recent study by the Children's Defense Fund has indicated that existing health systems are not adequate to facilitate the goals of EPSDT, the program has uncovered many previously undetected or untreated health problems among those children whom it has been able to reach.

EARLY INTERVENTION
Programs and services focusing on prevention by relieving family stress before child abuse and neglect occur; for example, helplines, Head Start, home health visitors, EPSDT, crisis nurseries.

ECCHYMOSIS (See INTRADERMAL HEMORRHAGE)

EDEMA
Swelling caused by an excessive amount of fluid in body tissue. It often follows a bump or bruise but may also be caused by allergy, malnutrition, or disease.

EMERGENCY CUSTODY (See CUSTODY)

EMERGENCY SERVICES
The focus of these services is protection of a child and prevention of further maltreatment through availability of a reporting mechanism on a 24-hour basis and immediate intervention. This intervention could include hospitalization of the child, assistance in the home including homemakers, or removal of the child from the home to a shelter or foster home. (See also COMPREHENSIVE EMERGENCY SERVICES)

EMOTIONAL ABUSE (See CHILD ABUSE AND NEGLECT)

EMOTIONAL NEGLECT (See CHILD ABUSE AND NEGLECT)

ENCOPRESIS
Involuntary passage of feces.

ENURESIS
Involuntary passage of urine.

EPIPHYSIS
Growth center near the end of a long bone.

EVIDENCE
Any sort of proof submitted to the court for the purpose of influencing the court's decision. Some special kinds of evidence are:

Circumstantial
Proof of circumstances which may imply another fact. For example, proof that a parent kept a broken appliance cord may connect the parent to infliction of unique marks on a child's body.

Direct
Generally consisting of testimony of the type such as a neighbor stating that he/she saw the parent strike the child with an appliance cord.

Hearsay

Second-hand evidence, generally consisting of testimony of the type such as, "I heard him say. . . ." Except in certain cases, such evidence is usually excluded because it is considered unreliable and because the person making the original statement cannot be cross-examined.

Opinion

Although witnesses are ordinarily not permitted to testify to their beliefs or opinions, being restricted instead to reporting what they actually saw or heard, when a witness can be qualified as an expert on a given subject, he/she can report his/her conclusions, for example, "Based upon these marks, it is my opinion as a doctor that the child must have been struck with a flexible instrument very much like this appliance cord." Lawyers are sometimes allowed to ask qualified experts "hypothetical questions," in which the witness is asked to assume the truth of certain facts and to express an opinion based on those "facts." (See also EXPERT TESTIMONY)

Physical

Any tangible piece of proof such as a document, X-ray, photograph, or weapon used to inflict an injury. Physical evidence must usually be authenticated by a witness who testifies to the connection of the evidence (also called an exhibit) with other facts in the case.

Evidentiary Standards

State laws differ in the quantum of evidence which is considered necessary to prove a case of child maltreatment. Three of the most commonly used standards are:

Beyond a Reasonable Doubt (the standard required in all criminal court proceedings). Evidence which is entirely convincing or satisfying to a moral certainty. This is the strictest standard of all.

Clear and Convincing Evidence. Less evidence than is required to prove a case beyond a reasonable doubt, but still an amount which would make one confident of the truth of the allegations.

Preponderance of the Evident (the standard in most civil court proceedings). Merely presenting a greater weight of credible evidence than that presented by the opposing party. This is the easiest standard of proof of all.

EXHIBIT

Physical evidence used in court. In a child abuse case, an exhibit may consist of X-rays, photographs of the child's injuries, or the actual materials presumably used to inflict the injuries. (See also EVIDENCE)

EXPERT TESTIMONY

Witnesses with various types of expertise may testify in child abuse or neglect cases; usually these expert witnesses are physicians or radiologists. Experts are usually questioned in court about their education or experience which qualifies them to give professional opinions about the matter in question. Only after the hearing officer determines that the witness is, in fact, sufficiently expert in the subject matter may that witness proceed to state his/her opinions. (See also EVIDENCE)

EXPERT WITNESS (See EXPERT TESTIMONY)

EXPLOITATION OF CHILDREN

1) Involving a child in illegal or immoral activities for the benefit of a parent or caretaker. This could include child pornography, child prostitution, sexual abuse, or forcing a child to steal.
2) Forcing workloads on a child in or outside the home so as to interfere with the health, education, and well-being of the child.

EXPUNGEMENT

Destruction of records. Expungement may be ordered by the court after a specified number of years or when the juvenile, parent, or defendant applies for expungement and shows that his/her conduct has improved. Expungement also applies to the removal of an unverified report of abuse or neglect that has been made to a central registry. (See also CENTRAL REGISTRY)

EXTRAVASATED BLOOD
Discharge or escape of blood into tissue.

FAILURE TO THRIVE SYNDROME (FTT)
A serious medical condition most often seen in children under one year of age. An FTT child's height, weight, and motor development fall significantly short of the average growth rates of normal children. In about 10% of FTT cases, there is an organic cause such as serious heart, kidney, or intestinal disease, a genetic error of metabolisin, or brain damage. All other cases are a result of a disturbed parent-child relationship manifested in severe physical and emotional neglect of the child. In diagnosing FTT as child neglect, certain criteria should be considered:
1) The child's weight is below the third percentile, but substantial weight gain occurs when the child is properly nurtured, such as when hospitalized.
2) The child exhibits developmental retardation which decreases when there is adequate feeding and appropriate stimulation.
3) Medical investigation provides no evidence that disease or medical abnormality is causing the symptoms.
4) The child exhibits clinical signs of deprivation which decrease in a more nurturing environment.
5) There appears to be a significant environmental psychosocial disruption in the child's family.

FAMILIES ANONYMOUS
1) Name used by the National Center for the Prevention and Treatment of Child Abuse and Neglect at Denver for self-help groups for abusive parents. These groups operate in much the same way as the more widely-known Parents Anonymous. (See also PARENTS ANONYMOUS)
2) Self-help groups for families of drug abusers.

FAMILIES-AT-RISK
May refer to families evidencing high potential for child abuse or neglect because of a conspicuous, severe parental problem, such as criminal behavior, substance abuse, mental retardation, or psychosis. More often refers to families evidencing high potential for abuse or neglect because of risk factors which may be less conspicuous but multiple. These include: 1) environmental stress such as unemployment or work dissatisfaction; social isolation; anomie; lack of child care resources; I and/or 2) family stress such as marital discord; chronically and/or emotionally immature parent with a history of abuse or neglect as a child; unwanted pregnancy; colicky, hyperactive, or handicapped baby or child; siblings a year or less apart; sudden changes in family due to illness, separation, or death; parentla ignorance of child care and child development. Increasingly, the maternal-infant bonding process at childbirth is evaluated and used as one means to identify families-at-risk. Families thus identified should be offered immediate and periodic assistance.

FAMILY
Two or more persons related by blood, marriage, or mutual agreement who interact and provide one another with mutual physical, emotional, social, and/or economic care. Families can be described as "extended," with more than one generation in a household; or "nuclear," with only parent(s) and child(ren). Families can also be described as "mixed" or "multiracial"; "multi-parent," as in a commune or collective; or "single-parent." These types are not mutually exclusive.
FAMILY COURT (See COURTS)

FAMILY DYNAMICS
Interrelationships between and among individual family members. The evaluation of family dynamics is an important factor in the

identification, diagnosis, and treatment of child abuse and neglect.

FAMILY DYSFUNCTION
Ineffective functioning of the family as a unit or of individual family members in their family role because of physical, mental, or situational problems of one or more family members. A family which does not have or use internal or external resources to cope with its problems or fulfill its responsibilities to children may be described as dysfunctional. Child abuse and neglect is evidence of family dysfunction.

FAMILY IMPACT STATEMENT
Report which assesses the effect of existing and proposed legislation, policies, regulations, and practices on family life. The purpose is to promote legislation and policies which work for, not against, healthy family life. At the federal level, this activity is being developed by the Family Impact Seminar, George Washington University Institute for Educational Leadership (1001 Connecticut Ave., N.W., Suite 732, Washington, D.C. 20036).

FAMILY LIFE EDUCATION
Programs focusing on educating, enlightening, and supporting individuals and families regarding aspects of family life; for example, child development classes, communication skills workshops, sex education courses, or money management courses. Family life education might well be part of every child abuse and neglect prevention program, and may be part of the treatment program for abusive or neglectful parents who lack this information.

FAMILY PLANNING
Information and counseling provided to assist in controlling family size and spacing of children, including referrals to various agencies such as Planned Parenthood.

As a condition of receiving federal funding for AFDC (see SOCIAL SECURITY ACT), states are required to offer family planning services to applicants designated as "appropriate."

Family planning should be part of a child abuse and neglect prevention program.

FAMILY POLICY
Generally refers to public social and economic policies that centrally affect families. There is considerable confusion about the term, with some persons believing that family policy should mean more direct policies affecting families, such as family planning policies. There is much more agreement that we should look at the impact of numerous policies on families, and that these should include a wide range of governmental policies. (See also FAMILY IMPACT STATEMENT)

FAMILY SHELTER
A 24-hour residential care facility for entire families. The setting offers around-the-clock care, and often provides diagnosis and comprehensive treatment on a short-term basis. In child abuse and neglect, a family shelter is used primarily for crisis intervention.

FAMILY SYSTEM
The concept that families operate as an interacting whole and are an open system, so that many factors in the environment affect the functioning of family members and the interaction among members. It is also conceptualized that the behavior of the family as an interacting unit has an effect on a number of factors in the outer environment.

FAMILY VIOLENCE
Abusive or aggressive behavior between parents, known as wife battering or spouse abuse; between children, known as sibling abuse; and/or between parents and children within a family, usually child abuse. This behavior is related to factors within the structure of a family system and/or society; for example, poverty, models of violent behavior displayed via mass media, stress due to excessive numbers of children, values of dominance and submissiveness, and attitudes toward discipline and punishment. It may also occur as a result of alcoholism or other substance abuse.

The terms family violence and domestic violence are sometimes used interchangeably but some persons exclude child abuse from the definition of domestic violence and limit it to violence between adult mates or spouses.

FEDERAL REGULATIONS
Guidelines and regulations developed by departments or agencies of the federal government to govern programs administered or funded by those agencies. Regulations specify policies and procedures outlined in a more general way in public laws or acts. Proposed federal regulations, or changes in existing regulations, are usually published in the *Federal Register* for public review and comment. They are subsequently published in the final form adopted by the governing agency.

FEDERAL STANDARDS (See STANDARDS)

FELONY
A serious crime for which the punishment may be imprisonment for longer than a year and/or a fine greater than $1,000. Distinguished from misdemeanor or infraction, both of lesser degree.

FIFTH AMENDMENT
The Fifth Amendment to the U.S. Constitution guarantees a defendant that he/she cannot be compelled to present self-incriminating testimony.

FONTANEL
The soft spots on a baby's skull where the bones of the skull have not yet grown together.

FORENSIC MEDICINE
That branch of the medical profession concerned withestablishing evidence for legal proceedings.

FOSTER CARE
A form of substitute care for children who need to be removed from their own homes. Usually this is a temporary placement in which a child lives with a licensed foster family or caretaker until he/she can return to his/her own home or until reaching the age of majority. Foster care all too often becomes a permanent method of treatment for abused or neglected children. Effective foster care ideally includes service to the child, service to the natural parents, service to the foster parents, and periodic review of the placement.

FOSTER GRANDPARENTS
Retired persons or senior citizens who provide nurturance and support for children to whom they are not related, including abused and neglected children, by babysitting or taking them for recreational outings. This enables parents to have some respite and allows retired or older persons an opportunity to become involved in community activities. Sometimes foster grandparents are volunteers and sometimes they are paid by an agency program.

FOUNDED REPORT
Any report of suspected child abuse or neglect made to the mandated agency which is confirmed or verified. Founded reports outnumber unfounded reports.

FRACTURE
A broken bone, which is one of the most common injuries found among battered children. The fracture may occur in several ways:
Chip Fracture
A small piece of bone is flaked from the major part of the bone.

Comminuted Fracture
Bone is crushed or broken into a number of pieces.

Compound Fracture
Fragment(s) of broken bone protrudes through the skin, causing a wound.

Simple Fracture
Bone breaks without wounding the surrounding tissue.

Spiral Fracture

Twisting causes the line of the fracture to encircle the bone like a spiral staircase.

Torus Fracture
A folding, bulging, or buckling fracture. See diagram on next page for names and locations of the major bones of the human skeleton.

FRONTAL
Referring to the front of the head; the forehead.

FUNDASCOPIC EXAM
Opthalmic examination to determine if irregularities or internal injuries to the eye exist.

GATEKEEPERS
Professionals and the agencies which employ them who are in frequent or periodic contact with families or children and who are therefore in an advantageous position to spot individual and family problems, including child abuse and neglect, and make appropriate referrals for early intervention or treatment.

GLUTEAL
Related to the buttocks, which are made up of the large gluteus maximus muscles.

GONORRHEA (See VENEREAL DISEASE)

GRAND ROUNDS
Hospital staff meetings for presentation and discussion of a particular case or medical problem.

GUARDIAN
Adult charged lawfully with the responsibility for a child. A guardian has almost all the rights and powers of a natural parent, but the relationship is subject to termination or change. A guardian may or may not also have custody and therefore actual care and supervision of the child.

GUARDIAN AD LITEM (GAL)
Adult appointed by the court to represent the child in a judicial proceeding. The *guardian ad litem* may be, but is not necessarily, an attorney. Under the Child Abuse Prevention and Treatment Act, a state cannot qualify for federal assistance unless it provides by statute "that in every case involving an abused or neglected child which results in a judicial proceeding a *guardian ad litem* shall be appointed to represent the child in such proceedings." Some states have begun to allow a GAL for children in divorce cases.

HEAD START
A nationwide comprehensive program for disadvantaged preschool children, funded by the HEW Administration for Children, Youth and Families to meet the educational, nutritional, and health needs of the children and to encourage parent participation in their children's development.

Through federal policy instructions (see *Federal Register,* January 26, 1977), all Head Start staff are mandated to report suspected cases of child abuse and neglect. These policy instructions supersede individual child abuse and neglect reporting laws in states which do not include Head Start staff as mandated reporters.

HEARING
Judicial proceeding where issues of fact or law are tried and in which both parties have a right to be heard. A hearing is synonymous with a trial.

HEARING OFFICER
A judge or other individual who presides at a judicial proceeding. The role of judge is performed in some juvenile court hearings by referees or commissioners, whose orders are issued in the name of the supervising judge. Acts of a referee or commissioner may be undone after the supervising judge has conducted a rehearing in the case.

HELPLINE
Usually a telephone counseling, information, and referral service characterized by caller anonymity, late hour availability, and the use

of trained volunteers as staff. The goal is usually early intervention in any kind of family stress, as well as crisis intervention in child abuse and neglect. Helplines relieve social isolation and offer ways of ventilating stress which are not destructive. Unlike hotlines, helplines generally cannot report cases of child abuse and neglect since they do not know the caller's name. Instead, the helpline attempts to have the caller himself/herself seek professional assistance and/or maintain a regular calling relationship for support and as an alternative to violent behavior. Helplines appear to be very cost effective in the preventive of child abuse and neglect. Major disadvantages are lack of visual cues to problems and limited opportunity for follow-up services. (See also HOTLINE)

HEMATEMESIS
Vomiting of blood from the stomach, often resulting from internal injuries.

HEMATOMA
A swelling caused by a collection of blood in an enclosed space, such as under the skin or the skull.

HEMATUREA
Blood in the urine.

HEMOPHILIA
Hereditary blood clotting disorder characterized by spontaneous or traumatic internal and external bleeding and bruising.

HEMOPTYSIS
Spitting or coughing blood from the windpipe or lungs.

HEMORRHAGE
The escape of blood from the vessels; bleeding.

HOME HEALTH VISITOR (See CHILD HEALTH VISITOR)

HOME START
A nationwide home-based program funded by the HEW Administration for Children, Youth and Families to strengthen parents as educators of their own children.

HOMEMAKER SERVICES
Provision of assistance, support, and relief for parents who may be unable or unwilling to fulfill parenting functions because of illness or being overwhelmed with parenting responsibilities. A homemaker is placed in a home on an hourly or weekly basis and assists with housekeeping and child care while demonstrating parenting skills and providing some degree of nurturance for parents and children.

HOSPITAL HOLD
Hospitalization for further observation and protection of a child suspected of being abused or neglected. This usually occurs when a suspected case is discovered in an emergency room. In most cases, holding the child is against the wishes of the parent or caretaker. (See also CUSTODY)

HOTLINE
Twenty-four hour statewide or local answering service for reporting child abuse or neglect and initiating investigation by a local agency. This is often confused with a helpline. (See also HELPLINE)

HYPERACTIVE
More active than is considered normal.

HYPERTHERMIA
Condition of high body temperature.

HYPHEMA
Hemorrhage within the anterior chamber of the eye, often appearing as a bloodshot eye. The cause could be a blow to the head or violent shaking.

HYPOACTIVE
Less active than is considered normal.

HYPOTHERMIA
Condition of low body temperature.

HYPOVITAMINOSIS

Condition due to the deficiency of one or more essential vitamins. (See also AVITAMINOSIS)

IDENTIFICATION OF CHILD ABUSE AND NEGLECT

Diagnosis or verification of child abuse and neglect cases by mandated agency workers or a diagnostic team following investigation of suspected child abuse and neglect (see INDICATORS OF CHILD ABUSE AND NEGLECT). Identification of child abuse and neglect therefore depends not only on professional diagnostic skill but also on the extent to which the public and professionals report suspected cases. Public awareness campaigns are important to effect identification, but at the same time it is important to have sufficient staff in the mandated agency to handle all the reports a public awareness campaign may generate (see COMMUNITY AWARENESS and COMMUNITY EDUCATION). More reporting and therefore identification will also occur as states strengthen their reporting laws so as to extend the number of persons who must report and penalize them more heavily if they don't. It is generally agreed that to date the identification of child abuse and neglect represents only a small proportion of the actual incidence of the problem. It is also generally agreed that a greater degree of identification occurs in minority and low income groups because these persons are more visible to agencies and professionals required to report. The incidence is probably as high in upper socio-economic groups, but identification is more difficult, particularly because private physicians generally dislike to report.

ILEUM

Final portion of the small intestine which connects with the colon.

IMMUNITY, LEGAL

Legal protection from civil or criminal liability.
1) Child abuse and neglect reporting statutes often confer immunity upon persons mandated to report, giving them an absolute defense to libel, slander, invasion of privacy, false arrest, and other lawsuits which the person accused of the act might file. Some grants of immunity are limited only to those persons who report in good faith and without malicious intent.
2) Immunity from criminal liability is sometimes conferred upon a witness in order to obtain vital testimony. Thereafter, the witness cannot be prosecuted with the use of information he/she disclosed in his/her testimony. If an immunized witness refuses to testify, he/she can be imprisoned for contempt of court.

IMPETIGO

A highly contagious, rapidly spreading skin disorder which occurs principally in infants and young children. The disease, characterized by red blisters, may be an indicator of neglect and poor living conditions.

IMPULSE-RIDDEN MOTHER

Term often used to describe one kind of neglectful parent who demonstrates restlessness, aggressiveness, inability to tolerate stress, manipulativeness, and craving for excitement or change. This parent may have a lesser degree of early deprivation than the apathetic-futile parent, but lacks self-control over strong impulses and/or has not learned limit-setting.

IN CAMERA

Any closed hearing before a judge in his chambers is said to be *in camera*.

IN LOCO PARENTIS

"In the place of a parent." Refers to actions of a guardian or other non-parental custodian.

INCEST

Sexual intercourse between persons who are closely related. Some state laws recognize incest only as sexual intercourse among consaguineous, or blood, relations; other states recognize incest as sexual relations between a variety of family members related by blood and/or law. In the U.S., the prohibition against incest is specified by many states' laws as well as by cultural tradition, with state laws usually defining incest as marriage or sexual relationships between relatives who are closer than second, or sometimes even more distant, cousins. While incest and sexual abuse are sometimes thought to be synonymous, it should be realized that incest is only one aspect of sexual abuse. Incest can occur within families between members of the same sex, but the most common form of incest is between father and daughters. It is generally agreed that incest is much more common than the number of reported cases indicates. Also, because society has not until the present done much about this problem, professionals have generally not had adequate training to deal with it, and the way the problem is handled may prove more traumatic for a child victim of incest than the incest experience itself. It should be noted that sexual relations between relatives may be defined as incest, but that in cest is not considered child sexual abuse unless a minor is involved. (See also CHILD ABUSE AND NEGLECT, SEXUAL ABUSE, SEXUAL MISUSE)

INCIDENCE

The extent to which a problem occurs in a given population. No accurate or complete data is available on the actual incidence of child abuse and neglect in the U.S. because major studies have not been able to obtain data from some states or have found the data not to be comparable. For continuing efforts to solve this problem, see NATIONAL STUDY ON CHILD ABUSE AND NEGLECT REPORTING. Informed estimates of incidence range from 600,000 to one million cases of child abuse and neglect per year in this country. It is generally agreed that child neglect is four to five or more times more common than child abuse. Incidence of actual child abuse and neglect should not be confused with the number of reported cases in a central registry, since the latter include reports of suspected but unconfirmed cases. On the other hand, it is generally agreed that because of insufficient reporting, the number of actual cases coming to the attention of local agencies is but a small proportion of the actual number of cases in the population. (See also CENTRAL REGISTRY and IDENTIFICATION OF CHILD ABUSE AND NEGLECT)

INDICATED CHILD ABUSE AND NEGLECT

1) In some state statutes, "indicated" child abuse and neglect means a confirmed or verified case.
2) Medically, "indicated" means a probable case.

INDICATORS OF CHILD ABUSE AND NEGLECT

Signs or symptoms which, when found in various combinations, point to possible abuse or neglect. See chart on next page for common indicators of child abuse and neglect.

INDICTMENT

The report of a grand jury charging an adult with criminal conduct. The process of indictment by secret grand jury proceedings bypasses the filing of a criminal complaint and the holding of a preliminary hearing in municipal court, so that prosecution begins immediately in superior court.

INFANTICIDE

The killing of an infant or many infants. Until modern times, infanticide was an accepted method of population control. It often took the form of abandonment. A few primitive cultures still practice infanticide.

Indicators of Child Abuse and Neglect

CATEGORY	CHILD'S APPEARANCE	CHILD'S BEHAVIOR	CARETAKER'S BEHAVIOR
Physical Abuse	–Bruises and welts (on the face, lips, or mouth; in various stages of healing; on large areas of the torso, back, buttocks, or thighs; in unusual patterns, clustered, or reflective of the instrument used to inflict them; on several different surface areas). –Burns (cigar or cigarette burns; glove or sock-like burns or doughnut shaped burns on the buttocks or genitalia indicative of immersion in hot liquid; rope burns on the arms, legs, neck or torso; patterned burns that show the shape of the item (iron, grill, etc.) used to inflict them). –Fractures (skull, jaw, or nasal fractures; spiral fractures of the long (arm and leg) bones; fractures in various states of healing; multiple fractures; any fracture in a child under the age of two). –Lacerations and abrasions (to the mouth, lip, gums, or eye; to the external genitalia). –Human bite marks.	–Wary of physical contact with adults. –Apprehensive when other children cry. –Demonstrates extremes in behavior (e.g., extreme aggressiveness or withdrawal). –Seems frightened of parents. –Reports injury by parents.	–Has history of abuse as a child. –Uses harsh discipline inappropriate to child's age, transgression, and condition. –Offers illogical, unconvincing, contradictory, or no explanation of child's injury. –Seems unconcerned about child. –Significantly misperceives child (e.g., sees him as bad, evil, a monster, etc.). –Psychotic or psychopathic. –Misuses alcohol or other drugs. –Attempts to conceal child's injury or to protect identity of person responsible.
Neglect	–Consistently dirty, unwashed, hungry, or inappropriately dressed. –Without supervision for extended periods of time or when engaged in dangerous activities. –Constantly tired or listless. –Has unattended physical problems or lacks routine medical care. –Is exploited, overworked, or kept from attending school. –Has been abandoned.	–Is engaging in delinquent acts (e.g., vandalism, drinking, prostitution, drug use, etc.) –Is begging or stealing food. –Rarely attends school.	–Misuses alcohol or other drugs. –Maintains chaotic home life. –Shows evidence of apathy or futility. –Is mentally ill or of diminished intelligence. –Has long-term chronic illnesses. –Has history of neglect as a child.
Sexual Abuse	–Has torn, stained, or bloody underclothing. –Experience pain or itching in the genital area. –Has bruises or bleeding in external genitalia, vagina, or anal regions. –Has venereal disease. –Has swollen or red cervix, vulva, or perineum. –Has semen around mouth or genitalia or on clothing. –Is pregnant.	–Appears withdrawn or engages in fantasy or infantile behavior. –Has poor peer relationships. –Is unwilling to participate in physical activities. –Is engaging in delinquent acts or runs away. –States he/she has been sexually assaulted by parent/caretaker.	–Extremely protective or jealous of child. –Encourages child to engage in prostitution or sexual acts in the presence of caretaker. –Has been sexually abused as a child. –Is experiencing marital difficulties. –Misuses alcohol or other drugs. –Is frequently absent from the home.
Emotional Maltreatment	–Emotional maltreatment, often less tangible than other forms of child abuse and neglect, can be indicated by behaviors of the child and the caretaker.	–Appears overly compliant, passive, undemanding. –Is extremely aggressive, demanding, or rageful. –Shows overly adaptive behaviors, either inappropriately adult (e.g., parents other children) or inappropriately infantile (e.g., rocks constantly, sucks thumb, is enuretic). –Lags in physical, emotional, and intellectual development. Attempts suicide.	–Blames or belittles child. –Is cold and rejecting. –Withholds love. –Treats siblings unequally. –Seems unconcerned about child's problem.

INSTITUTIONAL CHILD ABUSE AND NEGLECT

1) Abuse and neglect as a result of social or institutional policies, practices, or conditions. The rather widespread practice of detaining children in adult jails is one example. Usually refers to specific institutions or populations, but may also be used to mean societal abuse or neglect. (See also SOCIETAL ABUSE AND NEGLECT)

2) Child abuse and neglect committed by an employee of a public or private institution or group home against a child in the institution or group home.

INTAKE

Process by which cases are introduced into an agency. Workers are usually assigned to interview persons seeking help in order to determine the nature and extent of the problem(s). However, in child abuse and neglect, intake of reports of suspected cases is usually by telephone and an interview with the reporting person is not required. Child abuse and neglect workers who do intake must be skilled in getting as much information as possible from the reporter in order to determine whether the situation is an emergency requiring instant attention.

INTERDISCIPLINARY TEAM (See COMMUNITY TEAM)

INTRADERMAL HEMORRHAGE

Bleeding within the skin; bruise. Bruises are common injuries exhibited by battered children, and are usually classified by size:

Petechiae
Very small bruise caused by broken capillaries. Petechiae may be traumatic in nature or may be caused by clotting disorders.

Purpura
Petechiae occurring in groups, or a small bruise (up to 1 cm. in diameter).

Ecchymosis
Larger bruise.

INVOLUNTARY CLIENT

Person who has been referred or court-ordered for services but who has not asked for help. Most abusive and neglectful parents are initially involuntary clients and may not accept the need for services. They may deny that there is a problem and resist assistance. Motivation for change may be minimal or nonexistent; however, skillful workers have demonstrated that motivation can be developed and treatment can be effective.

INVOLUNTARY PLACEMENT

Court-ordered assignment of custody to an agency and placement of a child, often against the parents' wishes, after a formal court proceeding, or the taking of emergency or protective custody against the parents' wishes preceding a custody hearing. (See also CUSTODY)

JEJUNUM

Middle portion of the small intestine between the duodenum and the ileum.

JURISDICTION

The power of a particular court to hear cases involving certain categories of persons or allegations. Jurisdiction may also depend upon geographical factors such as the county of a person's residence. (See also COURTS)

JURY

Group of adults selected by lawyers who judge the truth of allegations made in a legal proceeding. Trial by jury is available in all criminal cases, including cases of suspected child abuse and neglect. Very few juvenile, probate, or domestic relations court cases can be tried before a jury and are instead decided by the presiding judge.

JUVENILE COURT (See COURTS)

JUVENILE JUDGE

Presiding officer of a juvenile court. Often in a juvenile court, there are several other hearing officers of lesser rank, usually called referees or commissioners. (See also HEARING OFFICER)

LABELING
The widespread public and professional practice of affixing terms which imply serious or consistent deviance to the perpetrators and/or victims of child abuse and neglect; for example, "child abuser." Since deviance may suggest that punishment is warranted, this kind of labeling decreases the possibility of treatment. This is unfortunate, because experts agree that 80% or 85% of all child abuse and neglect cases have the potential for successful treatment. Such labeling may also make parents see themselves in a negative, despairing way, and discourage them from seeking assistance.

LABORATORY TESTS
Routine medical tests used to aid diagnosis. Those particularly pertinent to child abuse are:

Partial Thromboplastin Time (PTT) Measures clotting factors in the blood.

Prothrombin Time (PT)
Measures clotting factors in the blood.

Urinalysis
Examination of urine for sugar, protein, blood, etc.

Complete Blood Count (CBC)
Measure and analysis of red and white blood cells.

Rumpel-Leede (Tourniquet) Test
Measures fragility of capillaries and/or bruisability.

LACERATION
A jagged cut or wound.

LATCH KEY CHILDREN
Working parents' children who return after school to a home where no parent or caretaker is present. This term was coined because these children often wear a house key on a chain around their necks.

LATERAL
Toward the side.

LAY THERAPIST (See PARENT AIDE)

LEAST DETRIMENTAL ALTERNATIVE
(See
BEST INTEREST OF THE CHILD)

LEGAL RIGHTS OF PERSONS IDENTIFIED IN REPORTS
Standards for legal rights stress the need for all persons concerned with child abuse and neglect to be aware of the legal rights of individuals identified in reports and to be committed to any action necessary to enforce these rights. According to the National Center on Child Abuse and Neglect *Revision to Federal Standards on the Prevention and Treatment of Child Abuse and Neglect (Draft),* these rights include the following:
1 Any person identified in a report as being suspected of having abused or neglected a child should be informed of his/her legal rights.
2) The person responsible for the child's welfare should receive written notice and be advised of his her legal rights when protective custody authority is exercised.
3) A child who is alleged to be abused or neglected should have independent legal representation in a child protection proceeding.
4) The parent or other person responsible for a child's welfare who is alleged to have abused or neglected a child should be entitled to legal representation in a civil or criminal proceeding.
5) The local child protective services unit should have the assistance of legal counsel in all child protective proceedings.
6) Each party should have the right to appeal protective case determinations.
7) Any person identified in a child abuse or neglect report should be protected from unauthorized disclosure of personal information contained in the report.

LESION

Any injury to any part of the body from any cause that results in damage or loss of structure or function of the body tissue involved. A lesion may be caused by poison, infection, dysfunction, or violence, and may be either accidental or intentional.

LIABILITY FOR FAILURE TO REPORT

State statutes which require certain categories of persons to report cases of suspected child abuse and/or neglect are often enforced by the imposition of a penalty, fine and/or imprisonment, for those who fail to report. Recent lawsuits have provided what may become an even more significant penalty for failure to report: when a report should have been made and a child comes to serious harm in a subsequent incident of abuse or neglect, the person who failed to report the initial incident may be held civilly liable to the child for the damages suffered in the subsequent incident. Such damages could amount to many thousands of dollars. (See also MANDATED REPORTERS)

LICENSING PARENTHOOD

Proposed method of assuring adequate parenting skills. Various proposals have been developed, including mandatory parenthood education in high school, with a certificate upon completion. Serious advocates compare the process with certification of driving capability by driver's licenses. Many consider the proposal unworkable.

LOCAL AUTHORITY

Local authority refers to two groups: 1) the social service agency (local agency) designated by the state department of social services (state department) and authorized by state law to be responsible for local child abuse and neglect prevention, identification, and treatment efforts, and 2) the community child protection coordinating council (community council). The standards on local authority, as specified in the National Center on Child Abuse and Neglect *Revision to Federal Standards on the Prevention and Treatment of Child Abuse and Neglect*

(Draft), include:

Administration and Organization

1   The local agency should establish a distinct child protective services unit with sufficient and qualified staff.
2   The local agency in cooperation with the state department should allocate sufficient funds and provide adequate administrative support to the local unit.
3   The local agency should initiate the establishment of a community council which is to be representative of those persons providing or concerned with child abuse and neglect prevention, identification, and treatment services.

Primary Prevention

4   The local unit and the community council should work together to establish formalized needs assessment and planning processes.

Secondary and Tertiary Prevention

5   The local unit and the community council should work together to develop a comprehensive and coordinated service delivery system for children-at-risk and families-at-risk to be presented in an annual plan.
6   The local unit and the community council should develop standards on the care of children which represent the minimum expectations of the community and provide the basis for the local unit's operational definitions and referral guidelines.
7   The local unit and the community council should establish a multidisciplinary child abuse and neglect case consultation team.
8   The local unit should provide or arrange for services to assist families who request help for themselves in fulfilling their parenting responsibilities.
9   The local unit should ensure that reports of child abuse and neglect can be received on a twenty-four hour, seven days per week basis.

10 The intake services worker should intervene immediately if a report is considered an emergency; otherwise, intervention should take place within seventy-two hours.

11 The intake services worker should ensure the family's right to privacy by making the assessment process time-limited.

12 The treatment services worker should develop an individualized treatment plan for each family and each family member.

13 The treatment services worker should arrange for, coordinate, and monitor services provided to a family.

Resource Enhancement

14 The agency and the community council should assist in the training of the local unit and other community service systems.

15 The agency should promote internal agency coordination.

16 The local unit should implement community education and awareness.

17 The agency should participate in or initiate its own research, review, and evaluation studies.

(See also STATE AUTHORITY)

LONG BONE
General term applied to the bones of the leg or the arm.

LONG TERM TREATMENT
Supportive and therapeutic services over a period of time, usually at least a year, to restore the parent(s) of an abused or neglected child and/or the child himself/herself to adequate levels of functioning and to prevent recurrence of child abuse or neglect.

LUMBAR
Pertaining to the part of the back and sides between the lowest ribs and the pelvis.

MALNUTRITION
Failure to receive adequate nourishment.

Often exhibited in a neglected child, malnutrition may be caused by inadequate diet (either lack of food or insufficient amounts of needed vitamins, etc.) or by a disease or other abnormal condition affecting the body's ability to properly process foods taken in.

MALTREATMENT
Actions that are abusive, neglectful, or otherwise threatening to a child's welfare. Frequently used as a general term for child abuse and neglect.

MANDATED AGENCY
Agency designated by state statutes as legally responsible for receiving and investigating reports of suspected child abuse and neglect. Usually, this agency is a county welfare department or a child protective services unit within that department. Police or sheriffs departments may also be mandated agencies. (See also STATE AUTHORITY and LOCAL AUTHORITY)

MANDATED REPORTERS or MANDATORY REPORTERS
Persons designated by state statutes who are legally liable for not reporting suspected cases of child abuse and neglect to the mandated agency. The persons so designated vary according to state law, but they are primarily professionals, such as pediatricians, nurses, school personnel, and social workers, who have frequent contact with children and families.

MARASMUS
A form of protein-calorie malnutrition occurring in infants and children. It is characterized by retarded growth and progressive wasting away of fat and muscle, but it is usually accompanied by the retention of appetite and mental alertness.

MATERNAL CHARACTERISTICS SCALE
Instrument designed to study personality characteristics of rural Appalachian mothers and the level of care they were providing their children. The purpose of this scale is to

sharpen caseworkers' perception of "apathetic-futile" or "impulse-ridden" mothers' personality characteristics for evaluation, diagnosis, and formulation of a treatment plan in cases of child neglect. Some authorities believe this scale has not been adequately validated.

MATERNAL-INFANT BONDING (See BONDING)

MEDIAL
Toward the middle or mid-line.

MEDICAID, TITLE 19 (See SOCIAL SECURITY ACT)

MEDICAL MODEL
Conceptualizing problems in terms of diagnosis and treatment of illness. With respect to child abuse and neglect, the medical model assumes an identifiable and therefore treatable cause of the abuse and/or neglect and focuses on identification and treatment in a medical or other health setting. For child abuse and neglect, some advantages of the medical model are financial support by the hospital, clinic, medical community; accessibility of medical services to the abused or neglected child; involvement of the physicians; and visibility and public acceptance. Possible disadvantages are overemphasis on physical abuse; overemphasis on physical diagnosis to the detriment of total treatment; and isolation from other professional and community resources. (Kempe)

MEDICAL NEGLECT (See CHILD ABUSE AND NEGLECT)

MENKES KINKY HAIR SYNDROME
Rare, inherited disease resulting in brittle bones and, eventually, death. It is found in infants and, because of the great number of fractures the child may exhibit, can be mistaken for child abuse.

MENTAL INJURY
Injury to the intellectual or psychological capacity of a child as evidenced by observable and substantial impairment in his/her ability to function within a normal range of performance and behavior, with due regard to his/her culture. The Child Abuse Prevention and Treatment Act and some state statutes include mental injury caused by a parent or caretaker as child abuse or neglect.

MESENTERY
Membrane attaching various organs to the body wall.

METABOLISM
The sum of all physical and chemical processes which maintain the life of an organism.

METAPHYSIS
Wider part of a long bone between the end and the shaft.

MINIMALLY ACCEPTABLE ENVIRONMENT
The emotional climate and physical surroundings necessary for children to grow physically, mentally, socially, and emotionally.

MINOR (See CHILD)

MIRANDA RULE
Legal provision that a confession is inadmissible in any court proceeding if the suspect was not forewarned of his/her right to remain silent before the confession was disclosed. (See also FIFTH AMENDMENT)

MISDEMEANOR
A crime for which the punishment can be no more than imprisonment for a year and/or a fine of $1,000. A misdemeanor is distinguished from a felony, which is more serious, and an infraction, which is less serious.

MODEL CHILD PROTECTION ACT
Guide for development of state legislation concerning child abuse and neglect and intended to enable legislators to provide a

comprehensive and workable law which will aid in resolving the problem. A draft *Model Child Protection Act* has been developed and is available from the National Center on Child Abuse and Neglect.

MONDALE ACT (See CHILD ABUSE PREVENTION AND TREATMENT ACT)

MONGOLIAN SPOTS
A type of birthmark that can appear anywhere on a child's body, most frequently on the lower back. These dark spots usually fade by age five. They can be mistaken for bruises.

MORAL NEGLECT (See CHILD ABUSE AND NEGLECT)

MORIBUND
Dying or near death.

MOTHERS ANONYMOUS
Original name of Parents Anonymous. (See PARENTS ANONYMOUS)

MULTIDISCIPLINARY TEAM
A group of professionals and possibly para-professionals representing a variety of disciplines who interact and coordinate their efforts to diagnose and treat specific cases of child abuse and neglect. A multidisciplinary group which also addresses the general problem of child abuse and neglect in a given community is usually described as a community team, and it will probably consist of several multidisciplinary teams with different functions (see COMMUNITY TEAM). Multidisciplinary teams may include, but are not limited to, medical, child care, and law enforcement personnel, social workers, psychiatrists and/or psychologists. Their goal is to pool their respective skills in order to formulate accurate diagnoses and to provide comprehensive coordinated treatment with continuity and follow-up for both parent(s) and child or children. Many multidisciplinary teams operate according to the Denver Model (see DENVER MODEL). Multidisciplinary teams may also be referred to as

cross-disciplinary teams, interdisciplinary teams, or SCAN teams (see SCAN TEAM). However, the Child Abuse Prevention and Treatment Act uses the term "multidisciplinary team."

NATIONAL ASSOCIATION OF SOCIAL WORKERS (NASW)
1425 H St., N.W.
Washington, D.C. 20005
A national organization of professional social workers who are enrolled in or have completed baccalaureate, master's, or doctoral programs in social work education. Members must subscribe to the NASW Code of Ethics, and NASW provides a policy for adjudication of grievances in order to protect members and promote ethical practices.

NATIONAL CENTER FOR CHILD ADVOCACY (NCCA)
P.O. Box 1182
Washington, D.C. 20013
The National Center for Child Advocacy is part of the Children's Bureau of the Administration for Children, Youth and Families within the Office of Human Development Services of HEW. NCCA supports research, demonstration, and training programs and provides technical assistance to state and local agencies with the goal of increasing and improving child welfare services. These services include in-home support to families, such as parent education and homemaker services; foster care, adoption, and child protective services; and institutional care of children. A major project of NCCA is the Child Welfare Resource Information Exchange. (See also CHILD WELFARE RESOURCE INFORMATION EXCHANGE)

NATIONAL CENTER FOR THE PREVENTION AND TREATMENT OF CHILD ABUSE AND NEGLECT
1205 Oneida St.
Denver, Colorado 80220
This center, which is affiliated with the Department of Pediatrics of the University of Colorado Medical School, was established in

the fall of 1972 to provide more extensive and up-to-date education, research, and clinical material to professionals working in the area of child abuse and neglect. The center's multidisciplinary staff has provided leadership in formulating the views that child abuse and neglect is symptomatic of troubled family relationships; that treatment must consider the needs of all family members; and that outreach to isolated, non-trusting families and the multidisciplinary approach are necessary. Funded by the State of Colorado, the HEW Administration for Children, Youth and Families, and private foundations, the center's work includes education, consultation and technical assistance, demonstration programs for treatment, program evaluation, and research. This center also serves as the HEW Region VIII Resource Center.

NATIONAL CENTER ON CHILD ABUSE AND NEGLECT (NCCAN)

P.O. Box 1182
Washington, D.C. 20013
Office of the federal government located within the Children's Bureau of the Administration for Children, Youth and Families (formerly the Office of Child Development), which is part of the Office of Human Development Services of HEW. Established in 1974 by the Child Abuse Prevention and Treatment Act, the functions of NCCAN are to:

1) Compile, analyze, and publish an annual summary of recent and current research on child abuse and neglect.
2) Develop and maintain an information clearinghouse on all programs showing promise of success for the prevention, identification, and treatment of child abuse and neglect.
3) Compile and publish training materials for personnel who are engaged or intend to engage in the prevention, identification, and treatment of child abuse and neglect.
4) Provide technical assistance to public and nonprofit private agencies and organizations to assist them in planning,

improving, developing, and carrying out programs and activities relating to the prevention, identification, and treatment of child abuse and neglect.
5) Conduct research into the causes of child abuse and neglect, and into the prevention, identification, and treatment thereof.
6) Make a complete and full study and investigation of the national incidence of child abuse and neglect, including a determination of the extent to which incidents of child abuse and neglect are increasing in number or severity.
7) Award grants to states whose child abuse and neglect legislation complies with federal legislation.

NCCAN is authorized to establish grants and contracts with public and private agencies and organizations to carry out the above activities. Grants and contracts may also be used to establish demonstration programs and projects which, through training, consultation, resource provision, or direct treatment, are designed to prevent, identify, and treat child abuse and neglect. (See also CHILD ABUSE PREVENTION AND TREATMENT ACT and REGIONAL RESOURCE CENTER)

NATIONAL CLEARINGHOUSE ON CHILD NEGLECT AND ABUSE (NCCNA) (See NATIONAL STUDY ON CHILD NEGLECT AND ABUSE REPORTING)

NATIONAL COMMITTEE FOR THE PREVENTION OF CHILD ABUSE

111 E. Wacker Drive
Suite 510
Chicago, Illinois 60601
The National Committee originated in Chicago in 1972 in response to increasing national incidence of deaths due to child abuse. It was formed to help prevent child abuse, which was defined as including non-accidental injury, emotional abuse, neglect, sexual abuse, and exploitation of children, at a time when most programs focused on identification and treatment. The commit-

tee's goals are to:
1) Stimulate greater public awareness of the problem.
2) Encourage public involvement in prevention and treatment.
3) Provide a national focal point for advocacy to prevent child abuse.
4) Facilitate communication about programs, policy, and research related to child abuse prevention.
5) Foster greater cooperation between existing and developing resources for child abuse prevention.

Activities of the committee include a national media campaign, publications, conference, research, and the establishment of state chapters of the committee.

NATIONAL REGISTER
Often confused with the National Study on Child Neglect and Abuse Reporting (National Clearinghouse), which compiles statistics on incidence of child abuse and neglect. A national register, which does not exist at this time, would operate in much the same way and with the same purposes as a state-level central register, but would collect reports of abuse and neglect nationwide. Collecting reports on a national scale would be highly problematic because of variance in state reporting laws and definitions of abuse and neglect. (See also CENTRAL REGISTER and NATIONAL STUDY ON CHILD NEGLECT AND ABUSE REPORTING)

NATIONAL STUDY ON CHILD NEGLECT AND ABUSE REPORTING
Formerly the National Clearinghouse on Child Neglect and Abuse, the National Study is funded by the National Center on Child Abuse and Neglect, Children's Bureau, HEW and is being conducted by the Children's Division of the American Humane Association. The study has been established to systematically collect data from official state sources on the nature, incidence, and characteristics of child abuse and neglect. Participating states receive reports generated from their own data on a quarterly basis so that they can monitor their own reporting mechanisms. At this time, about 40 states are submitting detailed incidence data to the study. It is hoped that the National Study will be able to produce accurate data on the national incidence of child abuse and neglect.

NEEDS ASSESSMENT
A formal or informal evaluation of what services are needed by abused and neglected children and their families within a specified geographical area or within another given population.

NEGLECT (See CHILD ABUSE AND NEGLECT)

NEGLECTED CHILD (See INDICATORS OF CHILD ABUSE AND NEGLECT)

NEGLIGENCE
Failure to act. May apply to a parent, as in child neglect, or to a person who by state statute is mandated to report child abuse and neglect but who fails to do so. Negligence lawsuits arising from failure to report are increasing, and any failure to obey the statutes proves negligence. Lawsuits claiming damages for negligence are civil proceedings.

NETWORKING
Formal or informal linkages of individuals, families, or other groups with similar social, education, medical, or other service needs with the public or private agencies, organizations, and/or individuals who can provide such services in their locale. Formal agreements are usually written and spell out under what circumstances a particular agency, group, or individual will provide certain services. Informal agreements are apt to be verbal and relate to a particular family or case.

NURTURANCE
Affectionate care and attention provided by a parent, parent substitute, or caretaker to promote the well-being of a child and encour-

age healthy emotional and physical development. Nurturance may also be needed by adults with inadequate parenting skills, or who were themselves abused or neglected as children, as a model for developing more positive relationships with their own children and as a way of strengthening their own self-esteem.

OCCIPITAL
Referring to the back of the head.

OMISSION, ACTS OF
Failure of a parent or caretaker to provide for a child's physical and/or emotional well-being. (See also CHILD ABUSE AND NEGLECT)

OSSIFICATION
Formation of bone.

OSTEOGENESIS IMPERFECTA
An inherited condition in which the bones are abnormally brittle and subject to fractures, and which may be mistakenly diagnosed as the result of child abuse.

OUTREACH
The process in which professionals, paraprofessionals, and/or volunteers actively seek to identify cases of family strees and potential or actual child abuse and neglect by making services known, accessible, and unthreatening. Effective outreach providing early intervention is important for the prevention of child abuse and neglect.

PA BUDDY
Term used by Parents Anonymous for a person who functions like a parent aide in relation to a Parents Anonymous member. (See also PARENTS ANONYMOUS and PARENT AIDE)

PARAPROFESSIONAL
Volunteer or agency employee trained to a limited extent in a particular profession. Since paraprofessionals are usually close in age, race, nationality, religion, or lifestyle to the clientele, they often have a greater likeli-

hood of developing a trusting relationship with a client than do some professionals. The role of the paraprofessional in protective service work is usually to provide outreach or nurturance and advocacy for the family, often as a case aide or parent aide. (See also PARENT AIDE)

PARENS PATRIAE
"The power of the sovereign." Refers to the state's power to act for or on behalf of persons who cannot act in their own behalf; such as, minors, incompetents, or some developmentally disabled.

PARENT
Person exercising the function of father and/or mother, including adoptive, foster, custodial, and surrogate parents as well as biological parents.

PARENT AIDE
A paraprofessional, either paid or voluntary, who functions primarily as an advocate and surrogate parent for a family in which child abuse or neglect is suspected or has been confirmed. The Parent Aide particularly serves the mother by providing positive reinforcement, emotional support, and nurturance, and by providing or arranging transportation, babysitting, etc., as necessary. Rather than serving as a homemaker, nutrition aide, or nurse, the parent aide's function is more like a friend to the family. Parent aides may also be referred to as case aides, lay therapists, or visiting friends.

PARENT EFFECTIVENESS TRAINING (PET)
An educational program developed by Dr. Thomas Gordon and presented in his book, *Parent Effectiveness Training* (New York, Peter H. Wyden, Inc., 1970). The program, taught by trained and certified PET instructors, focuses on improving communication between parents and children by teaching listening skills and verbal expression techniques to parents. The PET course has proven useful for parents who are motivated to change, who are able to give it a consider-

able amount of time, and who can afford the relatively high tuition. For these and other reasons, PET has not proven particularly useful in child abuse and neglect treatment, especially when used as the only mode of treatment.

PARENTAL STRESS SERVICES

Services aimed at relieving situational and/or psychological parental stress in order to relieve family dysfunction and to prevent parents from venting rage or frustration on their children. Service usually begins via a telephone helpline and may include home visits. Workers are usually trained volunteers or paraprofessionals who focus on providing warmth, nurturance, friendship, and resource referrals to the distressed parent. Some parental stress services promote development and use of Parents Anonymous chapters for their clients. Parental Stress Services may refer to specific programs such as in Chicago, Illinois, or Oakland, California, although there is no organizational linkage between them, or this may be a functional description of services provided within a larger agency program.

PARENTING SKILLS

A parent's competencies in providing physical care, protection, supervision, and psychological nurturance appropriate to a child's age and stage of development. Some parents, particularly those whose own parents demonstrated these skills, have these competencies without formal training, but adequacy of these skills may be improved through instruction.

PARENTS ANONYMOUS

22330 Hawthorne Blvd., #208
Torrance, California 90505
Self-help group for parents who want to stop physical, psychological, sexual, or verbal abuse of their children. Because members do not need to reveal their full names, they feel free to share concerns and provide mutual support. Members are accountable to the group for their behavior toward their children, and the group functions like a fam-

ily in supporting members' efforts to change. With chapters in every state, over 800 in all, Parents Anonymous has been formally evaluated as an effective method for treating child abuse. Unlike most other self-help groups with anonymous members, Parents Anonymous requires that each chapter have an unpaid professional sponsor who attends all meetings to facilitate discussion, provide a role model, and suggest appropriate community resources for members' problems. The Child Abuse Prevention and Treatment Act provides for funding of self-help groups, and Parents Anonymous is one of the few self-help organizations which has received funding from the federal government.

PARENTS' RIGHTS

Besides the rights protected by the Constitution for all adults, society accords parents the right to custody and supervision of their own children, including, among others, parents' rights to make decisions about their children's health care. This plus parents' rights to privacy may complicate investigations of suspected child abuse and neglect and treatment of confirmed cases. Parents' rights may be cited in court in order to prevent the state from taking custody of a child who is in danger in his/her own home. (See also CHILDREN'S RIGHTS)

PARENTS UNITED

Organization name sometimes used for self-help groups of parents in families in which sexual abuse has occurred. Begun in 1972, Parents United is one component of a model Child Sexual Abuse Treatment Program in Santa Clara County, California. (See also DAUGHTERS UNITED)

PASSIVE ABUSER

Parent or caretaker who does not intervene to prevent abuse by another person in the home.

PATHOGNOMONIC

A sign or symptom specifically distinctive or characteristic of a disease or condition from which a diagnosis may be made.

PERINATAL
Around the time of birth, both immediately before and afterward.

PERIOSTEAL ELEVATION
The ripping or tearing of the surface layer of a bone (periosteum) and the resultant hemorrhage, occuring when a bone is broken.

PERITONITIS
Inflammation of the membrane lining the abdomen (peritoneum); caused by infection.

PERJURY
Intentionally inaccurate testimony. Perjury is usually punishable as a felony, but only if the inaccuracy of the testimony and the witness's knowledge of the inaccuracy can be proven.

PETECHIAE (See INTRADERMAL HEMORRHAGE)

PETITION
Document filed in juvenile or family court at the beginning of a neglect, abuse, and/or delinquency case. The petition states the allegations which, if true, form the basis for court intervention.

PETITIONER
Person who files a petition. In juvenile and family court practice, a petitioner may be a probation officer, social worker, or prosecutor, as variously defined by state laws.

PHYSICAL ABUSE (See CHILD ABUSE AND NEGLECT)

PHYSICAL NEGLECT (See CHILD ABUSE AND NEGLECT)

PLEA BARGAINING
Settlement of a criminal prosecution, usually by the reduction of the charge and/or the penalty, in return for a plea of guilty. Plea bargains are sometimes justified by congested court calendars. They are attacked as devices which weaken the intended effect of penal statutes and which reduce the dignity of the criminal justice system. Far more than half of all criminal prosecutions in this country are resolved by plea bargaining.

POLICE HOLD (See CUSTODY)

POLYPHAGIA
Excessive or voracious eating.

PREDICTION OF CHILD ABUSE AND NEGLECT
There are no evaluation instruments or criteria to predict absolutely that child abuse or neglect will occur in specific families. Recently, experts have developed instruments and methods of evaluating the bonding process at childbirth in order to identify families where because of incomplete or inadequate bonding, it can be expected that without further appropriate intervention, child abuse or neglect may occur. Besides bonding, many other indicators can be used to identify families-at-risk for child abuse and neglect, but these factors are rarely sufficiently conclusive to enable absolute prediction. (See also BONDING and FAMILIES-AT-RISK)

PREPONDERANCE OF EVIDENCE (See EVIDENTIARY STANDARDS)

PRESENTMENT
The notice taken or report made by a grand jury of an offense on the basis of the jury's knowledge and without a bill of indictment. (See also INDICTMENT)

PRE-TRIAL DIVERSION
Decision of the district attorney not to issue charges in a criminal case where those charges would be provable. The decision is usually made on the condition that the defendant agrees to participate in rehabilitative services. In child abuse cases, this usually involves cooperation with child protective services and/or voluntary treatment, such as Parents Anonymous.

PREVENTION OF CHILD ABUSE AND NEGLECT
Elimination of the individual and societal causes of child abuse and neglect.

Primary Prevention
Providing societal and community policies and programs which strengthen all family functioning so that child abuse and neglect is less likely to occur.

Secondary Prevention
Intervention in the early signs of child abuse and neglect for treatment of the presenting problem and to prevent further problems from developing.

Tertiary Prevention
Treatment after child abuse and neglect has been confirmed.

Primary, and to varying degrees secondary and tertiary, prevention requires:

1) Breaking the tendency in the generational cycle wherein the abused or neglected child is likely to become the abusive or neglectful parent.
2) Helping a parent cope with a child who has special problems or special meaning to a parent.
3) Helping families cope with long term and immediate situational or interpersonal stress.
4) Linking families to personal and community sources of help to break their social isolation.
5) Eliminating or alleviating violence in our society, particularly sanctioned violence such as corporal punishment in the schools.

A major problem in preventing child abuse and neglect is the stigma attached to the problem and to receiving services from a county protective service agency. Therefore, prevention programs must include community education and outreach. Another problem is that stress is pervasive in our society, and ways must be found both to reduce it and deal with it if child abuse and neglect is to be prevented. (See also EARLY INTERVENTION)

PRIMA FACIE
A latin term approximately meaning "at first sight," "on the first appearance," or "on the face of it." In law, this term is used in the context of a "prima facie case." That is, the presentation of evidence at a trial which has been sufficiently strong to prove the allegations unless contradicted and overcome by other evidence. In a child maltreatment case, the allegations of maltreatment will be considered as proven unless the parent presents rebutting evidence.

PRIVILEGED COMMUNICATIONS
Confidential communications which are protected by statutes and need not or cannot be disclosed in court over the objections of the holder of the privilege. Lawyers are almost always able to refuse to disclose what a client has told them in confidence. Priests are similarly covered. Doctors and psychotherapists have generally lesser privileges, and their testimony can be compelled in many cases involving child abuse or neglect. Some social workers are covered by such statutes, but the law and practice vary widely from state to state. (See also CONFIDENTIALITY)

PROBABLE CAUSE
A legal standard used in a number of contexts which indicates a reasonable ground for suspicion or belief in the existence of certain facts. Facts accepted as true after a reasonable inquiry which would induce a prudent and cautious person to believe them. Also-Please note that the definitions on page 28 of EVIDENTIARY STANDARDS are incorrect. A suggested alternative follows:

PROBATE COURT (See COURTS)

PROBATION
Allowing a convicted criminal defendant or a juvenile found to be delinquent to remain at liberty, under a suspended sentence of imprisonment, generally under the supervi-

sion of a probation officer and under certain conditions. Violation of a condition is grounds for revocation of the probation. In a case of child abuse or neglect, a parent or caretaker who is convicted of the offense may be required, as part of his/her probation, to make certain promises to undergo treatment and/or to improve the home situation. These promises are made as a condition of the probation in which the child is returned home and are enforced with the threat of revocation of parental rights.

PROGRAM COORDINATION
Interagency of intra-agency communication for policy, program, and resource development for an effective service delivery system in a given locality. Program coordination for child abuse and neglect is usually implemented through a community council or community task force or planning committee under the direction of a program coordinator. The functions of these groups are:
1) Comprehensive planning, including identifying gaps and duplication in service and funding policies.
2) Developing interagency referral policies.
3) Educating members to new and/or effective approaches to child abuse and neglect.
4) Problem sharing.
5) Facilitating resolution of interagency conflicts.
6) Providing a forum where differing professional and agency expertise can be pooled.
7) Generating and lobbying for needed legislation.
(See also COMMUNITY TEAM)

PROTECTIVE CUSTODY (See CUSTODY)

PROTOCOL
A set of rules or guidelines prescribing procedures and responsibilities. Originally used primarily in medical settings, establishment of protocols is an increasingly important goal of the child abuse and neglect community team.

PROXIMAL
Near; closer to any point of reference; opposed to distal.

PSYCHOLOGICAL ABUSE (See CHILD ABUSE AND NEGLECT)

PSYCHOLOGICAL NEGLECT (See CHILD ABUSE AND NEGLECT)

PSYCHOLOGICAL PARENT
Adult who, on a continuing day-to-day basis, fulfills a child's emotional needs for nurturance through interaction, companionship, and mutuality. May be the natural parent or another person who fulfills these functions.

PSYCHOLOGICAL TESTS
Instruments of various types used to measure emotional, intellectual, and personality characteristics. Psychological tests should always be administered and interpreted by qualified personnel. Such tests have been used to determine potential for abuse or neglect, effects of abuse or neglect, or psychological makeup of parent or children.

PSYCHOTIC PARENT
A parent who suffers a major mental disorder where the individual's ability to think, respond emotionally, remember, communicate, interpret reality, or behave appropriately is sufficiently impaired so as to interfere grossly with his/her capacity to meet the ordinary demands of life. The term "psychotic" is neither very precise nor definite. However, the parent who is periodically psychotic or psychotic for extended periods and who abuses his/her children has a poor prognosis; permanent removal of the children is often recommended in this situation. It is estimated that well under 10% of all abusive or neglectful parents are psychotic.

PUBLIC AWARENESS (See COMMUNITY AWARENESS)

PUBLIC DEFENDER
Person paid with public funds to plead the cause of an indigent defendant.

PUBLIC LAW 93-247 (See CHILD ABUSE PREVENTION AND TREATMENT ACT)

PUNISHMENT
Infliction of pain, loss, or suffering on a child because the child has disobeyed or otherwise antagonized a parent or caretaker. Abusive parents may inflict punishment without cause, or may inflict punishment, particularly corporal punishment, in the belief that it is the only way to discipline children. Many parents confuse the difference between discipline and punishment. These differences are delineated under DISCIPLINE. (See also CORPORAL PUNISHMENT)

PURCHASE OF SERVICE
Provision for diagnosis and/or treatment of child abuse and neglect by an agency other than the mandated agency using mandated agency funds. The mandated agency subcontracts with the provider agency for specific services with specific clients, but the mandated agency retains statutory responsibility for the case. (See also CASE MANAGEMENT)

PURPURA (See INTRADERMAL HEMORRHAGE)

RADIOLUCENT
Permitting the passage of X-rays without leaving a shadow on the film. Soft tissues are radiolucent; bones are not.

RAREFACTION
Loss of density. On an X-ray photograph, an area of bone which appears lighter than normal is in a state of rarefaction, indicating a loss of calcium.

RECEIVING HOME
A family or group home for temporary placement of a child pending more permanent plans such as return to his/her own home, foster care, or adoption.

RECIDIVISM
Recurrence of child abuse and neglect. This happens relatively frequently because child protective service agencies heretofore have been mandated and staffed only to investigate and provide crisis intervention and not to provide treatment. Most cases where child abuse or neglect results in a child's death have been previously known to a child protection agency.

REFEREE (See HEARING OFFICER)

REGIONAL RESOURCE CENTER
With respect to child abuse and neglect, a regional resource center was funded as a demonstration project in each of the ten HEW regions under the 1974 Child Abuse Prevention and Treatment Act. These resource centers vary in program emphasis, but they all function to some degree as extensions of the National Center on Child Abuse and Neglect in Washington to help NCCAN fulfill the aims of the Child Abuse Prevention and Treatment Act (see NATIONAL CENTER ON CHILD ABUSE AND NEGLECT and CHILD ABUSE PREVENTION AND TREATMENT ACT). Besides regional centers, there are also state resource centers in Arizona, Maryland, New York, and North Carolina; and two national resource centers, operated by the Education Commission of the States and the National Urban League. The regional resource centers are:

Region I (Connecticut, Maine, Massachusetts, New Hampshire, Rhode Island, Vermont)
Judge Baker Guidance Center
295 Longwood Ave.
Boston, Massachusetts 02115
Region II (New Jersey, Puerto Rico, Virgin Islands)
College of Human Ecology Cornell University
MVR Hall
Ithaca, New York 14853
Region III (Pennsylvania, Virginia, Delaware, West Virginia, District of Columbia)
Institute for Urban Affairs and Research
Howard University

2900 Van Ness St., N.W.
Washington, D.C. 20008
Region IV (Alabama, Florida, Georgia, Kentucky, Mississippi, South Carolina, Tennessee)
Regional Institute of Social Welfare Research
P.O. Box 152
Heritage Building
468 N. Milledge Ave.
Athens, Georgia 30601
Region V (Illinois, Indiana, Michigan, Minnesota, Ohio, Wisconsin)
Midwest Parent-Child Welfare Resource Center
Center for Advanced Studies in Human Services
School of Social Welfare
University of Wisconsin-Milwaukee
Milwaukee, Wisconsin 53201
Region VI (Arkansas, Louisiana, New Mexico, Oklahoma, Texas)
Center for Social Work Research
School of Social Work
University of Texas at Austin
Austin, Texas 78712
Region VII (Iowa, Kansas, Missouri, Nebraska)
Institute of Child Behavior and Development
University of Iowa
Oakdale, Iowa 53219
Region VIII (Colorado, Montana, North Dakota, South Dakota, Utah, Wyoming)
National Center for the Prevention and Treatment of Child Abuse and Neglect
University of Colorado Medical Center
1205 Oneida St.
Denver, Colorado 80220
Region IX (California, Hawaii, Nevada, Guam, Trust Territories of the Pacific, American Samoa)
Department of Special Education
California State University
5151 State University Dr.
Los Angeles, California 90033
Region X (Alaska, Idaho, Oregon, Washington)
Northwest Federation for Human Services
157 Yesler Way, #208
Seattle, Washington 98104

REGISTRY (See CENTRAL REGISTER and NATIONAL REGISTER)

REHEARING
After a juvenile court referee or commissioner has heard a case and made an order, some states permit a dissatisfied party to request another hearing before the supervising judge of juvenile court. This second hearing is called a rehearing. If the original hearing was not recorded by a court reporter, the rehearing may have to be granted. If a transcript exists, the judge may read it and either grant or deny the rehearing.

REPARENTING
Usually describes a nurturing process whereby parents who have not received adequate nurturance during their own childhoods are provided with emotional warmth and security through a surrogate parent such as a parent aide. Abusive and neglectful parents are thus given an opportunity to identify with more positive role models.

REPORTING LAWS
State laws which require specified categories of persons, such as professionals involved with children, and allow other persons, to notify public authorities of cases of suspected child abuse and, sometimes, neglect. All 50 states now have reporting statutes, but they differ widely with respect to types of instances which must be reported, persons who must report, time limits for reporting, manner of reporting (written, oral, or both), agencies to which reports must be made, and the degree of immunity conferred upon reporters.

RES IPSA LOQUITOR
Latin expression meaning "the thing speaks for itself." It is a doctrine of law which, when applied to criminal law, means that evidence can be admitted which is acceptable despite the fact that no one actually saw what occurred, only the results. An example in

criminal law would be admitting into evidence in a child abuse case the medical reports of the injured child victim which reflect multiple broken bones and the doctor's opinion that said injuries could not have been caused by an accident. The court using the *res ipsa loquitor* doctrine can convict the person having had exclusive custody of the child without any direct testimony as to how, when, where, or why the injuries were inflicted.

RETINA
Inside lining of the eye. Injury to the head can cause bleeding or-detachment of the retina, possible causing blindness.

RICKETS
Condition caused by a deficiency of vitamin D, which disturbs the normal development of bones.

ROLE REVERSAL
The process whereby a parent or caretaker seeks nurturance and/or protection from a child rather than providing this for the child, who frequently complies with this reversal. Usually this process develops as a result of unfulfilled needs of the parent or caretaker.

SACRAL AREA
Lower part of the back.

SCAN TEAM
Suspected Child Abuse and Neglect team which has as its objective the assessment of a child and his/her family to determine if abuse and/or neglect has occurred and what treatment is indicated. The team usually includes a pediatrician, a social worker, and a psychiatrist or psychologist, but other professionals are often involved as well. A SCAN team or unit is generally located in a hospital or outpatient facility. (See also MULTIDISCIPLINARY TEAM and DENVER MODEL)

SCAPEGOATING
Casting blame for a problem on one who is innocent or only partially responsible; for example, a parent or caretaker abusing or neglecting a child as punishment for family problems unrelated to the child.

SCURVY
Condition caused by a deficiency of vitamin C (ascorbic acid) and characterized by weakness, anemia, spongy gums, and other symptoms.

SEALING
In juvenile court or criminal court practice, the closing of records to inspection by all but the defendant or minor involved. Sealing is provided by statute in some states and may be done after proof is made that the defendant or minor has behaved lawfully for a specified period of years. Note that juvenile court records are never public, as are the records of most other courts; access to juvenile court records is theoretically very restricted, even before sealing. (See also EXPUNGEMENT)

SEIZURES
Uncontrollable muscular contractions, usually alternating with muscular relaxation and generally accompanied by unconsciousness. Seizures, which vary in intensity and length of occurrence, are the result of some brain irritation which has been caused by disease, inherited condition, fever, tumor, vitamin deficiency, or injury to the head.

SELF-HELP GROUP
Groups of persons with similar, often stigmatized, problems who share concerns and experiences in an effort to provide mutual help to one another. Usually these groups are self-directed. (See also PARENTS ANONYMOUS)

SELF-INCRIMINATION
The giving of a statement, in court or during an investigation, which subjects the person giving the statement to criminal liability. (See also DUE PROCESS, FIFTH AMENDMENT, IMMUNITY, and MIRANDA RULE)

SENTENCING

The last stage of criminal prosecution in which a convicted defendant is ordered imprisoned, fined, or granted probation. This is equivalent in a criminal case , to the disposition in a juvenile court case.

SEQUELAE

After-effects; usually medical events following an injury or disease. In child abuse and neglect, sequelae is used to refer to psychological consequences of abusive acts and also the perpetuation of maltreatment behavior across generations, as well as specific aftereffects such as brain damage, speech impairment, and impaired physical and/or psychological growth.

SERVICES

(See EARLY INTERVENTION, EMERGENCY SERVICES, PREVENTION OF CHILD ABUSE AND NEGLECT, SUPPORTIVE SERVICES, TREATMENT OF CHILD ABUSE AND NEGLECT)

SEXUAL ABUSE

In order to encompass all forms of child sexual abuse and exploitation within its mandate, the National Center on Child Abuse and Neglect has adopted the following tentative definition of child sexual abuse: contacts or interactions between a child and an adult when the child is being used for the sexual stimulation of the perpetrator or another person. Sexual abuse may also be committed by a person under the age of 18 when that person is either significantly older than the victim or when the perpetrator is in a position of power or control over another child. (See also CHILD ABUSE AND NEGLECT)

SEXUAL ASSAULT

Unlawful actions of a sexual nature committed against a person forcibly and against his/her own will. Various degrees of sexual assault are established by state law and are distinguished by the sex of the perpetrator and/or victim, the amount of force used, the amount and type of sexual contact, etc. Sexual abuse is one form of sexual assault wherein the perpetrator is known by the victim and is usually a member of the family. (See also CHILD ABUSE AND NEGLECT)

SEXUAL EXPLOITATION

A term usually used in reference to sexual abuse of children for commercial purposes; such as child prostitution, sexual exhibition, or the production of pornographic materials. (See also CHILD PORNOGRAPHY, CHILD PROSTITUTION)

SEXUAL MISUSE

Alternative term for sexual abuse, but particularly reflects the point of view that sexual encounters with children, if properly handled, need not be as harmful as is usually assumed. Its implication is that children are not necessarily harmed by so-called sexually abusive acts themselves, but rather the abuse results from damage generated by negative social and cultural reactions to such acts. (See also CHILD MISUSE AND NEGLECT, INCEST, SEXUAL ABUSE)

SEXUALLY TRANSMISSIBLE DISEASE (STD) (See VENEREAL DISEASE)

SIMPLE FRACTURE (See FRACTURE)

SITUATIONAL CHILD ABUSE AND NEGLECT

Refers to cases of child abuse and particularly child neglect where the major causative factors cannot be readily eliminated because they relate to problems over which the parents have little control. (See also APATHY-FUTILITY SYNDROME)

SKELETAL SURVEY

A series of X-rays that studies all bones of the body. Such a survey should be done in all cases of suspected abuse to locate any old, as well as new, fractures which may exist.

SOCIAL ASSESSMENT (See ASSESSMENT)

SOCIAL HISTORY

1) Information compiled by a social worker about factors affecting a family's past and present level of functioning for use in diagnosing child abuse and neglect and developing a treatment plan.
2) Document prepared by a probation officer or social worker for the juvenile or family court hearing officer's consideration at the time of disposition of a case. This report addresses the minor's history and environment. Social histories often contain material which would clearly be inadmissible in most judicial proceedings, either because of hearsay or lack of verification or reliability. The informal use of such reports has often been attacked as in violation of due process rights of minors and parents.

SOCIAL REPORT (See SOCIAL HISTORY)

SOCIAL ISOLATION

The limited interaction and contact of many abusive and/or neglectful parents with relatives, neighbors, friends, or community resources. Social isolation can perpetuate a basic lack of trust which hinders both identification and treatment of child abuse and neglect.

SOCIAL SECURITY ACT

Established in 1935 as a national social insurance program, this federal legislation includes several sections particularly applicable to child and family welfare:

Title IV-Parts A, B, C, D (Aid to Families with Dependent Children, Child Welfare Services, Work Incentive Program, Child Support and Establishment of Paternity)
Part A, now included under Title XX as services for children, was designed to encourage families to care for dependent children in their own or relatives' homes by providing services to families below a specified income level. As a condition of receiving federal funding for this program, states must provide family planning services. Part B authorizes support to states for child welfare

services developed in coordination with the AFDC program to supplement or substitute for parental care and supervision. These services include day care, foster care, and other preventive or protective programs promoting child and family welfare. Part C offers job training and placement for AFDC parents in an effort to assist them in becoming self-supporting. Part D enforces the support obligations owed by absent parents to their children by locating absent parents, establishing paternity, and obtaining child support.

Title V-Maternal and Child Health and Applied Children's Services
Provides a broad range of health care services for mothers and children from low-income families in order to reduce maternal and infant mortality and to prevent illness.

Title XIX-Grants to States for Medical Assistance Programs (Medicaid or Title 19)
Designed to help families with dependent children and other low-income persons by providing financial assistance for necessary medical services. This act is additionally designed to provide rehabilitation and other psychotherapy services to help families and individuals retain or regain independence and self-sufficiency.

Title XX-Grants to States for Services
Provides grants to states for developing programs and services designed to achieve the following goals for families and/or children: economic self-support; self-sufficiency; prevention of abuse and neglect; preserving; rehabilitating, reuniting families; referring for institutional care when other services are not appropriate.

Mandated child protective service agency programs are primarily funded through Title IV-B and Title XX of the Social Security Act.

SOCIETAL CHILD ABUSE AND NEGLECT
Failure of society to provide social policies and/or funding to support the well-being of all families and children or to provide sufficient resources to prevent and treat child

abuse and neglect, particularly for minority populations such as migrant workers and Native Americans.

SPECIAL CHILD
A child who is abused or neglected or at risk of abuse or neglect because he/she has a special problem with which the parent(s) have difficulty coping or because the child has some psychologically negative meaning for the parent. Also referred to as "target child." If this child is abused, the cause may be referred to as "victim" precipitated abuse."

SPIRAL FRACTURE (See FRACTURE)

SPOUSE ABUSE
Non-accidental physical or psychological injury inflicted on either husband or wife by his/her marital partner. Some experts conjecture that husbands as well as wives are frequently abused, particularly psychologically, but the subject of husband abuse has not gained public or professional recognition to the extent that battered wives has. Domestic violence is the term used when referring to abuse between adult mates who may not be married. (See also BATTERED WOMEN)

STAFF BURNOUT
Apathy and frustration felt by protective service workers who are overworked, undertrained, and lacking agency or supervisory support. This is a common problem, and workers who do not leave protective services (see STAFF FLIGHT) or who do not have supervisory support often lose sensitivity to client needs. (Also referred to as Worker Burnout)

STAFF FLIGHT
Continous change of child protective services staff due to staff burnout (see STAFF BURNOUT). This creates the need to provide frequent training for new workers. Informed estimates place the overall national turnover rate of protective service workers at 85% annually.

STAFF SATISFACTION
Structuring a supportive and encouraging environment for protective service workers with regular periods when no new cases are assigned, thereby decreasing staff burnout and staff flight. Supervisors and administrators need to develop programs including the following elements: manageable caseloads, in-service training, participation in and responsibility for agency decision-making.

STANDARD OF PROOF (See EVIDENTIARY STANDARDS)

STANDARDS
Guides developed to ensure comprehensiveness and adequacy of programs or services. Issued by relevant agencies, such as the National Center on Child Abuse and Neglect for state and local level programs and the Child Welfare League of America for member agencies, standards have various levels of authority.

STATE AUTHORITY
State authority refers to the state department of social services (state department) and a state child protection coordinating committee (state committee). As designated in state law, these structures are to accept responsibility for child abuse and neglect prevention, identification, and treatment efforts. The standards on state authority, as specified in the National Center on Child Abuse and Neglect *Revision to Federal Standards on the Prevention and Treatment of Child Abuse and Neglect (Draft),* include:
Administration and Organization
1   The state department should establish child abuse and neglect policies that are consistent with the state law and conducive to state-wide delivery of uniform and coordinated services.
2   The state department should establish a distinct child protection division (state division) to facilitate the implementation of departmental policies.
3   The state department should designate child protective services units

(local units) within each regional and/or local social services agency.

4 The state committee, as required by state law, should be representative of those persons and agencies concerned with child abuse and neglect prevention, identification, and treatment.

Primary Prevention

5 The state division and the state committee should work together towards primary prevention of child abuse and neglect through formalized needs assessment and planning processes.

Secondary and Tertiary Prevention

6 The state division and the state committee should jointly develop a comprehensive and coordinated plan for delivery of services to high-risk children and families.

7 The state division should ensure that those persons who have reason to suspect child abuse or neglect can make a report at any time, twenty-four hours a day, seven days a week.

8 The state division should transmit reports to appropriate authority for assessment of the degree of risk to the child.

9 The state division should operate a central registry that facilitates state and local planning.

10 The state division's operation of the central registry should ensure that children and families' rights to prompt and effective services are protected.

Resource Enhancement

11 The state division should develop and provide public and professional education.

12 The state division should ensure that training is provided to all divisional, regional, and local staff.

13 The state division should conduct and/or sponsor research, demonstration, and evaluation projects.

(See also LOCAL AUTHORITY)

STATUS OFFENSE

An act which is considered criminal only because it is committed by a person of a particular status, such as a minor. If an adult did the same thing, it would not be an offense. For example, a minor staying out after curfew.

STIPULATION

A statement, either oral or written, between lawyers on both sides of a particular court case which establishes certain facts about the case that are agreed upon by both sides. The facts delineated usually involve such issues as the addresses of the persons involved in the case, their relationships to one another, etc.

STRESS FACTORS

Environmental and/or psychological pressures over a prolonged period which are associated with child abuse and neglect or which, without being prolonged, may be the precipitant event. While a certain amount of stress can be useful in motivating people to change, it is generally agreed that there is an overload of stress in our present society, perhaps because people feel decreasingly in control of the forces affecting their lives. Prevention of child abuse and neglect requires both reducing stress in society and helping people cope with it. Environmental stress which may influence child abuse and neglect includes, but is not limited to, unemployment, poverty, poor and overcrowded housing, competition for success, and "keeping up with the Joneses." Psychological stress besides that caused by environmental factors which may influence child abuse and neglect could include such problems as marital discord, in-law problems, unwanted pregnancy, role confusion resulting from the Women's Movement, and unresolved psychodynamic conflicts from childhood.

SUBDURAL HEMATOMA

A common symptom of abused children, consisting of a collection of blood beneath the outermost membrane covering the brain and spinal cord. The hematoma may be caused by a blow to the head or from shaking a baby or small child. (See also WHIP-

LASH-SHAKEN INFANT SYNDROME)

SUBPOENA
A document issued by a court clerk, usually delivered by a process server or police officer to the person subpoenaed, requiring that person to appear at a certain court at a certain day and time to give testimony in a specified case. Failure to obey a subpoena is punishable as contempt of court.

SUBPOENA DUCES TECUM
A subpoena requiring the person subpoenaed to bring specified records to court.

SUDDEN INFANT DEATH SYNDROME (SIDS)
A condition which can be confused with child abuse, SIDS affects infants from two weeks to two years old, but usually occurs in a child less than six months of age. In SIDS, a child who has been healthy except for a minor respiratory infection is found dead, often with bloody frothy material in his/her mouth. The cause of SIDS is not fully understood. The confusion with child abuse results from the bloody sputum and occasional facial bruises that accompany the syndrome. However, SIDS parents rarely display the guarded or defensive behavior that many abusive parents do.

SUMMONS
A document issued by a court clerk, usually delivered by a process server or police officer to the person summoned, notifying that person of the filing of a lawsuit against him/her and notifying that person of the deadline for answering the suit. A summons does not require the attendance at court of any person.

SUPERVISION
1) Provision of age-appropriate protection and guidance for a child by a parent or caretaker. This is a parental responsibility, but in some cases of child abuse and neglect or for other reasons, the state may have to assume responsibility for supervision. (See also CHILD IN NEED OF SUPERVISION)
2) Process in social work practice whereby workers review cases with supervisors to assure case progress, to sharpen the workers' knowledge and skill, and to assure maintenance of agency policies and procedures. Unlike many practitioners in law and medicine, social workers do not generally practice independently or make totally independent judgments. In general, social work supervisors hold Master's degrees, but in some local public agencies these supervisors may be just out of graduate school and have little experience. Since good supervision is a critical factor in reducing the problem of staff burnout and staff flight, it is important for child protective service agencies to provide training and continuing education opportunities for supervisors.

SUPPORTIVE SERVICES
Supportive services are a wide range of human services which provide assistance to families or individuals so that they are more nearly able to fulfill their potential for positive growth and behavior. The concept implies that individuals have basic strengths which need to be recognized, encouraged, and aided. Thus, a wide range of financial, educational, vocational, child care, counseling, recreational, and other services might be seen as supportive if they do indeed emphasize the strengths of people and de-emphasize their occasional needs for help in overcoming destructive and debilitating factors which may affect their lives.

SURROGATE PARENT
A person other than a biological parent who, living within or outside the target home, provides nurturance. This person may be self-selected or assigned to fulfill parental functions. A surrogate parent may nurture children or abusive or neglectful parents who were themselves abused as children and therefore are in need of a nurturing parental model. (See also PARENT AIDE)

SUSPECTED CHILD ABUSE AND NEGLECT

Reason to believe that child abuse or neglect has or is occurring in a given family. Anyone can in good faith report this to the local mandated agency, which will investigate and protect the child as necessary. However, all states have statutes which provide that members of certain professions must report and that failure to do so is punishable by fine or imprisonment. For specific criteria for suspecting child abuse or neglect, see INDICATORS OF CHILD ABUSE AND NEGLECT and FAMILIES-AT-RISK.

SUTURE

1) A type of immovable joint in which the connecting surfaces of the bones are closely united, as in the skull.
2) The stitches made by a physician that close a wound.

SYPHILIS (See VENEREAL DISEASE)

TARGET CHILD (See SPECIAL CHILD)

TEMPORAL

Referring to the side of the head.

TEMPORARY CUSTODY (See CUSTODY)

TEMPORARY PLACEMENT

Voluntary or involuntary short term removal of a child from his/her own home, primarily when a child's safety or well-being is threatened or endangered, or when a family crisis can be averted by such action. Temporary placement may be in a relative's home, receiving home or shelter, foster home, or institution. Temporary placement should be considered only if service to the child and family within the home, such as use of a homemaker or day care, is determined to be insufficient to protect or provide for the child or if it is unavailable. If the home situation does not improve while the child is in temporary placement, long term placement may be warranted. However, authorities agree that too many temporary placements unnecessarily become permanent place-

ments. (See also CUSTODY)

TERMINATION OF PARENTAL RIGHTS (TPR)

A legal proceeding freeing a child from his/her parents' claims so that the child can be adopted by others without the parents' written consent. The legal bases for termination differ from state to state, but most statutes include abandonment as a ground for TPR. (See also ABANDONMENT)

TESTIMONY

A declaration or statement made to establish a fact, especially one made under oath in court.

THREATENED HARM

Substantial risk of harm to a child, including physical or mental injury, sexual assault, neglect of physical and/or educational needs, inadequate supervision, or abandonment.

TITLE IV (See SOCIAL SECURITY ACT)

TITLE V (See SOCIAL SECURITY ACT)

TITLE XIX (TITLE 19, MEDICAID) (See SOCIAL SECURITY ACT)

TITLE XX (See SOCIAL SECURITY ACT)

TORUS FRACTURE (See FRACTURE)

TRABECULA

A general term for a supporting or anchoring strand of tissue.

TRAUMA

An internal or external injury or wound brought about by an outside force. Usually trauma means injury by violence, but it may also apply to the wound caused by any surgical procedure. Trauma may be caused accidentally or, as in a ease of physical abuse, non-acciden-tally. Trauma is also a term applied to psychological discomfort or symptoms resulting from an emotional shock or painful experience.

TRAUMA X

Designation used by some hospitals for a child abuse and neglect program.

TREATMENT FOSTER CARE

Foster care for children with diagnosed emotional and/or behavioral problems in which foster parents with special training and experience become part of a treatment team working with a particular child. Treatment foster care may be indicated for abused or severely neglected children.

TREATMENT OF CHILD ABUSE AND NEGLECT

1) Helping parents or caretakers stop child abuse and neglect and assisting them and their children to function adequately as a family unit. 2) Providing temporary placement and services as necessary for abused or neglected children until their parents can assume their parental responsibilities without threat to the children's welfare. 3) Terminating parental rights and placing the children in an adoptive home if the parents abandon the children or absolutely cannot be helped. Experts believe that 80% to 85% of abusive and neglectful parents can be helped to function without threat to their children's welfare and, more often than not, without temporary placement of the children if sufficient supportive services are available.

Treatment for child abuse and neglect should include treatment for the abused and neglected children as well as for the parents.

Treatment for child abuse and neglect includes both crisis intervention and long term treatment. The mandated agency may provide services directly or by purchase of service from other agencies. Since a multiplicity of services is often necessary, a case management approach to treatment is usually most effective (see CASE MANAGEMENT). Because mandated agencies necessarily focus on investigation of suspected cases and crisis intervention, long term treatment is best assured through use of a community team (see COMMUNITY TEAM).

Both crisis intervention and long term treatment will usually require a mix of supportive and therapeutic services. Supportive services could include homemakers, day care, foster grandparents, parent education, health care, family planning, recreational activities, housing assistance, transportation, legal services, employment training and placement, financial counseling and assistance. Therapeutic services could include psychotherapy, casework, lay therapy from parent aides, group therapy, family or couple therapy, and self-help such as Parents Anonymous.

TURGOR

Condition of being swollen and congested. This can refer to normal or other fullness.

TWENTY-FOUR HOUR EMERGENCY SERVICES

Local services available at all times to receive reports and make immediate investigations of suspected cases of child abuse and severe neglect and to perform crisis intervention if necessary. The mode of providing twenty-four hour emergency services varies in different localities. However, often mandated agency protective service workers are on call for specific evening and weekend assignments. Often the after-hours number rings the police or sheriffs department which then contacts the assigned worker. (See also COMPREHENSIVE EMERGENCY SERVICES)

UNFOUNDED REPORT

Any report of suspected child abuse or neglect made to the mandated agency for which it is determined that there is no probable cause to believe that abuse or neglect has occurred. Mandated agencies may or may not remove unfounded reports from their records after a period of time. (See also EXPUNGEMENT)

VASCULAR

Of the blood vessels.

VENEREAL DISEASE
Any disease transmitted by sexual contact. The two most common forms of venereal disease are gonorrhea and syphilis. Presence of a venereal disease in a child may indicate that the mother was infected with the disease during the pregnancy, or it may be evidence of sexual abuse.

VERBAL ABUSE (See CHILD ABUSE AND NEGLECT)

VERIFICATION OF CHILD ABUSE AND NEGLECT
Substantiation of child abuse or neglect following investigation of suspected cases by mandated agency workers and/or assessment by a diagnostic team. Also referred to as a founded report.

VICTIM-PRECIPITATED ABUSE (See SPECIAL CHILD)

VISITING FRIEND (See PARENT AIDE)

VITAL SIGNS
Signs manifesting life, such as respiratory rate, heartbeat, pulse, blood pressure, and eye responses.

VOIR DIRE
1   Procedure during which lawyers question prospective jurors to determine their biases, if any.
2   Procedure in which lawyers question expert witnesses regarding their qualifications before the experts are permitted to give opinion testimony.

VOLUNTARY PLACEMENT
Act of a parent in which custody of his/her child is relinquished without a formal court proceeding. Sometimes called voluntary relinquishment.

VOLUNTEER ROLES
1) Extension and enrichment of direct services to families by unpaid, screened, trained, and supervised persons who generally lack professional training. Common roles are parent aides, child care workers, outreach workers, or staff for helplines. 2) Development and advocacy of child abuse and neglect programs by unpaid persons through participation on community councils. agency boards, or community committees. Scarce resources in relation to the magnitude of the problem of child abuse and neglect demands that volunteers be used increasingly.

WANTON
Extremely reckless or malicious. Often used in court proceedings in conjunction with "willful" to establish certain kinds of unlawful behavior only vaguely distinguished from careless but lawful conduct.

WARRANT
Document issued by a judge, authorizing the arrest or detention of a person or the search of a place and seizure of specified items in that place. Although a judge need not hold a hearing before issuing a warrant and although the party to be arrested or whose property will be seized need not be notified, the judge must still be given "reasonable cause to believe" that a crime has occurred and that the warrant is necessary in the apprehension and conviction of the criminal.

WHIPLASH-SHAKEN INFANT SYNDROME
Injury to an infant or child that results from that child having been shaken, usually as a misguided means of discipline. The most common symptoms, which can be inflicted by seemingly harmless shakings, are bleeding and/or detached retinas and other bleeding inside the head. Repeated instances of shaking and resultant injuries may eventually cause mental and developmental disabilities. (See also SUBDURAL HEMATOMA)

WILLFUL
Done with understanding of the act and the intention that the act and its natural consequences should occur. Some conduct

becomes unlawful or negligent only when it is done willfully.

WITNESS

1   A person who has seen or heard something.

2   A person who is called upon to testify in a court hearing.

WORKER BURNOUT   (See Staff Burnout)

WORK-UP

Study of a patient, often in a hospital, in order to provide information for diagnosis. A full work-up includes past medical and family histories, present condition and symptoms, laboratory, and, possibly, X-ray studies.

WORLD OF ABNORMAL REARING (WAR)

A generational cycle of development in which abused or neglected children tend to grow up to be abusive or neglectful parents unless intervention occurs to break the cycle. The diagram which follows outlines the WAR cycle. (Heifer)

X-RAYS

Photographs made by means of X-rays. X-rays are one of the most important tools available to physicians in the diagnosis of physical child abuse or battering. With X-rays, or radiologic examinations, physicians can observe not only the current bone injuries of a child, but also any past injuries that may exist in various stages of healing. This historical information contributes significantly to the assessment of a suspected case of child abuse. Radiologic examination is also essential to distinguish organic diseases that may cause bone breakage from physical child abuse.

Acronyms

AAP	American Academy of Pediatrics
ACSW	Academy of Certified Social Workers
ACYF	Administration for Children, Youth and Families (formerly Office of Child Development), U.S. Department of Health, Education and Welfare
ADC	Aid to Dependent Children (Title IV-A of the Social Security Act) (also referred to as AFDC)
AF	Alleged Father
AFDC	Aid to Families with Dependent Children (Title IV-A of the Social Security Act) (also referred to as ADC)
AHA	American Humane Association
AMA	Against Medical Advice; American Medical Association
APA	American Psychiatric Association; American Psychological Association
APWA	American Public Welfare Association
CALM	Child Abuse Listening Mediation
CAN	Child Abuse and Neglect
CAP	Community Action Program
CDAHA	Children's Division of the American Humane Association
CDF	Children's Defense Fund
CES	Comprehensive Emergency Services
CHIPS	Child in Need of Protection and Supervision
CLL	Childhood Level of Living Scale
CNS	Central Nervous System
	Office of Human Development Services), U.S. Department of Health, Education and Welfare
OHDS	Office of Human Development Services (formerly Office of Human Development), U.S. Department of Health, Education and Welfare
PA	Parents Anonymous

PET	Parent Effectiveness Training
PINS	Person in Need of Supervision
CPS	Child Protective Services
CWLA	Child Welfare League of America
DART	Detection, Admission, Reporting, and Treatment (multidisciplinary team)
DD	Developmental Disability
DHEW	U.S. Department of Health, Education and Welfare (also referred to as HEW)
DPW	Department of Public Welfare
DSS	Department of Social Services
EPSDT	Early and Periodic Screening, Diagnosis, and Treatment
ER	Emergency Room
FTT	Failure to Thrive
GAL	*Guardian ad l item*
HEW	U.S. Department of Health, Education and Welfare (also referred to as DHEW)
IP	Identified Patient
LD	Learning Disability
MINS	Minor in Need of Supervision
NASW	National Association of Social Workers
NCCA	National Center for Child Advocacy
NCCAN	National Center on Child Abuse and Neglect
NIH	National Institutes of Health
NIMH	National Institute of Mental Health
OCD	Office of Child Development (now Adminstration for Children, Youth and Families). U.S. Department of Health, Education and Welfare
OHD	Office of Human Development (now
PL 93-247	Child Abuse Prevention and Treatment Act
SCAN	Suspected Child Abuse and Neglect

SIDS	Sudden Infant Death Syndrome	**VD**	Venereal Disease
STD	Sexually Transmissible Disease	**WAR**	World of Abnormal Rearing
TPR	Termination of Parental Rights	**WIN**	Work Incentive Program
UM	Unmarried Mother		

———